TO:

_____

FROM:

_____

DATE:

_____

TREASURY
of LOVE *and*
ROMANCE

A CLASSIC COLLECTION OF STORIES,

QUOTES, BALLADS, VERSES, AND POEMS

Honor Books
Tulsa, Oklahoma

Treasury of Love and Romance:
A Classic Collection of Stories,
Ballads, Verses, and Poems
ISBN 1-56292-560-1
Copyright © 1999 by Honor Books
P.O. Box 55388
Tulsa, Oklahoma 74155

Compiled and edited by Paul M. Miller

All possible efforts were made by Honor Books, to secure permission and insure
proper credit given for every entry within this book.

CONTENTS

THE GREATEST OF ALL

"Though I speak with the tongues of men and of angels, but have not love . . . I am nothing" (1 Corinthians 13:1-2).

St. Paul eloquently states that no human endeavor or accomplishment—not beautiful words, not wisdom, not faith, not even martyrdom—is equal to the simple and pure act of love.

The beauty of this treasury is that you need not choose between the tongues of angels or love. You will discover both beautiful words and the many facets of true love.

Sometimes deeply spiritual . . . sometimes humorous . . . sometimes poignant and sad . . . but always uplifting . . . you will cherish this keepsake collection of poems, stories, verses, songs and other expressions of love.

Whether you linger over the words of this treasury by yourself on a rainy Saturday afternoon, or read them aloud with the one you love over a cup of coffee in a bistro late on a Friday night, experience the wonder of love anew as you laugh, smile, shed a tear, and sigh over the greatest gift of all.

A Letter From
The Editor

For readers raised on the King James Version (1611) of the Holy Bible and the thirteenth chapter of First Corinthians, the word *charity* was held up as the virtue for which we should all be striving. For many, *charity* offered up visions of boxes for the poor, the Salvation Army, and perhaps the homeless man with a deformed leg who, along with his sleeping mutt, sat on a downtown street corner with a cigar "alms" box.

In his first letter to the Corinthians, St. Paul writes that *charity* was supposed to be greater than *faith* and *hope* all put together, but as a KJV-reading teenager I wasn't totally convinced about the charity bit.

Then, the first "modern language" New Testament made its entrance, and we discovered that *charity* really means *love*. That's when my Sunday school instruction began to make a little more sense. I had been unable to imagine any of the great lovers in the Holy Bible looking on their beloved with charity. At least, that wasn't what this fourteen-year-old thought it was all about, especially when we'd snicker through some rather detailed anatomical description in The Song of Solomon.

Now, as I compile and edit this treasury of love stories, poetry, essays, and unaccountable pieces of other literature, I am made aware of how much the English language lacks in its ability to articulate the many characteristics and types of love. The fact is, from the genteel writers like Shakespeare, the Brownings, William Blake, and those Bronte sisters, through the more rough and ready crowd, Mark Twain and Brett Harte, right down to the favorites of this century, there has been but one word to represent the many facets of love. Think of it, when we signed thank-you notes to grandma and Uncle Charlie with "Love, Paul," we used the same word with which we signed love letters to the current object of our deepest affections. When we try to express our great enthusiasm for our favorite sports hero, pastime or food, we are stuck with the same word we spoke in front of the altar in a tuxedo with the light of our life all dressed in white.

In reality, the Apostle Paul had a number of words for love at his disposal. The ancient Greek language provided several options for the affairs of life that affect the heart; there was the erotic for those kinds of lovers, the affectionate for good friends, and there was the self-giving *agape* love that became translated as *charity* in First Corinthians 13. You see, it makes a lot of sense to rank *agape* love higher on the Apostle's list of virtues than *faith* and *hope*. Besides, the erotic Old Testament love stories like Samson and Delilah, Ruth and Boaz, not to mention David and Bathsheba, were originally written in Hebrew.

So how does all this erudite information relate to the book in your hands? As I have read and re-read the selections that make up this anthology, I am convinced that genuine love between a man and a woman reflects all three of the words available to St. Paul; erotic love, friendly love, and self-giving love. They are all reflected in this treasury. Hopefully, they are all represented in your relationship to the one you call "my love."

A final word: take time to read selections from this book with the one you love. Read them aloud to each other. Enjoy the physical closeness of the one next to you, hear the sound of his or her voice, respond to the word pictures and endearing terms expressed in the texts, relate some to your own relationship.

In all of your faith and hoping, remember that love is the greatest.

PAUL M. MILLER

WHAT IS LOVE?

If I speak in the tongues of mortals and of angels, but do
not have love, I am a noisy gong or a clanging cymbal.

And if I have prophetic powers, and understand all mysteries
and all knowledge, and if I have all faith, so as to remove
mountains, but do not have love, I am nothing.

If I give away all my possessions, and if I hand over my body
so that I may boast, but do not have love, I gain nothing.

Love is patient;
Love is kind;
Love is not envious
or boastful
or arrogant
or rude.
It does not insist on its own way;
It is not irritable
or resentful;
It does not rejoice in wrongdoing,
But rejoices in the truth.
It bears all things,
believes all things,
hopes all things,
endures all things.
Love never ends. . . .

And now faith, hope, and love abide, these three;

And the greatest of these is love.

1 CORINTHIANS 13:1-8,13 NRSV

Chapter 1
LOVE THE LANGUAGE OF MORTALS

The parlance of love is probably the most personal and fragile of all topics in the languages of mankind. Forgetting language differences, just the familiar phrase "I love you" in dialects from Afrikaans to Zuni requires some understanding of culture as well as vocabulary and grammar.

For writers and readers of English, the words of love are as varied as the imaginations and passions of those who write and read them. Short of whispers and sighs, love letters and notes are certainly the most personal expressions of mortals. You will find a selection of them here and scattered throughout this treasury.

To many, Elizabeth Barrett Browning's Sonnets from the Portuguese contains some of most sublime love language to be found. Come in and revel in the languages of love.

Behold,

What manner of love

the Father hath

bestowed upon us.

1 John 3:1

IF THOU MUST LOVE ME, LET IT BE FOR NAUGHT

If thou must love me, let it be for naught

Except for love's sake only. Do not say

"I love her for her smile—her look—her way

Of speaking gently—for a trick of thought

That falls in well with mine, and certes brought

A sense of pleasant ease on such a day"—

For these things in themselves, Beloved, may

Be changed, or changed for thee—and love, so wrought,

May be unwrought so. Neither love me for

Thine own dear pity's wiping my cheeks dry—

A creature might forget to weep, who bore

Thy comfort long, and lose thy love thereby!

But love me for love's sake, that evermore

*Thou mayest love on, through love's eternity.*₁

ELIZABETH BARRETT BROWNING

THE PRESENCE OF LOVE

And in Life's noisiest hour,

There whispers still the ceaseless Love of Thee,

The heart's Self-solace and soliloquy.

You mould my Hopes, you fashion me within;

And to the leading Love—throb in the Heart

Thro' all my Being, thro' my pulses beat;

You lie in all my many Thoughts, like Light,

Like the fair light of Dawn, or summer Eve

On rippling Stream, or cloud-reflecting Lake.

And looking to the Heaven, that bends above you,

How oft! I bless the Lot, that made me love you.

SAMUEL TAYLOR COLERIDGE

TO JANE

The keen stars were twinkling,

And the fair moon was rising among them,

Dear Jane.

The guitar was tinkling,

But the notes were not sweet

till you sung them

Again.

As the moon's soft splendour

O'er the faint cold starlight of Heaven

Is thrown,

So your voice most tender

To the strings without soul had then given

Its own.

PERCY BYSSHE SHELLEY

LETTERS OF LOVE

A FRAGMENT FROM

MARY WORDSWORTH TO

HER HUSBAND WILLIAM WORDSWORTH

*Because poet William Wordsworth was a "serious writer,"
to his wife Mary, a love letter from William was a very special gift.*

AUGUST 1, 1810

Oh my William! it is not in my power to tell thee how I
have been affected by this dearest of all letters—it was so unexpected—so new a thing to see the breathing of thy inmost heart
upon paper that I was quite overpowered, and now that I sit
down to answer thee in the loneliness and depth of that love
which unites us and which cannot be felt but by ourselves, I am
so agitated and my eyes are so dimmed that I scarcely know
how to proceed . . .

AUTHOR JACK LONDON TO HIS WIFE

Jack London was the premier turn-of-the-century Northern
Californian novelist and short story writer whose romantic works deal
with nature and man's elemental struggle to survive. The Call of the
Wild *is probably London's best known work. This letter to the love-*
of-his-life, wife Charmian Kittredge, was written from Oakland.

OAKLAND
THURSDAY, SEPTEMBER 24, 1903

Nay, nay, dear Love, not in my eyes is this love of ours a
small and impotent thing. It is the greatest and most powerful
thing in the world. The relativity of things makes it so. That
I should be glad to live for you or to die for you is proof in itself
that it means more to me than life or death, is greater, far
greater, than life or death.

That you should be the one woman to me of all women;
that my hunger for you should be greater than any hunger for
food I have ever felt; that my desire for you should bite harder
than any other desire I have ever felt for fame and fortune and
such things;—all, all goes to show how big is this, our love.

As I tell you repeatedly, you cannot possibly know what you
mean to me. The days I do not see you are merely so many
obstacles to be got over somehow before I see you. Each night
as I go to bed I sigh with relief because I am one day nearer to
you. So it has been this week, and it is only Monday that I was
with you. Today I am jubilant, my work goes well. And I am
saying to myself all the time, "Tonight I shall see her! Tonight
I shall see her!"

My thoughts are upon you always, lingering over you always, caressing you always in a myriad of ways. I wonder if you feel those caresses sometimes!

Ah Love, it looms large. It wills my whole horizon. Wherever I look I feel you, see you, touch you, and know my need for you. . . . I love you, you only and wholly. . . . I clutch for you like a miser for his gold, because you are everything and the only thing.

I know I am 27, at the high-tide of my life and vigor. [I write these words] to show how large to me, in the scheme of life, bulks this love of ours.

VICTORIA ABOUT ALBERT

The journals of Britain's Queen Victoria, when writing about her Albert, read like love letters. For all the so-called-prudery of the Victorian Era, the queen herself appears to be a passionate woman.

15 OCTOBER 1839

At about half past twelve I sent for Albert; he came to the Closet where I was alone, and after a few minutes I said to him, that I thought he must be aware why I wished [to have him come] here, and that it would make me too happy if he would consent to do what I wished (to marry me); we embraced each other over and over again, and he was so kind, so affectionate; Oh! To feel I was, and am, loved by such an Angel as Albert was too great delight to describe! He is perfection; perfection in every way—in beauty—in everything! I told him I was quite unworthy of him and kissed his dear hand—he said he would be very happy and was so kind and seemed happy, that I really felt it was the happiest brightest moment in my life, which had made up for all I suffered and endured. Oh! How I adore and love him. I cannot say!! how I will strive to make him feel as little as possible the great sacrifice he has made; I told him it was a great sacrifice, which he wouldn't allow . . . I feel the happiest of human beings.

12 FEBRUARY 1840

Already the second day since our marriage; his love and gentleness is beyond everything, and to kiss that dear soft cheek, to press my lips to his, is heavenly bliss. I feel a purer more unearthly feel than I ever did. Oh! Was ever woman so blessed as I am.

13 FEBRUARY 1840

My dearest Albert put on my stockings for me. I went in and saw him shave; a great delight for me.

FROM RUSSIAN PLAYWRIGHT ANTON CHEKHOV, TO HIS WIFE OLGA

Olga was a beautiful young actress who had appeared in Anton's plays. This note from the playwright was written a few months after their marriage.

AUGUST 21, 1901

I kiss you firmly a hundred times, embrace you tenderly and am sketching in my imagination various pictures in which you and I figure, and nobody and nothing else.

—Anton

FROM MARK TWAIN (SAMUEL LANGHORNE CLEMENS) TO OLIVIA LANGDON, HIS FUTURE WIFE

As taciturn and curmudgeon—like Mark Twain appears to be in his
writings—this brief letter to the woman
who would one day be his wife, is surprisingly tender.

MAY 12, 1869

Out of the depths of my happy heart wells a great tide of love and prayer for this priceless treasure that is confided to my life-long keeping.

You cannot see its intangible waves as they flow toward you, darling, but in these lines you will hear, as if it were, the distant beating of its surf.

Forever yours,

Sam

JOHN STEINBECK TO HIS WIFE, GWENDOLYN

The Pulitzer-Prize-awarded American novelist, noted for realism,
writes during a lecture tour away from Northern California.

JULY, 1943

Darling, you want to know what I want of you. Many things of course, but chiefly these. I want you to keep this thing we have inviolate and waiting—the person who is neither I nor you but us.

German composer Robert Schumann lost his heart to Clara, a pianist
who became a principle interpreter of his piano works.
This is a pre-marriage note.

APRIL 15, 1838

I want you for always—days, years, eternities.

———————⟨⟩———————

A LETTER FROM ELIZABETH BARRETT TO

ROBERT BROWNING

Elizabeth Barrett, a thirty-two-year-old semi-invalid English poet,
had recently published a collection of her verse, in which she included a
tribute to the poetry of renowned Robert Browning. He enthusiasti-
cally wrote back, "I love your verses," and near the end of the letter
declared, "and I love you too." So began a two-year correspondence
that resulted in an exchange of some 600 letters. One year after
Robert's initial missive, Elizabeth writes . . .

JANUARY 10, 1846

Do you know, when you have told me to think of you, I have
been feeling ashamed of thinking of you so much, of thinking
only of you—which is too much, perhaps. Shall I tell you?
It seems to me to myself, that no man was ever before to any
woman what you are to me—the fullness must be in proportion,
you know, to the vacancy . . . and only I know what was behind—
the long wilderness without the blossoming rose . . . and the
capacity for happiness, like a black gaping hole, before this silver flooding.   Is it wonderful that I should stand as in a dream,
and disbelieve—not you—but my own fate? Was ever any one
taken suddenly from a lampless dungeon and placed upon the
pinnacle of a mountain, without the head turning round and the
heart turning faint, as mine do? And you love me more, you

say? Shall I thank you or God? Both—indeed—and there is no possible return from me to either of you! I thank you as the unworthy may . . . and as we all thank God. How shall I ever prove what my heart is to you? How will you ever see it as I feel it? I ask myself in vain.

Have so much faith in me, my only beloved, as to use me simply for your own advantage and happiness, and to your own ends without a thought of any others—that is all I could ask you without any disquiet as to the granting of it—May God bless you!—

Your

B.A.

ELIZABETH BARRETT TO ROBERT BROWNING

In 1846, in defiance to her father, Edward Barrett, Robert and Elizabeth Eloped to Italy, where they were united in what would become a fifteen-year marriage. Mr. Barrett never wrote or spoke to his daughter again. He died in 1857 without forgiving her. Elizabeth and Robert were never separated until the day Elizabeth died cradled in Robert's arms.

AUGUST 17, 1846

You have lifted my very soul up into the light of your soul, and I am not ever likely to mistake it for the common daylight.[2]

How do I love thee? Let me count the ways.

I love thee to the depth and breadth and height

My soul can reach, when feeling out of sight

For the ends of Being and ideal Grace.

I love thee to the level of everyday's

Most quiet need, by sun and candlelight.

I love thee freely, as men strive for Right;

I love thee purely, as they turn from Praise.

I love thee with the passion put to use

In my old griefs, and with my childhood's faith.

I love thee with a love I seemed to lose—

With my lost saints—I love thee with the breath,

Smiles, tears, of all my life!—and, if God choose,

*I shall but love thee better after death.*₃

ELIZABETH BARRETT BROWNING

From *Sonnets from the Portuguese*

ROMEO AND JULIET

WILLIAM SHAKESPEARE

The balcony scene Retold from Charles and Mary Lamb's
Tales from Shakespeare

Romeo Montague left the Capulet masquerade ball where he met and instantly fell in love with Juliet. Unable to forget the beautiful daughter of his family's sworn enemies, he returned to the Capulet house where he hoped for another glimpse of the girl.

He leaps the wall of the orchard which is at the back of Juliet's house. Here he had not been long, ruminating on his new love, when Juliet appeared above at a window, through which her great beauty seems to break like the light of the sun in the east; and the moon, which shines in the orchard with a faint light, appears to Romeo as if sick and pale with grief at the superior lustre of this new sun.

"But, soft! What light through yonder window breaks? It is the east, and Juliet is the sun. Arise, fair sun, and kill the envious moon."

Juliet leans at the casement with her hand upon her cheek. Romeo speaks,

"It is my lady, O, it is my love! O, that I were a glove upon her hand, that I might touch that cheek!"

Thinking herself alone, Juliet steps out onto the balcony and exclaims,

"Ah me!"

Romeo, enraptured to hear her speak responds softly,

"O speak again, bright angel! For thou art as glorious to this night as is a winged messenger of heaven."

She, not being aware of Romeo's presence, calls upon her lover by name:

"O Romeo, Romeo! Wherefore art thou Romeo? Deny thy father and refuse thy name, for my sake; or if thou wilt not, be but my sworn love, and I no longer will be a Capulet."

Romeo, having this encouragement, wishes to speak, but he wants to hear more.

The lady continues her passionate discourse by declaring that Romeo should put away that hated name Montague. "What's in a name?" she asks, "That which we call a rose by any other name would smell as sweet. O Romeo, doft thy name and take me."

At this loving word, Romeo can no longer keep silent. He bades her call him by another name—even "Love."

Juliet is alarmed to hear a man's voice in the garden, but then knows it to be Romeo's. She declares that he is in grave danger if any of her kinsmen should find him here, it would mean death to him, being a Montague.

"Alack," says Romeo, "there is more peril in your eyes than in twenty of their swords. Do you but look kindly upon me, lady, and I am proof against their enmity. Better my life should be ended by their hate, than that hated life should be prolonged to live without your love."

"How came you into this place," asked Juliet, "and by whose direction?"

"Love directed me."

A crimson blush comes over Juliet's face, unseen by Romeo by reason of the night. But he, being anxious that she exchange a vow of love with him that night, listened as his Juliet explained that she already had given him her vow of love before he requested it.

A cloud hides the moon, and Juliet's nurse calls for her to come to bed. From the vantage of her balcony Juliet leans toward Romeo and whispers,

"Good night, good night! Parting is such sweet sorrow, that I shall say good night till it be morrow."

Reaching up to his Juliet, Romeo pronounces a benediction,

"Sleep dwell upon thine eyes, peace in thy breast! Would I were sleep and peace, so sweet to rest!"

YOUNG AND IN LOVE

Young and in love—how magical the phrase!

How magical the fact! Who has not yearned

Over young lovers when to their amaze

They fall in love, and find their love returned,

And the lights brighten, and their eyes are

Clear

To see God's image in their common clay.

Is it the music of the spheres they hear?

Is it the prelude to that noble play

The drama of Joined Lives?[4]

ALICE DUER MILLER
From *The White Cliffs*

ANY WAY YOU SAY IT...

It is expressed with just three little words in English—"I love you." For people around the world those three words become one, two, three, or even six. Some of the languages below have up to sixteen ways to say the phrase. Try some of these on your loved one.

Afrikaans	Ek het jou liefe
Albanian	te dua
Arabic	Ana Behibak (spoken, to a male)
	Ana Behibek (spoken, to a female)
Bavarian	I mog di narrisch gern
Bengali	Ami tomAy bhAlobAshi
Bolivian Quechua	ganta munani
Bulgarian	Obicham te
Burmese	chit pa de
Cambodian	Bon sro lanh oon (spoken)
Cantonese	Moi oiy neya (spoken)
Chickasaw	chiholloli (first "i" nasalized)
Croatian	LJUBim te
Czech	miluji te
Danish	Jeg elsker dig
Dutch	Ik hou van jou
Esperanto	Mi amas vin
Estonian	Mina armmastan sind
Filipino	Iniibig Kita

Finnish	Mina" rakaastan sinua
French	Je t'aime
Gaelic	Ta gra agam ort
German	Ich liebe Dich
Greek	s'ayapo (spoken)
Greek (old)	(Ego) philo su
Greenlandic	Asavakit
Hawaiian	Aloha I'a Au Oe
Hebrew	Ani ohev otach
	(spoken, male to female)
	Ani ohevet otcha
	(spoken, female to male)
Hindi	Mai tumase pyar karata
	(spoken, male to female)
	Mai tumase pyar karati hun
	(spoken, female to male)
Hopi	Nu' umi unangwa'ta
Hungarian	Szeretlek te'ged
Icelandic	Eg elska thig
Iranian	Mahn doostaht doh-rahm
	(spoken)
Italian	ti amo
Japanese	Kimi o ai shiteru (spoken)
	Suki desu (spoken, start of
	relationship)
Klingon	gabang
Korean	Tangshin-ul Sarang Ha Yo
	(spoken, plus fifteen more)
Latin	Te amo
	Ego amo te (old)
Marathi	me tujhashi prem karto
	(spoken, male to female)
	me tujhashi prem karte
	(spoken, female to male)

Mohawk	Konoronhkwa
Navaho	Ayor anosh' ni
Norwegian	Eg elskar deg
Pakistani	Mujhe Tumse Muhabbat Hai (spoken)
Persian	Tora dost daram
Polish	Kocham Cie
Portuguese	Amo-te
Punjabi	Mai taunu pyar karda
Romanian	Te iu besc
Russian	Ya vas liubliu
Sioux	Techihhila
Slovak	lubim ta
Spanish	Te amo
Srilankan	Mama Oyata Arderyi
Swedish	Jag a"lskar dig
Thai	Khao Raak Thoe (spoken)
Tunisian	Ha eh bak (spoken)
Turkish	Seni Seviyurum (spoken)
Ukrainian	ja tebe koKHAju (spoken)
Urdu	Mujhe tumse mohabbat hai (spoken)
Vietnamese	Em ye^u anh (spoken, female to male) Anh ye^u em (spoken, male to female)
Welsh	'Rwy'n dy garu di
Yiddish	Ich libe dich
Zulu	Ngiyakuthanda!
Zuni	Tom ho' ichema

CYRANO DE BERGERAC

FROM ACT THREE
EDMOND ROSTAND

*One of the great love stories of all time, is that of poet
Cyrano de Bergerac and his love for the beautiful Roxane,
who in turn loves Christian, a handsome young soldier who
is unable to express his love as poetically as Cyrano.
In this scene Christian, with Cyrano lurking in the bushes,
enters Roxane's garden. She enters . . .*

ROXANE *(seeing Christian)*: You are here! *(She goes to him.)*
Evening is closing round . . . Not a passer in sight . . . Let us sit
here . . . Talk! . . . I will listen.

CHRISTIAN *(sits beside her on the bench. Silence.)*: I love you.

ROXANE *(closing her eyes)*: Yes. Talk to me of love.

CHRISTIAN: I love you.

ROXANE: Yes. That is the theme. Play variations upon it.

CHRISTIAN: I love . . .

ROXANE: Variations!

CHRISTIAN: I love you so much . . .

ROXANE: I do not doubt it. What further? . . .

CHRISTIAN: And further . . . I should be so happy if you loved
me! Tell me, Roxane, that you love me . . .

ROXANE *(pouting)*: You proffer cider to me when I was hoping
for champagne! . . . Now tell me a little *how* you love me.

CHRISTIAN: Why . . . very, very much.

ROXANE: Oh! . . . unravel, disentangle your sentiments!

CHRISTIAN: Your throat! . . . I want to kiss it! . . .

ROXANE: Christian!

CHRISTIAN: I love you! . . .

ROXANE *(attempting to rise)*: Again! . . .

CHRISTIAN *(hastily holding her back)*: No, I do not love you! . . .

ROXANE *(sitting down again)*: That is fortunate!

CHRISTIAN: I adore you!

ROXANE: *(rising and moving away)*: Oh! . . .

CHRISTIAN: Yes, . . .

ROXANE *(dryly)*: And I am displeased at it! as I should be displeased at your no longer being handsome.

CHRISTIAN: But . . .

ROXANE: Go, and rally your routed eloquence!

CHRISTIAN: I . . .

ROXANE: You love me. I have heard it. Good-evening. *(She goes toward the house.)*

CHRISTIAN: No, no, not yet! . . . I wish to tell you . . .

ROXANE *(pushing the door open to go in)*: That you adore me. Yes, I know. No! No! Go away! . . . Go! . . . Go! . . .

CHRISTIAN: But I . . .

(She closes the door in his face.)

CYRANO *(who has been on the scene a moment, unnoticed)*:
Unmistakably a success.

CHRISTIAN: Help me!

CYRANO: No, sir, no.

CHRISTIAN: I will go kill myself if I am not taken back into
favor at once . . . at once!

CYRANO: And how can I . . . how, the devil?. . . make you learn
on the spot . . .

CHRISTIAN *(seizing him by the arm)*: Oh, there! . . .
Look! . . . See!

(Light has appeared in the balcony window.)

CYRANO *(with emotion)*: Her window!

CHRISTIAN: Oh, I shall die!

CYRANO: Not so loud!

CHRISTIAN *(in a whisper)*: I shall die!

CYRANO: It is a dark night . . .

CHRISTIAN: Well?

CYRANO: All may be mended. But you do not deserve . . .
There! Stand there, miserable boy! . . . in front of the balcony!
I will stand under it and prompt you.

CHRISTIAN: But . . .

CYRANO: Do as I bid you!

CYRANO: Call her!

CHRISTIAN: Roxane!

CYRANO *(picking up pebbles and throwing them at the window-pane)*: Wait! A few pebbles . . .

ROXANE *(opening the window)*: Who is calling me?

CHRISTIAN: It is I . . .

ROXANE: Who is . . . I?

CHRISTIAN: Christian!

ROXANE *(disdainfully)*: Oh, you!

CHRISTIAN: I wish to speak with you.

CYRANO *(under the balcony, to* CHRISTIAN*)*: Speak low! . . .

ROXANE: No, your conversation is too common. You may go home!

CHRISTIAN: In mercy! . . .

ROXANE: No . . . you do not love me any more!

CHRISTIAN *(whom* CYRANO *is prompting)*: You accuse me . . . just Heaven! of loving you no more . . . when I can love you no more!

ROXANE *(who was about to close the window, stops)*: Ah, that is a little better!

CHRISTIAN *(same business)*: To what a . . . size has Love grown in my . . . sigh-rocked soul which the . . . cruel cherub has chosen for his cradle!

ROXANE (*stepping nearer to the edge of the balcony*): That is distinctly better! . . . But, since he is so cruel, this Cupid, you were unwise not to smother him in his cradle!

CHRISTIAN (*same business*): I tried to, but, madame, the . . . attempt was futile. This . . . new-born Love is . . . a little Hercules. . . .

ROXANE: Much, much better!

CHRISTIAN (*same business*): . . . Who found it merest baby-play to . . . strangle the two serpents . . . twain Pride and . . . Mistrust.

ROXANE (*leaning her elbows on the balcony rail*): Ah, that is very good indeed! . . . But why do you speak so slowly and stintedly? Has your imagination gout in its wings?

CYRANO (*drawing* CHRISTIAN *under the balcony, and taking his place*): Hush! It is becoming too difficult!

ROXANE: Tonight your words come falteringly . . . Why is it?

CYRANO (*talking low like* CHRISTIAN): Because of the dark. They have to grope to find your ear.

ROXANE: My words do not find the same difficulty.

CYRANO: They reach their point at once? Of course they do! That is because I catch them with my heart. My heart, you see, is very large, your ear particularly small. . . . Besides, your words drop . . . that goes quickly; mine have to climb . . . and that takes longer!

ROXANE: They have been climbing more nimbly, however, in the last few minutes.

CYRANO: They are becoming used to this gymnastic feat!

ROXANE: It is true that I am talking to you from a very mountaintop!

CYRANO: It is sure that a hard word dropped from such a height upon my heart would shatter it!

ROXANE *(with the motion of leaving)*: I will come down.

CYRANO *(quickly)*: Do not!

ROXANE *(pointing to the bench at the foot of the balcony)*: Then do you get up on the seat! . . .

CYRANO *(drawing away in terror)*: No!

ROXANE: How do you mean . . . no?

CYRANO *(with ever increasing emotion)*: Let us profit a little by this chance of talking softly together without seeing each other . . .

ROXANE: Without seeing each other? . . .

CYRANO: Yes, to my mind, delectable! Each guesses at the other, and no more. You discern but the trailing blackness of a mantle, and I a dawn-gray glimmer which is a summer gown. I am a shadow merely, a pearly phantom are you! You can never know what these moments are to me! If ever I was eloquent . . .

ROXANE: You were!

CYRANO: My words never till now surged from my very heart . . .

ROXANE: And why?

CYRANO: Because, till now, they must strain to reach you through . . .

ROXANE: What?

CYRANO: Why, the bewildering emotion a man feels who sees

[39]

you, and whom you look upon! . . . But this evening, it seems to me that I am speaking to you for the first time!

ROXANE: It is true that your voice is altogether different.

CYRANO *(coming nearer, feverishly)*: Yes, altogether different, because, protected by the dark, I dare at last to be myself. I dare . . . *(He stops, and distractedly.)* What was I saying? . . . I do not know . . . All this . . . forgive my incoherence! . . . is so delicious . . . is so new to me!

ROXANE: So new? . . .

CYRANO *(in extreme confusion, still trying to mend his expressions)*: So new . . . yes, new, to be sincere; the fear of being mocked always constrains my heart . . .

ROXANE: Mocked . . . for what?

CYRANO: Why, . . . for its impulses, its flights! . . . Yes, my heart always cowers behind the defense of my wit. I set forth to capture a star . . . and then, for dread of laughter, I stop and pick a flower . . . of rhetoric!

ROXANE: That sort of flower has its pleasing points . . .

CYRANO: But yet, tonight, let us scorn it!

ROXANE: Never before had you spoken as you are speaking! . . .

CYRANO: Ah, if far from Cupid-darts and quivers, we might seek a place of somewhat fresher things! If instead of drinking, flat sip by sip, from a chiseled golden thimble, drops distilled and dulcified, we might try the sensation of quenching the thirst of our souls by stooping to the level of the great river, and setting our lips to the stream!

ROXANE: But yet, wit . . . fancy . . . delicate conceits . . .

CYRANO: I gave my fancy leave to frame conceits, before, to

make you linger, . . . but now it would be an affront to this balm-breathing night, to Nature and the hour, to talk like characters in a pastoral performed at Court! . . . Let us give Heaven leave, looking at us with all its earnest stars, to strip us of disguise and artifice: I fear, . . . oh, fear! . . . lest in our mistaken alchemy sentiment should be subtilized to evaporation; lest the life of the heart should waste in these empty pastimes, and the final refinement of the fine be the undoing of the refined!

ROXANE: But yet, wit, . . . aptness, . . . ingenuity . . .

CYRANO: I hate them in love! Criminal, when one loves, to prolong overmuch that paltry thrust and parry! The moment, however, comes inevitably—and I pity those for whom it never comes!—in which, we apprehending the noble depth of the love we harbor, a shallow word hurts us to utter!

ROXANE: If . . . if, then, that moment has come for us two, what words will you say to me?

CYRANO: All those, all those, all those that come to me! Not in formal nosegay order, . . . I will throw them you in a wild sheaf! I love you, choke with love, I love you, dear. . . . My brain reels, I have can bear no more , it is too much. . . . Your name is in my heart the golden clapper in a bell; and as I know no rest, Roxane, always the heart is shaken, and ever rings your name! . . . Of you, I remember all, all have I loved! Last year, one day, the twelfth of May, in going out at morning you changed the fashion of your hair. . . . I have taken the light of your hair for my light, and as having stared too long at the sun, on everything one sees a scarlet wheel, on everything when I come from my chosen light, my dazzled eyes set swimming golden blots! . . .

ROXANE (in a voice unsteady with emotion): Yes . . . this is love . . .

CYRANO: Ah, verily! The feeling which invades me, terrible and jealous, is love . . . with all its mournful frenzy! It is love, yet self-forgetting more than the wont of love! Ah, for your happiness now readily would I give mine, though you should never know it, might I but, from a distance, sometimes, hear the happy laughter brought on by my sacrifice! Every glance of yours breeds in me new strength, new valor! Are you beginning to understand? Tell me, do you grasp my love's measure? Does some little part of my soul make itself felt of you there in the darkness? . . . Oh, what is happening to me this evening is too sweet, too deeply dear! I tell you all these things, and you listen to me, you! Not in my least modest hoping did I ever hope so much! I have now only to die! It is because of words of mine that she is trembling among the dusky branches! For you are trembling, like a flower among leaves! Yes, you tremble, . . . for whether you will or no, I have felt the worshipped trembling of your hand all along this thrilled and blissful jasmine bough!

(He madly kisses the end of a pendent bough.)

ROXANE: Yes, I tremble . . . and weep . . . and love you. . . and am yours! . . . For you have carried me away . . . away! . . .

CYRANO: Then, let death come! I have moved you, I! . . . There is but one thing more I ask . . .

CHRISTIAN *(under the balcony)*: A kiss!

ROXANE *(drawing hastily back)*: What?

CYRANO: Oh!

ROXANE: You ask? . . .

CYRANO: Yes . . . I . . . *(to* CHRISTIAN*)* You are in too great haste!

CHRISTIAN: Since she is so moved, I must take advantage of it!

CYRANO *(to* ROXANE*)*: I . . . Yes, it is true I asked . . . but, merciful heavens! . . . I knew at once that I had been too bold.

ROXANE *(a shade disappointed)*: You insist no more than so?

CYRANO: Indeed, I insist . . . without insisting! Yes! yes! but your modesty shrinks! . . . I insist, but yet . . . the kiss I begged . . . refuse it me!

CHRISTIAN *(to* CYRANO, *pulling at his cloak)*: Why?

CYRANO: Hush, Christian!

ROXANE *(bending over the balcony rail)*: What are you whispering?

CYRANO: Reproaches to myself for having gone too far; I was saying "Hush, Christian!"

CHRISTIAN: Insist upon the kiss! . . .

CYRANO: No, I will not!

CHRISTIAN: Sooner or later . . .

CYRANO: It is true! It must come, the moment of inebriation when your lips shall imperiously be impelled toward each other, because the one is fledged with youthful gold and the other is so soft a pink! . . . *(To himself.)* I had rather it should be because . . .

ROXANE *(returning to the balcony)*: Are you there? We were speaking of . . . of . . . of a . . .

CYRANO: Kiss. The word is sweet. Why does your fair lip stop at it? If the mere word burns it, what will be of the thing itself? Do not make it into a fearful matter, and then fear! Did you not a moment ago insensibly leave playfulness behind and slip without trepidation from a smile to a sigh, from a sigh to a tear? Slip but a little further in the same blessed direction: from a tear to a kiss there is scarcely a dividing shiver!

ROXANE: Say no more!

CYRANO: A kiss! When all is said, what is a kiss? An oath of allegiance taken in closer proximity, a promise more precise, a seal on a confession, a rose-red dot upon the letter i in loving; a secret which elects the mouth for ear; an instant of eternity murmuring like a bee; balmy communion with a flavor of flowers; a fashion of inhaling each other's heart, and of tasting, on the brink of the lips, each other's soul!

ROXANE: Say no more . . . no more!

CYRANO: A kiss, madame, is a thing so noble that the Queen of France, on the most fortunate of lords, bestowed one, did the queen herself!

ROXANE: If that be so . . .

CYRANO *(with increasing fervor)*: Like Buckingham I have suffered in long silence, like him I worship a queen, like him I am sorrowful and unchanging . . .

ROXANE: Like him you enthrall through the eyes the heart that follows you!

CYRANO *(to himself, sobered)*: True, I am handsome . . . I had forgotten!

ROXANE: Come then and gather it, the supreme flower . . .

CYRANO *(pushing* CHRISTIAN *toward the balcony)*: Go!

ROXANE: . . . tasting of the heart.

CYRANO: Go!

ROXANE: . . . murmuring like a bee . . .

CYRANO: Go!

CHRISTIAN *(hesitating)*: But now I feel as if I ought not!

ROXANE: . . . making eternity an instant . . .

CYRANO *(pushing* CHRISTIAN*)*: Scale the balcony, you donkey!

(CHRISTIAN *springs toward the balcony, and climbs by means of the bench, the vine, the posts and balusters.)*

CHRISTIAN: Ah, Roxane! *(He clasps her to him, and bends over her lips.)*

CYRANO: Ha! . . . What a turn of the screw to my heart! . . . Kiss, banquet of love at which I am Lazarus, a crumb drops from your table even to me, here in the shade. . . . Yes, in my outstretched heart a little falls, as I feel that upon the lip pressing her lip Roxane kisses the words spoken by me!₅

"THOUGH I GIVE MY BODY TO BE BURNED . . ."

I beg would-be missionaries to remember that though you give your bodies to be burned, and have not love, it profits nothing—nothing! You can take nothing greater to the unchurched world than the marks and reflection of the love of God on your own character. That is the universal language. It will take you years to speak Chinese, or the dialects of India. From the day you land, however, that language of love, understood by all, will be pouring forth its unconscious eloquence. It is the man or woman who is the missionary, it is not his or her words. Character is the message.[6]

HENRY DRUMMOND

From *The Greatest Thing in the World*

VARIATIONS ON THE WORD LOVE

There is a word we use to plug

holes with. It's the right size for those warm

blanks in speech, for those red heart-

shaped vacancies on the page that look nothing

like real hearts. Add lace

and you can sell it.

We insert it also in one empty

space on the printed form

that comes with no instructions. There are whole

magazines with not much in them

but the word love, *you can*

rub it all over your body and you

can cook with it too. How do we know

it isn't what goes on at the cool

debaucheries of slugs under damp

pieces of cardboard? As for weed-

seedlings nosing their tough snouts up

among the lettuces, they shout it.

Love! Love! sing the soldiers, raising

their glittering knives in salute.

Then there's the two

of us. This word

is far too short for us, it has only

four letters, too sparse

to fill those deep bare

vacuums between the stars

that press on us with their deafness.

It's not love we don't wish

to fall into, but that fear.

This word is not enough but it will

have to do. It's a single

vowel in this metallic

silence, a mouth that says

O again and again in wonder

and pain, a breath, a finger-

grip on a cliffside. You can

hold on or let go.[7]

MARGARET ATWOOD

SHE WALKS IN BEAUTY

She walks in beauty, like the night
Of cloudless climes and starry skies;
And all that's best of dark and bright
Meet in her aspect and her eyes:
Thus mellowed to that tender light
Which heaven to gaudy day denies.

One shade the more, one ray the less,
Had half impaired the nameless grace
Which waves in every raven tress,
Or softly lightens o'er her face;
Where thoughts serenely sweet express
How pure, how dear their dwelling place

And on that cheek, and o'er that brow,
So soft, so calm, yet eloquent,
The smiles that win, the tints that glow,
But tell of days in goodness spent,

A mind at peace with all below,
A heart whose love is innocent.[8]

LORD BYRON

A MIDSUMMER NIGHT'S DREAM

ON FALLING IN LOVE

"LORD, WHAT FOOLS THESE MORTALS BE!"
ROBERT LOUIS STEVENSON

There is only one event in life which really astonishes a man and startles him out of his prepared opinions. Everything else befalls him very much as he expected. Event succeeds to event, with an agreeable variety indeed, but with little that is either startling or intense; they form together no more than a sort of background, or running accompaniment to the man's own reflections; and he falls naturally into a cool, curious, and smiling habit of mind, and builds himself up in a conception of life which expects tomorrow to be after the pattern of today and yesterday. He may be accustomed to the vagaries of his friends and acquaintances under the influence of love. He may sometimes look forward to it for himself with an incomprehensible expectation. But it is a subject in which neither intuition nor the behavior of others will help the philosopher to the truth. There is probably nothing rightly thought or rightly written on this matter of love that is not a piece of the person's experience. I remember an anecdote of a well-known French theorist, who was debating a point eagerly in his *cénacle*. It was objected against him that he had never experienced love. Whereupon he arose, left the society, and made it a point not to return to it until he considered that he had supplied the defect. "Now," he remarked, on entering, "now I am in a position to continue the discussion." Perhaps he had not penetrated very deeply into the subject after all; but the story indicates right thinking, and may serve as an epilogue to readers of this essay.

When at last the scales fall from his eyes, it is not without something of the nature of dismay that the man finds himself in such changed conditions. He has to deal with commanding emotions instead of the easy dislikes and preferences in which he has hitherto passed his days; and he recognizes capabilities

"BUT ON THIS OCCASION ALL IS DIFFERENT."

for pain and pleasure of which he had not yet suspected the existence. Falling in love is the one illogical adventure, the one thing of which we are tempted to think as supernatural, in our trite and reasonable world. The effect is out of all proportion with the cause. Two persons, neither of them, it may be, very amiable or very beautiful, meet, speak a little, and look a little into each other's eyes. That has been done a dozen or so of times in the experience of either with no great result. But on this occasion all is different. They fall at once into that state in which another person becomes to us the very gist and center-point of God's creation, and demolishes our laborious theories with a smile; in which our ideas are so bound up with the one master-thought that even the trivial cares of our own person become so many acts of devotion, and the love of life itself is translated into a wish to remain in the same world with so precious and desirable a fellow-creature. And all the while their acquaintances look on in stupor, and ask each other, with almost passionate emphasis, what so-and-so can see in that woman, or such-an-one in that man? I am sure, gentlemen, I cannot tell you. For my part, I cannot think what the women mean. It might be very well, if the Apollo Belvedere should suddenly glow all over into life, and step forward from the pedestal with that godlike air of his. But of the misbegotten changelings who call themselves men, and prate intolerably over dinner tables, I never saw one who seemed worthy to inspire love—no, nor read of any, except Leonardo da Vinci, and perhaps Goethe in his youth. About women I entertain a somewhat different opinion; but there, I have the misfortune to be a man.

"LOVE SHOULD RUN OUT TO MEET LOVE WITH OPEN ARMS."

There are many matters in which you may waylay Destiny, and bid him stand and deliver. Hard work, high thinking, adventurous excitement, and a great deal more that forms a part of this or the other person's spiritual bill of fare, are within the reach of almost anyone who can dare a little and be patient. But it is by no means in the way of everyone to fall in love. You know the difficulty Shakespeare was put into when Queen Elizabeth asked him to show Falstaff in love. I do not believe that Henry Fielding was ever in love. Scott, if it were not for a passage or two in *Rob Roy*, would give me very much the same effect. These are great names and (what is more to the purpose) strong, healthy, highstrung, and generous natures, of whom the reverse might have been expected. As for the inumerable army of anemic and tailorish persons who occupy the face of this planet with so much propriety, it is palpably absurd to imagine them in any such situation as a love affair. A wet rag goes safely by the fire; and if a man is blind, he cannot expect to be much impressed by romantic scenery. Apart from all this, many lovable people miss each other in the world, or meet under some unfavorable star. There is the nice and critical moment of declaration to be got over.

From timidity or lack of opportunity a good half of possible love cases never get so far, and at least another quarter do there cease and determine. A very adroit person, to be sure, manages to prepare the way and out with his declaration in the nick of time. And then there is a fine solid sort of man, who goes on from snub to snub; and if he has to declare forty times, will continue imperturbably declaring, amid the astonished consideration of men and angels, until he has a favorable answer. I daresay, if one were a woman, one would like to marry a man who was capable of doing this, but not quite one who had done so. It is just a little bit abject, and somehow just a little bit gross; and marriages in which one of the parties has been thus battered into consent scarcely form agreeable subjects for meditation. Love should run out to meet love with open arms. Indeed, the ideal story is that of two people who go into love step for step, with a fluttered consciousness, like a pair of children venturing together into a dark room.

"...AS THE MAN KNOWS WHAT IT IS IN HIS OWN HEART..."

From the first moment when they see each other, with a pang of curiosity, through stage after stage of growing pleasure and embarrassment, they can read the expression of their own trouble in each other's eyes. There is here no declaration properly so called; the feeling is so plainly shared, that as soon as the man knows what it is in his own heart, he is sure of what it is in the woman's.

This simple accident of falling in love is as beneficial as it is astonishing. It arrests the petrifying influence of years, disproves cold-blooded and cynical conclusions, and awakens dormant sensibilities. Hitherto the man had found it a good policy to disbelieve the existence of any enjoyment which was out of his reach; and thus he turned his back upon the strong, sunny parts of nature, and accustomed himself to look exclusively on

> "THERE LET HIM SIT AWHILE TO HATCH
>
> DELIGHTFUL HOPES
>
> AND PERILOUS ILLUSIONS."

what was common and dull. He accepted a prose ideal, let himself go blind of many sympathies by disuse; and if he were young and witty, or beautiful, willfully forewent these advantages. He joined himself to the following of what, in the old mythology of love, was prettily called *nonchaloir;* and in an odd mixture of feelings, a fling of self-respect, a preference for selfish liberty, and a great dash of that fear with which honest people regard serious interests, kept himself back from the straightforward course of life among certain selected activities. And now, all of a sudden, he is unhorsed, like St. Paul, from his infidel affectation. His heart, which has been ticking accurate seconds for the last year, gives a bound and begins to beat high and irregularly in his breast. It seems as if he had never heard or felt or seen until that moment; and by the report of his memory, he must have lived his past life between sleep or waking, or with the preoccupied attention of a brown study. He is practically incommoded by the generosity of his feelings, smiles much when he is alone, and develops a habit of looking rather blankly upon the moon and stars.

But it is not at all within the province of a prose essayist to give a picture of this hyperbolical frame of mind; and the thing has been done already, and that to admiration.

In *Adelaide*, in Tennyson's *Maud*, and in some of Heine's songs, you get the absolute expression of this midsummer spirit. Romeo and Juliet were very much in love; although they tell me some German critics are of a different opinion, probably the same who would have us think Mercutio a dull fellow. Poor Antony was in love, and no mistake. That lay figure Marius, in *Les Misérables*, is also a genuine case in his own way, and worth observation. A good many of George Sand's people are thoroughly in love; and so are a good many of George Meredith's.

Altogether, there is plenty to read on the subject. If the root of the matter be in him, and if he has the requisite chords to set in vibration, a young man may occasionally enter, with the key of art, into that land of Beulah which is upon the borders of Heaven and within sight of the City of Love. There let him sit awhile to hatch delightful hopes and perilous illusions.

"THE PRESENCE OF THE TWO LOVERS IS SO ENCHANTING TO EACH OTHER . . ."

One thing that accompanies the passion in its first blush is certainly difficult to explain. It comes (I do not quite see how) that from having a very supreme sense of pleasure in all parts of life—in lying down to sleep, in waking, in motion, in breathing, in continuing to be—the lover begins to regard his happiness as beneficial for the rest of the world and highly meritorious in himself.

Our race has never been able contentedly to suppose that the noise of its wars, conducted by a few young gentlemen in a corner of an inconsiderable star, does not re-echo among the courts of Heaven with quite a formidable effect. In much the same taste, when people find a great to-do in their own breasts, they imagine it must have some influence in their neighborhood. The presence of the two lovers is so enchanting to each other that it seems as if it must be the best thing possible for everybody else. They are half inclined to fancy it is because of them and their love that the sky is blue and the sun shines. And certainly the weather is usually fine while people are courting.

. . . In point of fact, although the happy man feels very kindly towards others of his own sex, there is apt to be something too much of the magnifico in his demeanor. If people grow presuming and self-important over such matters as a dukedom or the Holy See, they will scarcely support the dizziest elevation in life without some suspicion of a strut; and the dizziest elevation is to love and be loved in return.

Consequently, accepted lovers are a trifle condescending in their address to other men. An overweening sense of the passion and importance of life hardly conduces to simplicity of manner. To women, they feel very nobly, very purely, and very generously, as if they were so many Joan-of-Arc's; but this does not come out in their behavior; and they treat them to Grandisonian airs marked with a suspicion of fatuity. I am not quite certain that women do not like this sort of thing; but really, after having bemused myself over *Daniel Deronda*, I have given up trying to understand what they like.

If it did nothing else, this sublime and ridiculous superstition, that the pleasure of the pair is somehow blessed to others, and everybody is made happier in their happiness, would serve at least to keep love generous and greathearted. Nor is it quite a baseless superstition after all. Other lovers are hugely interested. They strike the nicest balance between pity and approval, when they see people aping the greatness of their own sentiments.

"...THE PLEASURE OF THE PAIR IS SOMEHOW BLESSED..."

[57]

It is an understood thing in the play that while the young gentlefolk are courting on the terrace, a rough flirtation is being carried on, and a light, trivial sort of love is growing up, between the footman and the singing chambermaid.

As people are generally cast for the leading parts in their own imaginations, the reader can apply the parallel to real life without much chance of going wrong. In short, they are quite sure this other love-affair is not so deep-seated as their own, but they like dearly to see it going forward. And love, considered as a spectacle, must have attractions for many who are not of the confraternity. The sentimental old maid is a commonplace of the novelists; and he must be rather a poor sort of human being, to be sure, who can look on at this pretty madness without indulgence and sympathy. For nature commends itself to people with a most insinuating art; the busiest is now and again arrested by a great sunset; and you may be as pacific or as cold-blooded as you will, but you cannot help some emotion when you read of well-disputed battles, or meet a pair of lovers in the lane.

Certainly, whatever it may be with regard to the world at large, this idea of beneficent pleasure is true as between the sweethearts. To do good and communicate is the lover's grand intention. It is the happiness of the other that makes his own most intense gratification. It is not possible to disentangle the different emotions, the pride, humility, pity, and passion, which are excited by a look of happy love or an unexpected caress.

To make one's self beautiful, to dress the hair, to excel in talk, to do anything and all things that puff out the character and attributes and make them imposing in the eyes of others, is not only to magnify one's self, but to offer the most delicate homage at the same time. And it is in this latter intention that they are done by lovers; for the essence of love is kindness; and indeed it may be best defined as passionate kindness: kindness, so to speak, run mad and become importunate and violent. Vanity in a merely personal sense exists no longer. The lover takes a perilous pleasure in privately displaying his weak points and having them, one after another, accepted and condoned. He wishes to be assured that he is not loved for this or that good quality, but for himself, or something as like himself as he can contrive to set forward.

"WORDS AND ACTS ARE EASILY WRENCHED FROM THEIR TRUE SIGNIFICANCE . . ."

For, although it may have been a very difficult thing to paint the marriage of Cana, or write the fourth act of *Antony and Cleopatra*, there is a more difficult piece of art before every one in this world who cares to set about explaining his own character to others. Words and acts are easily wrenched from their true significance; and they are all the language we have to come and go upon. A pitiful job we make of it, as a rule.

For better or worse, people mistake our meaning and take our emotions at a wrong valuation. And generally we rest pretty content with our failures; we are content to be misapprehended by cackling flirts; but when once a man is moonstruck with this affection of love, he makes it a point of honor to clear such dubieties away. He cannot have the Best of her Sex misled upon a point of this importance; and his pride revolts at being loved in a mistake.

He discovers a great reluctance to return on former periods of his life. To all that has not been shared with her, rights and duties, bygone fortunes and dispositions, he can look back only by a difficult and repugnant effort of the will. That he should have wasted some years in ignorance of what alone was really important, that he may have entertained the thought of other women with any show of complacency, is a burden almost too heavy for his self-respect. But it is the thought of another past that rankles in his spirit like a poisoned wound. That he himself made a fashion of being alive in the bald, beggarly days before a certain meeting, is deplorable enough in all good conscience. But that She should have permitted herself the same liberty seems inconsistent with a Divine providence.

A great many people run down jealousy, on the score that it is an artificial feeling, as well as practically inconvenient. This is scarcely fair; for the feeling on which it merely attends, like an ill-humored courtier, is itself artificial in exactly the same sense and to the same degree. I suppose what is meant by that objection is that jealousy has not always been a character of man; formed no part of that very modest kit of sentiments with which he is supposed to have begun the world; but waited to make its appearance in better days and among richer natures.

And this is equally true of love, and friendship, and love of country, and delight in what they call the beauties of nature, and most other things worth having. Love, in particular, will not endure any historical scrutiny: to all who have fallen across it, it is one of the most incontestable facts in the world; but if you begin to ask what it was in other periods and countries, in Greece for instance, the strangest doubts begin to spring up, and everything seems so vague and changing that a dream is logical in comparison. Jealousy, at any rate, is one of the consequences of love; you may like it or not, at pleasure; but there it is.

It is not exactly jealousy, however, that we feel when we reflect on the past of those we love. A bundle of letters found after years of happy union creates no sense of insecurity in the present; and yet it will pain a man sharply. The two people entertain no vulgar doubt of each other: but this preexistence of both occurs to the mind as something indelicate. To be altogether right, they should have had twin birth together, at the same moment with the feeling that unites them. Then indeed it would be simple and perfect and without reserve or afterthought. Then they would understand each other with a fullness impossible otherwise. There would be no barrier between them of associations that cannot be imparted. They would be led into none of those comparisons that send the blood back to the heart. And they would know that there had been no time lost, and they had been together as much as was possible.

For besides terror for the separation that must follow some time or other in the future, men feel anger, and something like remorse, when they think of that other separation which endured until they met.[9]

Someone has written that love makes people believe in immortality, because there seems not to be room enough in life for so great a tenderness, and it is inconceivable that the most masterful of our emotions should have no more than the spare moments of a few years. Indeed, it seems strange; but if we call to mind analogies, we can hardly regard it as impossible.

"The blind bow-boy," who smiles upon us from the end of terraces in old Dutch gardens, laughingly hails his bird-bolts among a fleeting generation. But for as fast as ever he shoots, the game dissolves and disappears into eternity from under his falling arrows; this one is gone ere he is struck; the other has but time to make one gesture and give one passionate cry; and they are all the things of a moment. When the generation is gone, when the play is over, when the thirty years' panorama has been withdrawn in tatters from the stage of the world, we may ask what has become of these great, weighty, and undying loves, and the sweethearts who despised mortal conditions in a fine credulity; and they can only show us a few songs in a bygone taste, a few actions worth remembering, and a few children who have retained some happy stamp from the disposition of their parents.9

XXXVIII
FIRST TIME HE KISSED ME

First time he kissed me, he but only kissed

The fingers of this hand wherewith I write;

And ever since it grew more clean and white,

Slow to world-greetings, quick with its "Oh, list,"

When the angels speak. A ring of amethyst

I could not wear here, plainer to my sight,

Than that first kiss. The second passed in height

The first, and sought the forehead, and half missed,

Half falling on the hair. O beyond meed!

That was the chrism of love, which love's own crown,

With sanctifying sweetness, did precede.

The third upon my lips was folded down

In perfect, purple state; since when, indeed,

I have been proud and said, "My Love, my own."₁₀

ELIZABETH BARRETT BROWNING

From *Sonnets from the Portuguese*

Chapter 2

FIRST LOVE

Two ten year-old girls sit in the shade under the kitchen window. They have no idea that anyone hears their conversation.

"I think Jeff likes me."

"How come?"

"'Cuz he said his mom was going to buy me a special Valentine."

"What special Valentine?"

"Oh, you know, the kind that you buy one at a time at the drug store."

"Ugh, I wouldn't want a boy to do that for me."

There is a long reflective pause.

"Hey, come on, let's jump rope."

Jeff and Valentines are forgotten with the slap of the rope on the cement driveway. Pretty soon another little girl joins them and then there are three piping voices chanting a jump rope rhyme that little girls have chanted for a hundred years:

"First comes love . . .
Then comes marriage . . .
Then comes a baby in a baby carriage."

First love is not always chronological. Poets and novelists have expressed the beauty of this experience through the years. The one common denominator for all who make this discovery away from childhood is, "It makes me feel so young."

THE OWL AND THE PUSSY-CAT

The Owl and the Pussy-Cat went to sea
In a beautiful pea-green boat.
They took some honey, and plenty of money,
Wrapped up in a five pound note.
The Owl looked up to the stars above,
And sang to a small guitar,
"O lovely Pussy! O Pussy, my love,
What a beautiful Pussy you are,
You are,
You are!
What a beautiful Pussy you are!"

Pussy said to the Owl, "You elegant fowl!
How charmingly sweet you sing!
O let us be married! Too long we have tarried:
But what shall we do for a ring?"
They sailed away for a year and a day,
To the land where the Bong-Tree grows,
And there in the wood a Piggy-wig stood,
With a ring at the end of his nose,
His nose,
His nose,
With a ring at the end of his nose.

"Dear Pig, are you willing to sell for one shilling
Your ring?" Said the Piggy, "I will."
So they took it away, and were married next day
By the Turkey who lives on the hill.
They dined on mince, and slices of quince,
Which they ate with a runcible spoon;
And hand in hand, on the edge of the sand,
They danced by the light of the moon,
The moon,
The moon,
They danced by the light of the moon.

TOM MEETS BECKY

MARK TWAIN
From *The Adventures of Tom Sawyer*

*As punishment for stopping to talk with Huckleberry Finn and consequently
being late to school, the master has Tom sit at an empty desk on the girls' side
of the room, where Tom spies two long tails of yellow hair hanging down a
back. There is an empty spot at the desk next to her.*

The titter that rippled around the room appeared to abash
the boy, but in reality that result was caused rather more by his
worshipful awe of his unknown idol. . . . He sat down upon the
end of the pine bench and the girl hitched herself away from
him with a toss of her head. Nudges and winks and whispers
traversed the room, but Tom sat still with his arms upon the
long, low desk before him, and seemed to study his book.

By and by attention ceased from him, and the accustomed
school murmur rose upon the dull air once more. Presently the
boy began to steal furtive glances at the girl. She observed it,
"made a mouth" at him and gave him the back of her head for
the space of a minute. When she cautiously faced around again,
a peach lay before her. She thrust it away. Tom gently put it
back. She thrust it away again, but with less animosity. Tom
patiently returned it to its place. Then she let it remain. Tom
scrawled on his slate, "Please take it—I got more." The girl

glanced at the words, but made no sign. Now the boy began to draw something on the slate, hiding his work with his left hand. For a time the girl refused to notice, but her human curiosity presently began to manifest itself by hardly perceptible signs. The boy worked on, apparently unconscious. The girl made a sort of noncommittal attempt to see it, but the boy did not betray that he was aware of it. At last she gave in and hesitantly whispered: "Let me see it."

Tom partly uncovered a dismal caricature of a house with two gable ends to it and a corkscrew of smoke issuing from the chimney. Then the girl's interest began to fasten itself upon the work and she forgot everything else. When it was finished, she gazed a moment, then whispered: "It's nice—make a man."

The artist erected a man in the front yard, that resembled a derrick. He could have stepped over the house; but the girl was not hypercritical; she was satisfied with the monster, and whispered:

"It's a beautiful man—now make me coming along."

Tom drew an hourglass with a full moon and straw limbs to it and armed the spreading fingers with a portentous fan. The girl said:

"It's ever so nice—I wish I could draw."

"It's easy," whispered Tom, "I'll learn you."

"Oh, will you? When?"

"At noon. Do you go home to dinner?"

"I'll stay if you will."

"Good—that's a whack. What's your name?"

"Becky Thatcher. What's yours? Oh, I know. It's Thomas Sawyer."

"That's the name they lick me by. I'm Tom when I'm good. You can call me Tom, will you?"

"Yes."

Now Tom began to scrawl something on the slate, hiding the words from the girl. But she was not backward this time. She begged to see. Tom said: "Oh, it ain't anything."

"Yes, it is."

"No, it ain't. You don't want to see."

"Yes, I do, indeed I do. Please let me."

"You'll tell."

"No I won't—'deed and 'deed and double 'deed I won't."

"You won't tell anybody at all? Ever, as long as you live?"

"No, I won't ever tell anybody. Now let me."

"Oh, you don't want to see!"

"Now that you treat me so, I *will* see." And she put her small hand upon his and a little scuffle ensued, Tom pretending to resist in earnest but letting his hand slip by degrees till these words were revealed, "*I love you.*"

"Oh, you bad thing!" And she hit his hand a smart rap, but reddened and looked pleased nevertheless.

Just at this juncture the boy felt a slow, fateful grip closing on his ear, and a steady lifting impulse. In that vise he was borne across the room and deposited in his own seat, under a peppering fire of giggles from the whole school. Then the master stood over him during a few awful moments, and finally moved away to his throne without saying a word. But although Tom's ear tingled, his heart was jubilant.

JENNY KISSED ME

Jenny kissed me when we met,

Jumping from the chair she sat in;

Time, you thief, who love to get

Sweets into your lists, put that in!

Say I'm weary, say I'm sad,

Say that health and wealth have missed me;

Say I'm growing old—but add,

Jenny kissed me. [11]

LEIGH HUNT

THE COUPLE FROM NAZARETH

PAUL M. MILLER

We are on our way up to The City. It's a feast time and we are
camped out in a field. There are people everywhere. While I've
said nothing to my parents, Joseph's tent is near ours. If they
knew, we'd probably pull up the stakes and find a new camp site.
I'm so glad Joseph is near-by. I've spent most of the morning
hoping I'll run into him. I've barely noticed how beautiful the
temple is with the morning sun making it look like alabaster.
The City is set on a hill.

One of the rabbis read from whom Joseph calls "Our Prince of
Prophets"—Isaiah. The Messiah passage was read. I could tell
that people took great hope in God's promise of a deliverer.

We are on our way home. Mother is getting suspicious about
what I feel toward Joseph. She said she could tell I watched for
him at our camp site. I finally gave up trying to hide my feelings toward him; I put my head on Mother's well-padded shoulder and finally admitted for the first time to anyone but myself,
that I love Joseph. Her reply was a bit reserved, "Joseph is a
good man;" but I could tell she was pleased.

It's official—Joseph and I are betrothed. We have registered our happy intentions with the rabbi. He gave us his blessing and reminded us that we were not married yet. I am sure I blushed, and Joseph nodded gravely.

I am so in love. When Joseph comes over to our house, which is almost every night, he and my father sit at the table and talk about dreams. Joseph's great dream is to see his carpentry shop expand and receive much larger jobs—maybe even from the province. He and Father often discuss the hopes of Israel. Mother and I sit together and listen to the men. We are both sewing for my trousseau. A peddler came through Nazareth last week with lengths of fabric already dyed. There was a blue that I know Joseph will love to see me in.

I have never been so shocked in all of my years. I'm not even sure if it really happened or not. Last night as I knelt for my evening prayer, a messenger from heaven appeared to me. He was like a bright light, but I could also make out a form. Then the most surprising thing happened—he spoke to me. And, what he said made me tremble.

First he greeted me and called me blessed. (If I hadn't been so frightened I would have said, "Oh, I know I'm blessed!") Then in a kindly voice, he told me not to be fearful. This was to prepare me for what was to follow. The angel messenger said God is pleased with me and that I am going to become pregnant—*pregnant!*, and that I will be the mother of Messiah.

"But I am a virgin," I whispered to the angel, "I still live in my father's house. Joseph and I have not come together. How can I be pregnant?" Then the angel answered my question, "With God, all things are possible."

As you can imagine, I did not close my eyes the whole night through. All I could think of was my beloved Joseph and how he would react to this news. Toward morning, I finally said, "Your will be done, Lord."

My soul is in ecstasy! Can it be? Could a lowly person like me become mother of Messiah? Who can I tell? The High Priest in Jerusalem? No, I would be laughed to scorn. I longed to tell Mother this morning, but I couldn't. She'd say I'm putting on airs.

And Joseph, my beloved Joseph—how will he ever understand?

I've been away from Nazareth visiting with my cousin Elizabeth for three months. We had a glorious time together. We both have a secret.

When I left Elizabeth's home today it was easy to tell I was pregnant. People stared and pointed me out as I walked home to Nazareth. When I was close to town, friends, neighbors, and total strangers realized that the girl betrothed to Joseph was already with child.

Now I am home and safe in my own bedroom. My parents know the whole story. Mother is most comforting, but my father won't talk about it. Joseph is coming by tonight. I have not told him a thing about the heavenly messenger. Oh, dear, dear practical Joseph, will you still love me?

When Joseph knocked, I fled to my room and wept. Mother came in and wept with me. I did not see Joseph. Mother tried to explain, but could not. He had heard of my condition from his brethren and the neighbors and came to confront me with it. He had even brought along a witness, in case he was needed. My beloved finally left in great distress. He told my parents that he plans to send me away until the baby comes. That's what happened to Rachel two doors down from us. But she was guilty of fornication, and I am not.

How long will you forget me, O Lord? How long will you hide your face from me? Consider and hear me, O Lord my God.

The Lord has heard my cry! Blessed be His name! Joseph came to me while my parents were gone. There was a knock at the door, I did not know it was him. I smoothed my hair and went to see who it was. It was Joseph! I nervously invited him in. When the door closed he dropped to his knees and sobbed, "My darling Mary, please forgive me. I have been so wrong."

"Then you understand," I said.

"An angel appeared to me in a dream," he answered, "and the angel said to me, 'Joseph, you son of David, do not be afraid to take Mary. For that which has been conceived in her is of the Holy Spirit. She will give birth to a son. You are to name Him Jesus, because He will save His people from their sins.'"

Then, while still on his knees, Joseph took both my hands and begged, "My little Mary. Can you ever forgive me?"

Together we bowed in silence; then Joseph prayed brokenly: "Return to your rest, Oh my soul; for the Lord has dealt bountifully with us, and we shall walk uprightly before the Lord all of our days."

"All of our days"—with Joseph at my side and little Jesus in my arms . . . well, we will face that later.

FIRST LOVE

I ne'er was struck before that hour
With love so sudden and so sweet,
Her face it bloomed like a sweet flower
And stole my heart away complete.

My face turned pale as deadly pale,
My legs refused to walk away,
And when she looked, what could I ail?
My life and all seemed to turn to clay.

And then my blood rushed to my face
And took my eyesight quite away,
The trees and bushes round the place
Seemed midnight at noonday.

I could not see a single thing,
Words from my eyes did start—
They spoke as chords do from the string,
And blood burnt round my heart.

Are flowers the winter's choice?
Is love's bed always snow?
She seemed to hear my silent voice,
Not love's appeals to know.

I never saw so sweet a face
As that I stood before.
My heart has left its dwelling place
And can return no more. ₁₂

JOHN CLARE

Sleep, my child, lie still and slumber,

All through the night;

Guardian angels God will lend thee,

All through the night;

Soft the drowsy hours are creeping,

Hill and vale in slumber sleeping,

Mother dear her watch is keeping,

All through the night.

God is here, thou'lt not be lonely,

All through the night;

'Tis not I who guards thee only.

All through the night.

Night's dark shade will soon be over,

Still my watchful care shall hover,

God with me His watch is keeping,

All through the night.

ANONYMOUS

THE LAMB

Little lamb, who made thee?
Dost thou know who made thee?
Gave thee life, and bid thee feed,
By the streams and o'er the mead;
Gave thee clothing of delight,
Softest clothing, woolly, bright;
Gave thee such a tender voice,
Making all the vales rejoice?

Little lamb, who made thee?
Dost thou know who made thee?

Little lamb, I'll tell thee;
Little lamb, I'll thee.
He is called by thy name,
For He calls Himself a Lamb;
He is meek and He is mild,
He became a little child.
I a child, and thou a lamb,
We are called by His name.

Little lamb, God bless thee!
Little lamb, God bless thee![13]

WILLIAM BLAKE

THE FLEA

And here's the happy bounding flea—
You cannot tell the he from she.
The sexes look alike, you see;
But she can tell, and so can he.

ROLAND YOUNG

YOUNG LOVE

RICHARD EXLEY

From *Forever in Love*

I was only six years old the first time I fancied myself in love. That was more than 40 years ago, and try as I might I can't remember her name, the color of her eyes, or how she looked. I do remember the day she gave me a small gift-wrapped box, proudly announcing that she had bought it with her own money. Inside was a pair of cuff links and 37 shiny copper pennies.

Having never seen cuff links, I had no idea what to do with them. Finally, I decided to give them to my best friend. The pennies I kept. Every afternoon on the way home from school, I stopped by the corner store and treated myself to an infinite variety of penny candies. For nearly a month, the booty of love made me the richest kid on the block.

This was just the first in a series of young loves. In the sixth grade I fell hard for a pretty girl named Leah. That lasted until I went to church camp during summer vacation. There I lost my heart to a young lady with copper-colored hair. In time she was replaced by the girl I sat behind in my eighth-grade English class.

When I was 16, I went swimming in the South Platte River on a hot August afternoon with a pretty girl who would one day become my wife. Carelessly we splashed in the river, oblivious to the sun's deadly rays. Later that evening I rubbed Noxema skin cream on her sunburned shoulders, and to this day Noxema skin cream smells like love to me.

By now you are probably remembering your own young loves—and with a bit of chagrin no doubt. Don't be embarrassed. There is nothing wrong with puppy love—not if you are in the first grade, or the fifth grade, or even 15 years old. The thing that concerns me, though, is that many couples never seem to outgrow their childish fantasies. Years later they continue to believe in Prince Charming, Cinderella, and living "happily after."

Unfortunately, life in the real world is not at all like a fairy tale. Prince Charming puts on 25 pounds and his dirty clothes are lying around. Cinderella discovers that homemaking isn't all that it is cracked up to be. With laundry, housecleaning, and child care, there is little time or energy left for being romantic. And on those rare occasions when she is feeling amorous, Prince Charming is engrossed in Monday night football or barricaded behind the evening paper.

Given this all too familiar scenario, many couples conclude that they don't love each other any more. In truth, only young love has died with its unrealistic expectations. If they can accept this fact and move past it, they will likely discover a new and deeper love. It will be a more mature love, based on real commitment, rather than mere emotion.

Jacob was in love with Rachel and said [to her father], "I'll work for you seven years in return for your younger daughter Rachel" Laban said, "It's better that I give her to you than to some other man. Stay here with me." So Jacob served seven years to get Rachel, but they seemed like only a few days to him because of his love for her (Gen. 29:18-20, NIV).14

A QUOI BON DIRE

Seventeen years ago you said

Something that sounded like Good-bye;

And everybody thinks that you are dead,

But I.

So I, as I grow stiff and cold

To this and that say Good-bye too;

And everybody sees that I am old

But you.

And one fine morning in a sunny lane

Some boy and girl will meet and kiss and swear

That nobody can love their way again

While over there

You will have smiled, I shall have tossed your hair.[15]

CHARLOTTE MEW

THE FIRST DAY

I wish I could remember the first day,

First hour, first moment of your meeting me;

If bright or dim the season, it might be

Summer or winter for aught I can say.

So unrecorded did it slip away,

So blind was I to see and to forsee,

So dull to mark the budding of my tree

That would not blossom yet for many a May.

If only I could recollect it! Such

A day of days! I let it come and go

As traceless as a thaw of bygone snow.

It seemed to mean so little, meant so much!

If only now I could recall that touch,

First touch of hand in hand!—Did one but know.

CHRISTINA ROSSETTI

Saint Valentine's

"Show her how much you love her
with red roses—$75.00 per dozen."

"It Isn't Valentine's Day without a
Five Pound Box of exquisite candy!"

Can you remember when Valentine's Day was a celebration of
construction paper red hearts with pasted paper dollies and
those little pastel heart candies with love sayings printed on
them—you know, things like "Be Mine" and "Hug Me"? There
were larger candy hearts with epic messages,
"2 good 2B 4got10."
Remember those?

POETRY

AND THEN THERE WAS VALENTINE POETRY.
SIMPLE VERSES THAT SEEMED TO SPRING OUT
OF THE SIMPLE FOUR LINES,

Roses are red,

Violets are blue,

Sugar is sweet,

And so are you.

THEN SOME CLOWN GOT HOLD OF THAT
TRADITIONAL QUATRAIN, AND TURNED IT INTO,

Roses are red,

Violets are blue,

Monkeys like you,

Belong in the zoo.

TODAY, VALENTINE POETRY IS LESS
DIRECT AND CERTAINLY MORE
TO THE POINT OF LOVE,

Let me give you my hand;
May it ever be there for you.
Let me give you my shoulder;
May it always comfort you.
Let me give you my arms;
May they only hold you.
Let me give you my heart;
May it only love you.

ANONYMOUS

L E G E N D S

THERE ARE THREE LEGENDS CONCERNING
THE ORIGINS OF ST. VALENTINES DAY.

I

The first involves a man named Valentine who secretly married young couples, even though the Roman Empire had banned the rite of marriage in an attempt to inscript all able-bodied men into the army and away from sentiment and romance. When the Emperor discovered Valentine's crime, he had him banished to prison.

I I

Another Valentine was imprisoned for his underground work with the Christian community. While in prison, says legend, he fell in love with the Emperor's blind daughter and healed her vision. Before his execution, Valentine wrote a love letter to the young woman, which he signed, "From your Valentine."

I I I

The third legend of a man named Valentine says that he adored all children and often gave them flowers and sweets. When he was imprisoned with other Christians, the children whose lives he touched wrote little notes and threw them through the prison bars to Valentine. It is believed that one of these Christian saints was executed on February 14.

Other traditions from long ago are also believed to have influenced Valentine's Day. Lovebirds were believed to have mated on February 14. And, young people in France and England would gather together on St. Valentine's Day. The boys would put their names in a box and the name each girl selected became their Valentine.

TRADITIONS

ROSES ARE RED, VIOLETS ARE BLUE

There was a time when girls and boys wrote their own Valentine
sentiments on homemade cards. Even with smears of white paste
and a misspelled word or two, these were popular verses:

Forget me not;
Forget me never
Until the sun
Has set forever.

I wish thee health;
I wish thee wealth;
I wish thee gold a store;
I wish thee Heaven after
death—
What could I wish thee more?

Cupid took aim—
Zing went the dart.
Every day is a valentine
With you in my heart!

There are good ships,
There are bad ships;
But the best ship,
Is friendship.

Roses were made to blossom;
Cheeks were made to blush;
Arms were made to rest in;
Lips were made to . . . Oh, hush!

First comes love,
Then comes marriage,
Then comes Sally
With a baby carriage.

Forget me not;
Forget me never
Until the sun
Has set forever.

ON SAINT
VALENTINE'S DAY

Hearts speak to hearts
of Valentine's Day;
Love is displayed
in a personal way.
Candy and flowers
and big lacy hearts
Are mementos of sweetness
the occasion imparts.

Each little gift says,
"I love you . . . I care,"
And the spirit of romance
floats in the air.
Sweet sentimental verses convey
Gifts from the heart
on Saint Valentine's Day.

AUTHOR UNKNOWN

Give her a hug this morning,
Give her the old-time kiss—
From the calendar's first to final,
There's only one day like this.

Rumple her hair a little,
In the old-time tender way,
Show her you haven't forgotten . . . This is
St. Valentine's Day.

Never take love for granted,
Don't be afraid to speak—
While you are pouring his coffee,
Fondle his whiskered cheek.

And over his shoulder bending,
"I love you," be sure to say.
Now is the time to do it . . .
This is St. Valentine's Day.

If lovers at times seem foolish,
As cynics will agree,
Then this is the very morning
When foolish it's wise to be.

We all need a lot more loving,
And more of true love's display,
So, let's be a little silly . . .
This is St. Valentine's Day. 16

EDGAR A. GUEST

Your First Sweet-Heart

From an Old Turn-of-the-Century Scrapbook

You never can forget her. She was so very young and innocent and pretty. She had such a way of looking at you over her
hymn book in church. She alone, of all the world, did not think
you a boy of eighteen, but wondered at your size, and your
learning, and of your faint foreshadowing of a sandy mustache,
and believed you every inch a man. When at those stupid
evening parties, when boys who should have been in the nursery
and girls who should have eaten suppers of bread and milk and
gone to sleep hours before, waltzed and flirted, and made themselves ill over oysters and late suppers, you were favored by a
glance of her eye or a whisper from her lips, you ascended to the
seventh heaven immediately. When once upon a certain memorable eve she polkaed with the druggist's clerk, and never
looked at you, how miserable you were. It is funny to think of
now, but it was not so funny then, for you were awfully in
earnest.

Once, at a picnic, she wore a white dress, and had roses
twined in her...hair, and she looked so like a bride that you

fairly trembled. Some time, you thought, in such a snowy costume, with just such blossoms in her hair, she might stand beside the altar, and you, most blessed of all mortals, might place a golden ring upon her finger; and when you were left alone with her for a moment some of your thoughts would form themselves into words, and though she blushed and ran away, and would not let you kiss her, she did not seem angry.

And then you were parted, somehow, for a little while, and when you met again she was walking with a gentleman of twenty-eight or thirty, and had neither word nor smile for you. Shortly after this some well-meaning gossip informed you that she was engaged to the tall gentleman and that it was a "splendid match." It was terrible news to you, and sent you off to the great city, where after a good deal of youthful grief, and many resolutions to die and haunt her, you recovered your equanimity, and began to make money and to call love stuff and nonsense.

You have a wife of your own now, and grown children—aye, even two or three toddling grandchildren about your hearth; your hair is gray, and you lock your heart up in the fireproof safe at your countinghouse when you go home at night. And you thought you had forgotten that little episode of your nineteenth year, until the other day when you read of her death. You know she had come to be a rather stout matron who wore glasses, but your heart went back and you saw her smiling and blushing, with her golden hair, dreaming of wedding robes and rings, and you laid your old gray head upon your office desk and wept for the memory of your first sweetheart.

Chapter 3
NOTHING WITHOUT LOVE

"To love is to be vulnerable," says C. S. Lewis, a gentle man and acquainted with both sides of that statement; not being loved can make a man inaccessible as well as lonely. Lewis was an Oxford educated, much-read author of some 40 books, Christian apologist, and confirmed bachelor who believed that the love of a woman had passed him by, that is until Joy Davidman Gresham came into his life. We who have seen the wonderful play and film about that romance, realize that the C. S. Lewis romance and eventual marriage had a bitter-sweet ending, that confirms the old maxim, "Better to have loved and lost, than never to have loved at all."

Tradition declares that the Apostle Paul was a

bachelor. What was in his mind when he wrote his

first letter to the Christians in Corinth, and said,

"If I have enough faith to move mountains, but do

not have love, I am nothing." Perhaps this was

the apostle's way of reminding the Corinthians,

C. S. Lewis, and the rest of us that one must give

love before one can realize being loved.

The selections in this chapter are an assortment of

expressions of finding love, and then sometimes

being parted from the object of that love.

TO LOVE

Love anything and your heart will be wrung
and possibly broken.
If you want to make sure of keeping it intact
you must give it to no one,
not even an animal. Wrap it carefully round with
hobbies and little luxuries;
avoid all entanglements. Lock it up safe in the casket or
coffin of your selfishness.
But in that casket—safe dark, motionless,
airless—it will change.
It will not be broken; it will become unbreakable,
impenetrable, irredeemable.

To love is to be vulnerable. [17]

C. S. LEWIS

To whom I owe the leaping delight

That quickens my senses in our wakingtime
And the rhythm that governs the repose of our sleepingtime,
The breathing in unison

Of lovers whose bodies smell of each other
Who think the same thoughts without need of speech
And bubble the same speech without need of meaning.

No peevish winter wind shall chill
No sullen tropic sun shall wither
The roses in the rose-garden which is ours and ours only.

But this dedication is for others to read:
These are private words addressed to you in public.[18]

T. S. ELIOT

IDEAS FOR ANNIVERSARY CONVERSATION STARTERS

D R . J A M E S D O B S O N

From *Love for a Lifetime: Building a Marriage
That will Go the Distance*

THE WATCHWORDS HERE ARE *POSITIVE, NON-
THREATENING*, AND *FORWARD-LOOKING*. THIS IS AN
EVENING TO ENJOY! STEER AWAY FROM TOPICS
THAT RAISE BLOOD PRESSURE, RESURRECT OLD
ARGUMENTS, STIR UP BITTERNESS, OR SLOG
THROUGH THE MURK OF UNHAPPY MEMORIES. THE
OBJECT IS TO ENJOY ONE ANOTHER'S COMPANY
WHILE MOVING YOUR RELATIONSHIP IN
A POSITIVE, HOPEFUL DIRECTION.

What two or three things would you love to see develop in
our relationship in the coming years?

What are three major goals you would like to
accomplish this year?

On a scale of 1 to 10 (10 being the highest), where are you
in your spiritual life? How might we better encourage
one another in this area?

What are three things God has taught you over the
past couple of years?
What friendships would we like to foster as a couple?

What one thing could I do more of this year to serve you?

What could we do to encourage another couple
(spiritually, financially, emotionally) during the
coming year?

How can we find more time to communicate, day by day,
week by week?

Reflecting on this past year . . . what has been the most
memorable experience you've had? How about the most fun or
most silly? What is the best book you've read and why?

Did your family have "traditions" as you were growing up?
What was your favorite? What family traditions
might we establish?

What have you learned that's new about me? About yourself?

Are you satisfied with the time commitments you've made dur-ing this past year? What would you change if you could change?

If you could visit five countries or cities in the whole world (and had the money to go in style!) which would they be and why?

What is one thing you always wished you knew how to do—and is it really too late to learn?[19]

DON'T LET THE ENJOYMENT END WITH THIS CELEBRATION! GET OUT A CALENDAR AND SCHEDULE THREE SPECIAL WEEKENDS TOGETHER DURING THE UPCOMING YEAR; SET DATES, PLACES, AND DISCUSS BABYSITTING OPTIONS IF NECESSARY.

WHEN THE HEART IS FULL OF LOVE

There is beauty in the forest

When the trees are green and fair.

There is beauty in the meadows

When wild flowers scent the air.

There is beauty in the sunlight

And the soft blue beams above.

Oh, the world is full of beauty

When the heart is full of love.

AUTHOR UNKNOWN

WHEN I WAS ONE AND TWENTY

When I was one-and-twenty

I heard a wise man say,

"Give crowns and pounds

 and guineas

But not your heart away;

Give pearls away and rubies

But keep your fancy free."

But I was one-and-twenty,

No use to talk to me.

When I was one-and-twenty

I heard him say again,

"The heart out of the bosom

Was never given in vain;

'Tis paid with sighs a plenty

And sold for endless rue."

And I am two-and-twenty,

And oh, 'tis true, 'tis true.[20]

A. E. HOUSMAN

THE HIGHWAY MAN

ALFRED NOYES

I

The wind was a torrent of darkness among the gusty trees,
The moon was a ghostly galleon tossed upon cloudy seas,
The road was a ribbon of moonlight over the purple moor,
And the highwayman came riding
Riding, riding,
The highwayman came riding, up to the old inn door.

He'd a French cocked-hat on his forehead, a bunch of lace at
his chin,
A coat of the claret velvet, and breeches of brown doe-skin;
They fitted with never a wrinkle; his boots were up to the
thigh!
And he rode with a jeweled twinkle,
His pistol butts a-twinkle,
His rapier hilt a-twinkle, under the jeweled sky.

Over the cobbles he clattered and clashed in the dark inn-yard,
And he tapped with his whip on the shutters, but all was locked
and barred;
He whistled a tune to the window, and who should be
waiting there
But the landlord's black-eyed daughter,
Bess, the landlord's daughter,
Plaiting a dark red love-knot into her long black hair.

And dark in the dark old inn-yard a stable-wicket creaked
Where Tim the hostler listened; his face was white and peaked;
His eyes were hollows of madness, his hair like moldy hay,
But he loved the landlord's daughter,
The landlord's red-lipped daughter
Dumb as a dog he listened, and he heard the robber say:

"One kiss, my bonny sweetheart, I'm after a prize tonight,
But I shall be back with the yellow gold before the morning light;
Yet, if they press me sharply, and harry me through the day,
Then look for me by moonlight,
Watch for me by moonlight,
I'll come to thee by moonlight, though hell should bar the way."

He rose upright in the stirrups; he scarce could reach her hand,
But she loosened her hair i' the casement! His face burnt like a
brand
As the black cascade of perfume came tumbling over his breast;
And he kissed its waves in the moonlight,
(Oh, sweet black waves in the moonlight!)
Then he tugged at his rein in the moonlight, and galloped away
to the West.

II

He did not come in the dawning: he did not come at noon;
And out o' the tawny sunset, before the rise of the moon,
When the road was a gypsy's ribbon, looping the purple moor,
A redcoat troop came marching,
Marching, marching,
King George's men came marching, up to the old inn-door.

They said no word to the landlord, they drank his ale instead,
But they gagged his daughter and bound her to the foot of her
narrow bed;
Two of them knelt at her casement, with muskets at their side!
There was death at every window;
And hell at one dark window;
For Bess could see through her casement, the road that *he*
would ride.

They had tied her up to attention, with many a sniggering jest;
They had bound a musket beside her, with the barrel beneath
her breast!
"Now keep good watch!" and they kissed her.
She heard the dead man say—
Look for me by moonlight
Watch for me by moonlight,
I'll come to thee by moonlight, though hell should bar the way!

She twisted her hands behind her; but all the knots held good!
She writhed her hands till her fingers were wet with sweat
or blood!
They stretched and strained in the darkness, and the hours
crawled by like years,
Till, now, on the stroke of midnight,
Cold, on the stroke of midnight,
The tip of one finger touched it! The trigger at least was hers!

The tip of one finger touched it; she strove no more for the rest!
Up, she stood up to attention, with the barrel beneath her
breast,
She would not risk their hearing! she would not strive again;
For the road lay bare in the moonlight,
Blank and bare in the moonlight;
And the blood of her veins in the moonlight throbbed to her
love's refrain.

Tlot-tlot, tlot-tlot! Had they heard it? The horse-hoofs
ringing clear;
Tlot-tlot, tlot-tlot, in the distance? Were they deaf that they did
not hear?
Down the ribbon of moonlight, over the brow of the hill,
The highwayman came riding,
Riding, riding!
The red-coats looked to their priming! She stood up, straight
and still!

Tlot-tlot, in the frosty silence! *Tlot-tlot*, in the echoing night!
Nearer he came and nearer! Her face was like a light!
Her eyes grew wide for a moment! she drew one last
deep breath,

Then her finger moved in the moonlight,
Her musket shattered the moonlight,
Shattered her breast in the moonlight and warned him—with
her death.

He turned; he spurred to the West; he did not know she stood
Bowed, with her head o'er the musket, drenched with her own
red blood!
Not till the dawn he heard it; his face grew gray to hear
How Bess, the landlord's daughter,
The landlord's black-eyed daughter,
Had watched for her love in the moonlight, and died in the
darkness there.

Back, he spurred like a madman, shrieking a curse to the sky,
With the white road smoking behind him and his rapier bran-
dished high!
Blood-red were his spurs i' the golden noon; wine red was his
velvet coat,
When they shot him down on the highway,
Down like a dog on the highway,
And he lay in his blood on the highway, with the bunch of lace
at his throat.

And still of a winter's night, they say, when the wind is in the
trees,
When the moon is a ghostly galleon tossed upon cloudy seas,
When the road is a ribbon of moonlight over the purple moor,
A highwayman comes riding,
Riding, riding,
A highwayman comes riding, up to the old inn-door.

Over the cobbles he clatters and clangs in the dark inn-yard;
He taps with his whip on the shutters, but all is locked and
barred;
He whistles a tune to the window, and who should be waiting
there
But the landlord's black-eyed daughter,
Bess, the landlord's daughter,
Plaiting a dark red love-knot into her long black hair.[21]

LOVE'S
PHILOSOPHY

The fountains mingle with the river
And the rivers with the Ocean,
The winds of Heaven mix forever
With a sweet emotion;
Nothing in the world is single;
All things by a law divine
In one spirit meet and mingle.
Why not I with thine?—

See the mountains kiss high Heaven
And the waves clasp one another;
No sister-flower would be forgiven
If it disdained its brother,
And the sunlight clasps the earth
And the moonbeams kiss the sea:
What are all these kissings worth
*If thou kiss not me?*₂₂

PERCY BYSSHE SHELLEY

WHAT IS LOVE?

To love very much is to love inadequately;
we love—that is all. Love cannot be
modified without being nullified. Love
is a short word but it contains every-
thing. Love means the body, the soul,
the life, the entire being. We feel love as
we feel the warmth of our blood, we
breathe love as we breathe the air, we
hold it in ourselves as we hold our
thoughts. Nothing more exists for us.
Love is not a word; it is a wordless state
indicated by four letters . . .

GUY DE MAUPASSANT

MR. ROCHESTER PROPOSES TO JANE

CHARLOTTE BRONTE

From *Jane Eyre*

Jane Eyre is a strong-willed orphan who, after surviving miserable years at a charity school, becomes governess to the ward of the mysterious Edward Rochester, master of Thornfield estate. She and Mr. Rochester fall in love, but before they can be married . . . The following passage is from chapter 23.

"Jane, do you hear that nightingale singing in the wood? Listen!"

In listening, I sobbed convulsively; for I could repress what I endured no longer; I was obliged to yield, and I was shaken from head to foot with acute distress. When I did speak, it was only to express an impetuous wish that I had never been born, or never come to Thornfield.

"Because you are sorry to leave it?"

The vehemence of emotion, stirred by grief and love within me, was claiming mastery, and struggling for full sway; and asserting a right to predominate: to overcome, to live, rise, and reign at last; yes—and to speak.

"I grieve to leave Thornfield; I love Thornfield—I love it, because I have lived in it a full and delightful life, momentarily at least. I have not been trampled on. I have not been petrified. I have not been buried with inferior minds, and excluded from every glimpse of communion with what is bright and energetic, and high. I have talked, face to face, with what I reverence; with what I delight in, with an original, a vigorous, an expanded mind. I have known you, Mr. Rochester, and it strikes me with terror and anguish to feel I absolutely must be torn from you forever. I see the necessity of departure; and it is like looking on the necessity of death."

"Where do you see the necessity?" he asked, suddenly.

"Where? You, sir, have placed it before me."

"In what shape?"

"In the shape of Miss Ingram; [an attractive friend from other days] a noble and beautiful woman—your bride."

"My bride! What bride? I have no bride!"

"But you will have."

"Yes, I will! I will!" He set his teeth.

"Then I must go; you have said it yourself."

"No: you must stay! I swear it—and the oath shall be kept."

"I tell you I must go!" I retorted, roused to something like passion. "Do you think I can stay to become nothing to you? Do you think I'm an automaton? a machine without feelings? and can bear to my morsel of bread snatched from my lips, and my drop of living water dashed from my cup? Do you think, because I am poor, obscure, plain, and little, I am soulless and heartless? You think wrong! I have as much soul as you—and full as much heart! And if God had gifted me with some beauty, and much wealth, I should have made it as hard for you to leave me, as it is now for me to leave you. I am not talking to you now through the medium of custom, conventionalities, or even of mortal flesh—it is my spirit that addresses your spirit, just as if both had passed through the grave, and we stood at God's feet, equal, as we are!"

"As we are!" repeated Mr. Rochester, "so," he added, enclosing me in his arms, gathering me to his breast, pressing his lips on my lips, "so, Jane!"

"Yes, so, sir," I rejoined, "and yet not so; for you are a married man—or as good as a married man, and wed to one inferior to you—to one with whom you have no sympathy—whom I do not believe you truly love; for I have seen and heard you sneer at her. I would scorn such a union, therefore I am better than you—let me go."

"Where, Jane?" To Ireland?"

"Yes—to Ireland. I have spoken my mind, and can go anywhere now."

"Jane, be still; don't struggle so, like a wild, frantic bird that is rending its own plumage in its desperation."

"I am no bird; and no net ensnares me; I am a free human being with an independent will, which I now exert to leave you."

Another effort set me at liberty, and I stood erect before him.

"And your will shall decide your destiny," he said. "I offer you my hand, my heart, and a share of all my possessions."

"You play a farce, which I merely laugh at."

"I ask you to pass through life at my side—to be my second self and best earthly companion."

"For that fate you have already made your choice, and I must abide by it."

"Jane, be still a few moments, you are overexcited. I will be still too."

A waft of wind came sweeping down the laurel-walk, and trembled through the boughs of the chestnut; it wandered away—away—to an indefinite distance—it died. The nightingale's song was then the only voice of the hour; in listening to it, I again wept. Mr. Rochester sat quiet, looking at me gently and seriously. Some time passed before he spoke; he at last said,

"Come to my side, Jane, and let us explain and understand one another."

"I will never come to your side; I am torn away now, and cannot return."
"But Jane, I summon you as my wife, it is only you I intend to marry."

I was silent; I thought he mocked me.

"Come, Jane—come hither."

"Your bride stands between us."

He rose, and with a stride, reached me.

"My bride is here," he said, again drawing me to him, "because my equal is here, and my likeness. Jane, will you marry me?" Still I did not answer, and still I writhed myself from his grasp—for I was still incredulous.

"Do you doubt me, Jane?"

"Entirely."

"You have no faith in me?"

"Not a whit."

"Am I a liar in your eyes?" he asked passionately. "Little skeptic, you *shall* be convinced. What love have I for Miss Ingram? None—and that you know. What love has she for me? None—as I have taken pains to prove: I caused a rumor to reach her that my fortune was not a third of what she supposed, and after that I presented myself to see the result; it was coldness both from her and her mother. I would not—I could not—marry Miss Ingram. You—you strange—you almost unearthly thing!—I love as my own flesh. You—poor and obscure, and small and plain as you are—I entreat to accept me as a husband."

"What, me!" I ejaculated, beginning in his earnestness—and especially in his incivility—to credit his sincerity, "me who have not a friend in the world but you, if you are my friend, not a shilling but what you have given me?"

"You, Jane. I must have you for my own—entirely my own. Will you be mine? Say yes, quickly."

"Mr. Rochester, let me look at your face—turn to the moonlight."

"Why?"

"Because I want to read your countenance; turn!"

"There; you will find it scarcely more legible than a crumpled, scratched page. Read on, only make haste, for I suffer."

His face was very much agitated and very much flushed, and there were strong workings in the features, and strange gleams in the eyes.

"Oh, Jane, you torture me!" he exclaimed. "With that searching and yet faithful and generous look, you torture me!"

"How can I do that? If you are true and your offer real, my only feelings to you must be gratitude and devotion—they cannot torture."

"Gratitude," he ejaculated; and added wildly—"Jane, accept me quickly. Say Edward—give me my name—Edward will marry you."

"Are you in earnest?—Do you truly love me?—Do you sincerely wish me to be your wife?"

"I do; and if an oath is necessary to satisfy you, I swear it."

"Then, sir, I will marry you."

"Edward—my little wife!"

"Dear Edward!"

"Come to me—come to me entirely now," he said, and added in his deepest tone, speaking in my ear as his cheek was laid on mine, "Make my happiness—I will make yours."[23]

A KISS

And what is a kiss, when all is done?

A promise given under seal—a vow

A signature acknowledged—a rosy dot

Over the i of Loving—a secret whispered

To listening lips apart—a moment made

Immortal, with a rush of wings unseen—

A sacrament of blossoms, a new song

Sung by two hearts to an old simple tune—

The ring of one horizon around two souls

Together, all alone![24]

EDMOND ROSTAND

From *Cyrano de Bergerac*

THE HALLS OF HIGHEST HUMAN HAPPINESS

CATHERINE MARSHALL

From *A Man Called Peter*

For two full years I [Catherine] had longed to know this young Scotsman [Peter Marshall] whom I had frequently heard preach. Who could have had heard such sermons as "Agnostics and Azaleas" or "A Rosary of Remembrance" and failed to glimpse the poetry in this man's soul or the deep earnestness of his desire to take men and women by the hand and lead them to God? Both attributes appealed to me strongly; for at this stage (I might as well admit) I was in love with love, fancied myself a poet, and more important, was groping to find my way out of an inherited Christianity into a spiritual experience of my own.

One of my youthful self-indulgences was a journal in which I poured out my hopes and dreams and let my poetic urge have full reign. In it I had written earlier: "I am neither right with myself nor with God . . . I can never enjoy life until I learn *why* I am here and *where* I am going. . . ." And then a few pages on: "I have never met anyone whom I so want to know as Mr. Marshall."

MY LETTERS TO MY PARENTS IN
THE LITTLE TOWN OF KEYSER,
WEST VIRGINIA, WHERE MY FATHER
WAS PASTOR OF THE PRESBYTERIAN
CHURCH, HAD ALSO BEEN INCLUD-
ING COMMENTS ABOUT PETER
MARSHALL FOR SOME TIME. IN
JANUARY, 1934, I HAD WRITTEN
TO THEM:

Carol (one of my New England friends) *and I went to Westminster* [Church] *again yesterday to hear Peter Marshall.*

Westminster is a rather small church—but very quiet and worshipful. Mr. Marshall conducts beautiful services, and I like him more each time I go. He's only twenty-eight [I was mistaken. Peter was actually thirty-one at the time] *and has had just four years of experience, but believe me, he's something already.*

I have never heard such prayers in my life. It's as if, when he opens his mouth, there is a connected line between you and God. I know this sounds silly, but I've got to meet that man. . . .

There was however no apparent way to meet him. To me, a college girl, Peter Marshall, the clergyman, seemed almost as inaccessible as a man from Mars. Since I was very young and quite transparent, it must have been obvious to my parents that all my idealism, as well as my natural girlish romanticism, was rapidly centering upon this young Scottish minister.

You see [I explained in another letter], *as far as Mr. Marshall is concerned, he doesn't even know I exist. . . . I've never met such a young man with so much real power. You feel it the minute you step inside his church. He's oh, so Scotch, and very dignified, but he has a lovely sense of humor.* [Then I added self-consciously,] *All this is awfully silly, isn't it? Oh, shucks, I wish I'd stop thinking about the man!*

The night of the prohibition rally [where both Catherine and Peter Marshall were speaking] was, therefore, very important to me. At long last I was going to meet Peter Marshall. My romantic soul said that the event must have the proper setting. I had suggested to Dr. Robinson [college professor] that he pick me up in the Alumnae garden. In my imagination I could see Mr. Marshall march down between the rose arbors to get me, while I waited for him, holding in one graceful hand a copy of *Sonnets from the Portuguese* and dreamily trailing the other through the lily pond.

Dr. Robinson picked me up in the garden all right, but merely tooted his horn; so I climbed into the back seat by the boy from Emory. Mr. Marshall was sitting beside Dr. Robinson in front. I expected him to be thinking about his speech. Instead, he immediately turned around to ask, "What's this I hear about my being engaged? Dr. Robinson says that you said—"

I flushed and stammered, "I—I did hear some rumors to that effect."

"Don't believe everything you hear, my dear girl. I certainly am not even about to be married."

"He pronounced the word "mar-r-ied" with a very broad "a" and a rolling of the "r's."

I remembered then another story I had heard about him. One night in Prayer Meeting, he had been talking about gossip and had remarked that everyone in the church seemed to know better than he *when* he was going to be "mar-r-ied" and *whom* he was going to "mar-r-y."

"I'd like this clearly understood," he went on, grinning like a small boy, "I'm not going to get mar-r-ied till I'm good and ready. I'm good enough now, but I'm not ready." This remark soon went the rounds.

The village to which we were going was some twenty miles away and seemed to have a general store, six houses, and a schoolhouse set in a grove of trees. A large group of farmers and their wives from the surrounding countryside came, bringing with them numerous assorted wriggling children and some babies in arms. They apparently had some curiosity to know why we thought the county should go wet. Free schoolbooks had been cannily promised by the local politicians out of the tax for beer.

The night was blustery, with a wind from the south and frequent flashes of lightning. Soon the schoolroom was filled with people packed in around the old potbellied stove.

The choir was solicited from the audience by a gray-haired man who assured all bashful recruits that the choir was not going to sing an anthem. For this mercy we were grateful. He managed to get together an assortment of folks who looked as if they had stepped out of a Dickens novel. After they had self-consciously filed into the rows of cane chairs facing the audience, the meeting began, as it was to end, with the singing of revival hymns strange to us. The gray-haired man kept waving his arms and urging the choir on. The bass, a large red-faced man in the back row, tried harder, and, as a result, looked as if he might have a stroke any minute. The tremolo of the tall, thin woman in the front row became almost turbulent under his heckling.

Peter, standing beside me, managed to read the music, growing more and more lusty, finally entering into the spirit of the evening and enjoying himself immensely. Whenever I stumbled over the unfamiliar music, he would give me a nudge of encouragement to "car-r-y on."

One by one, we were then elaborately introduced, listened to patiently, and given more applause than we deserved. Frankly, I can't remember much about what we said. The county promptly went dry.

On the way home Peter said, "May I see you sometime this week? I've wanted to know you for a long time." And when I clearly showed my astonishment, he added, "Not even ministers are blind, you know."

Six dates, four chaperones, and a dozen months later we were engaged.

How it came about I still regard as one of God's nicest miracles and the first big evidence of God's hand on my life. . . .

BEFORE THEY WERE MARRIED, CATHERINE WENT TO
TEACH SCHOOL IN THE MOUNTAINS OF WEST VIRGINIA,
DESCRIBED SO ELOQUENTLY IN HER BOOK, CHRISTY.
LETTER WRITING BECAME AN OCCUPATION FOR BOTH
CATHERINE AND PETER.

[HERE] BEGAN A CORRESPONDENCE RARE IN THE ANNALS
OF LOVE-MAKING. CERTAINLY, THERE HAVE BEEN PLENTY
OF PASSIONATE LOVE LETTERS BEFORE. LITERATURE HAS
ALSO PRESERVED A FEW IN WHICH THERE RUNS A DEEP
SPIRITUAL NOTE. THERE HAVE BEEN LOVERS
SUFFICIENTLY DETACHED TO WRITE IN A HUMOROUS
VEIN. BUT I DOUBT IF MANY SERIES OF LETTERS,
BEFORE OR SINCE, HAVE MORE UNIQUELY COMBINED
ALL THREE ATTRIBUTES.

Dearest Catherine,

How last week dragged on leaden feet—while I was waiting to hear from you. I really did not expect to hear until Friday afternoon or Saturday morning, but when no letter or card had arrived on Saturday morning, I explored all the torments of the lovelorn. I thought all kinds of things! I suffered agonies of secret pain. You see, I was waiting for the first expression, the first reassurance.

You will never know with what transports of joy I received your precious letter sent special delivery. It came about 10:30 last night, as I was working on my evening sermon. I read it with a bursting heart. I could have wept and did—a little—and I thanked the Lord right then and there for giving me such happiness and such a wonderful sweetheart. Never in my life have I known such happiness and joy and peace. I cannot help thinking of the words of the hymn: "Peace, peace, the wonderful gift of God's love."

Everything is turning out so much better than I could have planned it, because He is planning it. It was far better to get your wonderful letter at 10:30 last night than in the morning. It meant more to me then, for I hoped all day and longed!

It was hard leaving you on Tuesday night. I stood gazing after you a long time. . . . I can never be the same again. I am a different person now, praise the Lord, and you have made all the difference. My heart is in your keeping forever and ever. I live from now on to serve Him and to make you happy. Life can hold nothing more satisfying or more glorious than this—the joy of building with you, a home that will be a temple of God, a haven and a sanctuary, a place of peace and love, of trust and joy. . . .[25]

ON THE ROAD TO THE SEA

CHARLOTTE MEW

We passed each other, turned and stopped for half an hour,
then went our way,
I who make other women smile did not make you—
But no man can move mountains in a day.
So this hard thing is yet to do.
But first I want your life—before I die I want to see
The world that lies behind the strangeness of your eyes,
There is nothing gay or green there for my gathering, it may be,
Yet on brown fields there lies
A haunting purple bloom: is there not something in the grey
skies
And in the grey sea?
I want what world there is behind your eyes,
I want your life and you will not give it to me.
Now, if I look, I see you walking down the years,
Young, and through August fields—a face, a thought,
a swinging dream
perched on a stile—;
I would have liked (so vile we are!) to have taught you tears
But most to have made you smile.
Today is not enough or yesterday: God sees it all—
Your length on sunny lawns, the wakeful rainy nights—;
tell me—;
(how vain to ask), but it is not a question—just a call—;
Show me then, only your notched inches climbing up the
garden wall,
I like you best when you are small.

Is this a stupid thing to say
Not having spent with you one day?
No matter; I shall never touch your hair
Or hear the little tick behind your breast,
Still it is there,
And as a flying bird
Brushes the branches where it may not rest
I have brushed your hand and heard
The child in you: I like that best
So small, so dark, so sweet; and were you also then
too grave and wise?
Always I think. Then put your far off little hand in mine;—
Oh! let it rest;
I will not stare into the early world beyond the opening eyes,
Or vex or scare what I love best.
But I want your life before mine bleeds away—
Here—not in the heavenly hereafters—soon,—
I want your smile this very afternoon,
(This last of all my vices, pleasant people used to say,
I wanted and sometimes I got—the Moon!)
You know, at dusk, the last bird's cry,
And round the house the flap of the bat's low flight,
Trees that go black against the sky
And then—how soon the night!
No shadow of you on any bright road again,
And at the darkening end of this—what voice? whose kiss? As
if you'd say!
It is not I who have walked with you, it will not be I who
take away
Peace, peace, my little handful of the gleaners grain
From your reaped fields at the shut of day.
Peace! Would you not rather die
Reeling, —with all the cannons at your ear?
So, at least, would I,
And I may not be here
To-night, to-morrow morning or next year.
Still I will let you keep your life a little while,
See dear?
I have made you smile.[26]

My Better Half

For better, for worse, in
Johannesburg, South Africa

My better half
Love nest well
in hard times
together
in difficulties
Cool drinks
both of us
down the bottom
Of hardship
had times
Mafanya life
Money there
Money here
In good times
buy a cool drink
both of us
Joburg our home
Our stable
Window pane
drink it cool
My better half
We build a home
On top of a rock
Our Joburg home
In hard times
in difficulties together
Come rain come
thou thunderstorms
My better half
Thou shall never wither[27]

IKE MUILA
AND ISABELLA
MOTADINYANE

RUTH AND BILLY'S COURTSHIP AND MARRIAGE

BILLY GRAHAM
From *Just As I Am*

"Saturday nights I dedicate to prayer and study, in preparation for the Lord's day."

What kind of a romance could a college man have with a woman who said a thing like that? Dating Ruth Bell had to be creative. And I did my best. For example, on one occasion we took a long walk in the countryside surrounding Wheaton to a graveyard, where we read tombstone epitaphs! It was a far cry from careening through Charlotte in a jalopy.

Ruth, born in China, had spent her first seventeen years in Asia. Her father, Dr. L. Nelson Bell, was a medical missionary in the eastern Chinese province of Northern Kiangsu, and her family lived in the hospital compound. Theirs was a hard existence, and certainly not a sheltered one. She remembers it as a happy, interesting childhood with strict but loving parents, among happy Christians, both fellow missionaries and Christian Chinese friends and helpers. But they were all exposed to everything from monsoons, sandstorms, and epidemics to bandit attacks and civil war. For high school, Ruth went to the Foreign School in Pyongyang, Korea (now North Korea).

In more ways than one, she was one of the belles of Wheaton campus. This I learned from a fellow I met at the Lane home, John Streater. To pay his way through college, Johnny ran his own trucking service. For a price, he would haul anything in his little yellow pickup. I gladly accepted his offer of work at 50-cents an hour and spent many afternoons at hard labor, moving furniture and other items around the western Chicago suburbs.

Johnny was a little older than I and had been in the Navy before coming to Wheaton. He had a vision for the mission field and felt that God had called him to serve in China, where he intended to go as soon as he graduated. He told me about a girl in the junior class— one of the most beautiful and dedicated Christian girls he had ever met. Sounded like my type. I paid attention.

One day we were hanging around in our sweaty work clothes in front of Williston Hall, the girls' dorm, getting ready to haul some furniture for a lady in Glen Ellyn, the next town over, when Johnny let out a whoop. "Billy, here's the girl I was telling you about," he said. "It's Ruth Bell."

I straightened up, and there she was. Standing there, looking right at me, was a slender, hazel-eyed movie starlet! I said something polite, but I was flustered and embarrassed. It took me a month to muster the courage to ask her out for a date.

The Christmas holidays were fast approaching, and the combined glee clubs were presenting Handel's *Messiah*. One day in the library of Blanchard Hall, I saw Ruth studying at one of the long tables. Johnny Streater and Howard Van Buren urged me to make my pitch to her right there. The expression of the librarian at the desk turned to a frown as we whispered among ourselves. Undaunted, I sauntered nonchalantly across to Ruth and scribbled my proposal for a date to the concert. To my surprise and delight, she agreed to go.

That Sunday afternoon was cold and snowy. With Ruth Bell sitting beside me in Pierce Chapel, I did not pay much attention to the music. Afterward we walked over to the Lane house for a cup of tea, and we had a chance to talk. I just could not believe that anyone could be so spiritual and so beautiful at one and the same time.

Ruth went back to her room (she told me later), got on her knees, and told the Lord that if she could spend the rest of her life serving Him with me, she would consider it the greatest privilege imaginable. So why did she make it so hard for me to get her to say yes out loud?

If I had not been smitten with love at the first sight of Ruth Bell, I would certainly have been the exception. Many of the men at Wheaton thought she was stunning. Petite, vivacious, smart, talented, witty, stylish, amiable, and unattached. What more could a fellow ask for?

"Billy, hold your horses!" I fell so head-over-heels in love with her that Johnny had to caution me, "You're going too fast."

And there was one minor problem that kept coming up. She wanted me to go with her as a missionary to Tibet! My mind was not closed to such a possibility. Not completely. After all, I had chosen to major in anthropology with just such a contingency in mind. But missionary work was a lot more comfortable to consider in the global abstract than in the Tibetan concrete.

In that list of good adjectives I just assigned to Ruth, I omitted one: *determined*. She felt that God had called her to be a missionary to the remote borders of Tibet just as strongly as a I felt that He had called me to preach the gospel. In my case, though, there was not a geographical stipulation.

Ruth was deeply impressed by the life of Amy Carmichael, that single—and indeed singular—woman who God had called to devote herself to the children of Dohnavur, in Southern India.

She reinforced her case by telling me about Mildred Cable, who had just rejected the young man she loved because marriage to him would have cut across her call from God to do pioneer work in China.

Two things I felt sure of: first, that Ruth was bound to get married someday; and second, that I was the man she would marry. Beyond that, I did not try to pressure her or persuade her—that is to say, not *overly* much. I let God do my courting for me.

But as the months went by, I asked her to at least consider me. It would not have been right to let her assume that what seemed to be my heroic understanding of her concerns was a lack of interest or expectation on my part. We had lots of discussions about our relationship. I wouldn't call them arguments exactly, but we certainly did not see eye to eye.

One Sunday evening after church, I walked into the parlor of the Gestung home, where I was rooming, and collapsed into a chair. That dear professor of German and his wife, with three boys of their own, were getting accustomed to my moods and always listened patiently. This time I bemoaned the fact that I did not stand a chance with Ruth. She was so superior to me in culture and poise. She did not talk as much as I did, so she seemed superior in her intelligence, too. "The reason I like Ruth so much," I wrote home to Mother, "is that she looks and reminds me of you."

By now I had directly proposed marriage to Ruth, and she was struggling with her decision. At the same time, she encouraged me to keep an open mind about the alternative of my going to the mission field. She was coming to realize, though, that the Lord was not calling me in that direction.

One day I posed a question to Ruth point-blank: "Do you believe that God brought us together?"

She thought so, without question.

"In that case," I said, "God will lead me, and you'll do the following."

She did not say yes to my proposal right then and there, but I knew she was thinking it over.

A test of our bond came when her sister Rosa was diagnosed as having tuberculosis. Ruth dropped out of school in the middle of my second semester to care for her. Rosa was placed in a hospital in New Mexico, and Ruth stayed with her the next fall too.

While I was in Florida, preaching . . . I got a thick letter from Ruth postmarked July 6, 1941. One of the first sentences made me ecstatic, and I took off running. "I'll marry you," she wrote.

When I went back to my room, I read that letter over and over until church time. On page after page, Ruth explained how the Lord had worked in her heart and she said she felt He wanted her to marry me. That night I got up to the pulpit and preached. When I finished and sat down, the pastor turned to me.

"Do you know what you just said?" he asked.

"No," I confessed.

"I'm not sure the people did either!"

After I went to bed, I switched my little lamp on and off all night, rereading that letter probably another dozen times.

At the close of a preaching series just after that at Sharon Presbyterian Church in Charlotte, those dear people gave me, as I recall, an offering of $165. I raced out and spent almost all of it on an engagement ring with a diamond so big you could almost see it with a magnifying glass! I showed it off at home, announcing that I planned to present it to Ruth over in Montreat in the middle of the day. But daytime was not romantic enough, I was told.

Ruth was staying part of that summer at the cottage of Buck Currie and his wife . . . Their house on Craigmont Road in Black Mountain was built near a stream and had swings that went out over the water.

As I turned off the main road and drove toward the house, which was some distance off, I saw a strange creature walking down the road. She had long, straight hair sticking out all over, an awful looking faded dress, bare feet, and what looked to be very few teeth. I passed her by, but when I suddenly realized it was Ruth playing a trick on me—her teeth blacked out so that she looked toothless—I slammed on the brakes. She got in and we went on to the Currie house deep in the woods.

I had the ring with me.

We went up to what is now the Blue Ridge Parkway. The sun was sinking on one side of us and the moon rising on the other. I kissed Ruth on the lips for the first time. I thought it was romantic, but she thought, or so she told me later, that I was going to swallow her.

"I can't wear the ring until I get permission from my parents," she said apologetically.

They were away, so she sent them a telegram: "Bill has offered me a ring. May I wear it?"

"Yes," they wired back, "if it fits."

Ruth was the woman of my dreams. . . . Our relationship deepened in the next year. . . . During this time, after Rosa got better and Ruth returned to Wheaton, there came into Ruth's mind a serious doubt about me, centered on my uncertainty about my calling (if any) to the mission field. She even reached the point of feeling that we ought to quit dating and not see each other for a while. I said I'd appreciate having the ring back, in that case. She could not accept that, though. She was emotional about the ring and would not give it back to me. And that was the end of her doubt.

In June 1943, Ruth and I graduated from Wheaton College in the same class. (Although she was a junior when I entered as a second-semester freshman, we ended up graduating in the same class. She fell behind because of the time she took out for Rosa's illness.)

We were married in August, on the night of Friday the thirteenth, with a full moon in the sky. In Gaither Chapel at eight-thirty in the evening, amid candles and clematis, my beloved Florida mentor, Dr. John Minder, pronounced us husband and wife. . . . It was the most memorable day of my life.[28]

SPECIAL PLEADING

Time, hurry my Love to me:
Haste, haste! Lov'st not good company?
Here's but a heartbreak sandy waste
'Twixt Now and Then.
Why, killing haste
Were best, dear Time, for thee, for thee!
Oh, would that I might divine
Thy name beyond the zodiac sign
Wherefrom our times-to-come descend.
He called thee
Sometime.
Change it, friend:
Now-time sounds so much more fine!
Sweet Sometime, fly fast to me:
Poor Now-time sits in the Lonesome-tree
And broods as gray as any dove,
And call,
When wilt thou come, O Love?
And pleads across the waste to thee.
Good Moment, that giv'st him me,
Wast ever in love?
Maybe, maybe
Thou'lt be this heavenly velvet time
When Day and Night as rhyme and rhyme
Set lip to lip dusk-modestly
Or haply some noon afar,
—O life's top bud, mixt rose and star,
How ever can thine utmost sweet
Be star-consummate, rose-complete,
Till thy rich reds full opened are?
Well, be it dusk-time or noon-time,
I ask but one small boon, Time:
Come thou in night, come thou in day,
I care not, I care not: have thine own way.
But only, but only, come soon, Time.[29]

SIDNEY LANIER

LOVE SERVICEABLE

What measure Fate to him did mete

Is not the lover's noble care;

He's heartsick with a longing sweet

To make her happy as she's fair.

Oh, misery, should she him refuse,

And so her dearest good mistake!

His own success he thus pursues

With frantic zeal for her sole sake.

To lose her were his life to blight,

Being lost to hers; to make her his,

Except as helping her delight,

He calls but accidental bliss;

And, holding life as so much pelf

To buy her posies, learns this lore:

He does not rightly love himself

Who does not love another more.

COVENTRY PATMORE

Chapter 4

LOVE IS PATIENT

To the English speaking world, the tender love story of David Copperfield and his beloved Dora is the favorite of all Charles Dickens' novels. From it has come a cast of characters who have become personality icons. Remember Uriah Heap and his hand-wringing, "We are so very 'umble"? The epitome of patience has always been exemplified by Mr. Barkis, who regularly expresses his spurned love for Mrs. Gummidge by declaring, "Barkis is willin'." Finally, when asked about his long patience, Barkis replies, "When a man says he's willin', it's as much as to say, that a man's waitin' for an answer."

One of the attributes of love, according to St. Paul, is patience. The kind of longevity that Jacob exhibited when he labored seven years for the hand of his beloved Rachel.

In more contemporary terms, an impatient poet, Diane Di Prima, admits to her husband, "I suppose it hasn't been easy living with me either." And in M. V. Caruther's "Prayer of Any Husband" there is a masculine plea for patience, "And let her make allowance—now and then / That we are only grown-up boys, we men."

Among the gems on the following pages you will find the Anderson fairy tale of a patient tin soldier, Abraham Lincoln's letter of marriage proposal, and other examples of love that know no lessening in the face of trials or imperfections.

POEM IN PRAISE OF MY HUSBAND (TAOS)

I suppose it hasn't been easy living with me either,

with my piques, and ups and downs, my need for privacy

leo pride and weeping in bed when you are trying to sleep

and you, interrupting me in the middle of a thousand poems

did I call the insurance people? the time you stopped a poem

in the middle of our drive over the nebraska hills and

into colorado, odetta singing, the whole world singing in me

the triumph of our revolution in the air

me about to get that down, and you

you saying something about the carburetor

so that it all went away

but we cling to each other

as if each thought the other was a raft

and he adrift alone, as in this mud house

not big enough, the walls dusting down around us, a fine dust rain

counteracting the good, high air, and stuffing our nostrils

we hang our pictures of the several worlds:

new york collage, and san francisco posters,

set out our japanese dishes, chinese knives

hammer small indian marriage cloths into the adobe

we stumble thru silence into each other's gut

blundering thru from one long place to the next

like kids who snuck out to play on a boat at night

and the boat slipped from it moorings, and they look at the stars

about which they know nothing, to find out

where they are going₃₀

DIANE DI PRIMA

Come Where My Love Lies Dreaming

Come where my love lies dreaming,
Dreaming the happy hours away,
In visions bright redeeming
The fleeting joys of day;
Dreaming the happy hours,
Dreaming the happy hours away
Come where my love lies dreaming,
Is sweetly dreaming the happy hours away.

Come where my love lies dreaming,
Is sweetly dreaming,
Her beauty beaming;
Come where my love lies dreaming,
Is sweetly dreaming the happy hours away.

Come with a lute, come with a lay,
My own love is sweetly dreaming,
Her beauty beaming;
Come where my love lies dreaming,
Is sweetly dreaming the happy hours away.

Soft is her slumber;
Thoughts bright and free
Dance through her dreams
Like gushing melody;
Light is her young heart,
Light may it be:
Come where my love lies dreaming.

STEPHEN FOSTER

PRAYER OF ANY HUSBAND

Lord, may there be no moment in life
When she regrets that she became my wife,
And keep her dear eyes just a trifle blind
To my defects, and to my failings kind!

Help me to do the utmost that I can
To prove myself her measure of a man,
But, if I often fail as mortals may,
Grant that she never sees my feet of clay!

And let her make allowance—now and then—
That we are only grown-up boys, we men,
So loving all our children, she will see,
Sometimes, a remnant of the child in me!

Since years must bring to all their load of care,
Let us together every burden bear,
And when Death beckons one its path along,
May not the two of us be parted long![31]

MAZIE V. CARUTHERS

THE CONCERT

No, I will go alone.
I will come back when it's over.
Yes, of course I love you.
No, it will not be long.
Why may you not come with me?—
You are too much my lover.
You would put yourself
Between me and song.

I go alone,
Quiet and suavely clothed,
My body will die in its chair,
And over my head a flame,
A mind that is twice my own,
Will mark with icy mirth
The wise advance and retreat
Of armies without a country,
Storming a nameless gate,

Hurling terrible javelins down
From the shouting walls of a singing town
Where no women wait!
Armies clean of love and hate,
Marching lines of pitiless sound
Climbing hills to sun and hurling
Golden spears to the ground!
Up the lines a silver runner
Bearing a banner whereon is scored
The milk and steel of a bloodless wound
Healed at length by the sword!

You and I have nothing to do with music.
We may not make of music a filigree frame,
Within which you and I,
Tenderly glad we came,
Sit smiling, hand in hand.

Come now, be content.
I will come back to you, I swear I will;
And you will know me still.
I shall be only a little taller
Than when I went.[32]

EDNA ST. VINCENT MILLAY

THE STEADFAST TIN SOLDIER

HANS CHRISTIAN ANDERSON

There was a time, before television, when young children got their ideas about romance and love from fairy tales, especially the stories of Hans Christian Anderson. Perhaps this age-old tale of steadfastness and hope will inspire other young lovers.

There were once twenty-five tin soldiers, all brothers, for they were the offspring of the same old tin spoon. Each man shouldered his gun, kept his eyes well to the front, and wore the smartest red and blue uniform imaginable. The first thing they heard in their new world when the lid was taken off the box, was a little boy clapping his hands and crying, "Soldiers, soldiers!"

It was his birthday and they had just been given to him, so he lost no time in setting them up on the table. All the soldiers were exactly alike with one exception, and he differed from the rest in having only one leg. For he was made last, and there was not quite enough tin left to finish him. However, he stood just as well on his one leg as the others did on two. In fact he was the very one who became famous.

On the table where they were being set up were many other toys, but the chief thing which caught the eye was a delightful paper castle. You could see through the tiny windows right into the rooms. Outside there were some little trees surrounding a small mirror, representing a lake, whose surface reflected the waxen swans, which were swimming about on it. It was altogether charming, but the prettiest thing of all was a little maiden standing at the open door of the castle.

She too was cut out of paper, but she wore a dress of the lightest gauze, a dainty little blue ribbon over her shoulders, by way of a scarf, set off by a brilliant spangle as big as her whole face. The little maid was stretching out both arms, for she was a dancer. And in the dance one of her legs was raised so high into the air that the tin soldier could see absolutely nothing of it, and supposed that she like himself had but one leg.

"That would be the very perfect wife for me!" he thought, "but she is much too grand. She lives in a palace, while I only have a box, and then there are twenty-five of us of us to share it. No, that would be no place for her. But I must try to make her acquaintance!" Then he lay down full length behind a snuffbox which stood on the table. From that point he could have a good look at the lady, who continued to stand on one leg without losing her balance.

Late in the evening the other soldiers were put into their box, and the people of the house went to bed. . . .Then the clock struck 12, when pop! Up flew the lid of the snuffbox, but there was no snuff in it. No! There was a little black goblin, a sort of jack-in-the-box.

"Tin soldier," said the goblin, "have the goodness to keep your eyes to yourself." But the tin soldier pretended not to hear.

"Ah! You just wait till tomorrow," said the goblin.

In the morning when the children got up, they put the tin soldier on the window sill, and whether it was caused by the goblin or by a puff of wind, I do not know, but all at once the window burst open and the soldier fell headfirst from the third story.

It was a terrific descent, and he landed at last with his leg in the air and resting on his hat, with his bayonet fixed between two paving stones. The maidservant and the little boy ran down to look for him, but although they almost stepped on him they could not see him.

Presently it began to rain, and the drops fell faster and faster till there was a regular torrent. When it was over two street boys came along. "Look out!" said one. "There's a tin soldier. Let's give him a sail."

So they made a boat by folding a newspaper and put the soldier in the middle of it, and he sailed down the gutter. Both boys ran alongside clapping their hands. . . . The paper boat rocked up and down in the gutter current. A shudder ran through the tin soldier, but he remained undaunted and did not move a muscle. He only looked straight ahead with his gun shouldered. All at once the boat drifted under a long wooden tunnel, and it became dark as it was in his box.

"Where on earth am I going now?" he thought. "It is all the fault of that goblin! Oh, if only the little maiden were with me in the boat, it might be twice as dark for all I should care."

At this moment a big water rat, who lived in the tunnel, came up. "Have you a pass?" asked the rat. "Hand over your pass."

The tin soldier did not speak, but clung still tighter to his gun. The boat rushed on, the rat close behind. Phew, how he gnashed his teeth and shouted, "Stop him! Stop him! He hasn't paid his toll. He hasn't shown his pass."

But the current grew stronger and stronger. The tin soldier could already see daylight before him at the end of the tunnel, but he also heard a roaring sound, fit to strike terror to the bravest heart. Just imagine: where the tunnel ended, the stream rushed straight into the big canal. That would be just as dangerous for him as it would be for us to shoot a great rapid.

He was so near the end now that it was impossible to stop. The boat dashed out. The poor tin soldier held himself as stiff as he could. No one should say of him that he even winced!

The boat swirled around three or four times and filled with water to the edge; it must sink. The tin soldier stood up to his neck in water, and the boat sank deeper and deeper. The paper became limp and soggy, and at last the water went over his head. Then he thought of the pretty little dancer whom he was never to see again, and this refrain rang in his ears:

"Onward! Onward! Soldier!
For death thou canst not shun."

At last the paper gave way entirely and the soldier fell through, but at the same moment he was swallowed by a big fish.

Oh, how dark it was inside the fish! It was worse even than being in the tunnel. And then it was so narrow! But the tin soldier was as dauntless as ever and lay full length, shouldering his gun.

The fish rushed about and made the most frantic movements. At last it became quiet, and after a time a flash like lightning pierced it. The soldier was once more in the broad daylight, and someone called out loudly, "A tin soldier!" The fish had been caught, taken to market, sold, and brought into the kitchen, where the cook cut it open with a large knife. She took the soldier up by the waist with two fingers and carried him into the parlor, where everyone wanted to see the wonderful man who had traveled about in the stomach of a fish. But the tin soldier was not at all proud. They set him up on the table, and—wonder of wonders! He found himself in the very same room that he had been in before. He saw the very same children, and the toys were still standing on the table, as well as the beautiful castle with the pretty little dancer.

She still stood on one leg and held the other up in the air. You see, she also was unbending. The soldier was so much moved that he was all ready to shed tears of tin, but that would not have been fitting. He looked at her and she looked at him, but they said never a word. At this moment one of the little boys took up the tin soldier, and without rhyme or reason threw him into the fire. No doubt the little goblin in the snuffbox was to blame for that. The tin soldier stood there, lighted up by the flame and in the most horrible heat, but whether it was the heat of the fire or the warmth of his feelings, he did not know. He had lost all his color. It might have been from his perilous journey, or it might have been from grief. Who can tell?

He looked at the little maiden and she looked at him, and he felt that he was melting away, but he still managed to keep himself standing, shouldering his gun bravely.

A door was suddenly opened. A draft of wind caught the little dancer and she fluttered straight into the fire, to the soldier, blazed up and was gone.

By this time the soldier was reduced to a mere lump, and when the maid took away the ashes next morning she found him in the shape of a small tin heart. All that was left of the beautiful dancer was the spangle, and that was burned as black as coal.[33]

JAMIE COME TRY ME

Jamie, come try me,

Jamie, come try me!

If thou would win my love,

Jamie, come try me!

If thou should ask my love,

Could I deny thee?

If thou would win my love,

Jamie, come try me!

If thou should kiss me, love,

Wha' could espy thee?

If thou would be my love,

Jamie, come try me!

ROBERT BURNS

Lincoln's Proposal

Probably this is the strangest love letter on record, and the most remarkable offer of marriage ever made. It is a love letter without a word of love, and a proposal for marriage that does not propose.

My dear Mary:

You must know that I cannot see you or think of you with entire indifference; and yet it may be that you are mistaken in regard to what my real feelings toward you are. If I knew that you were not, I should not trouble you with this letter. Perhaps any other man would know enough without further information, but I consider it my peculiar right to plead ignorance and your bounden duty to allow the plea. I want in all cases to do right, and most particularly so in all cases with women. I want at this particular time more than anything else to do right with you, and if I knew it would be doing right, as I rather suspect it would, to let you alone, I would do it. And for the purpose of making the matter as plain as possible I now say you can drop the subject, dismiss your thoughts—if you ever had any—from me forever, and leave this letter unanswered without calling forth one accusing murmur from me. And I will even go further and say that if it will add anything to your comfort and peace of mind to do so, it is my sincere wish that you should.

Do not understand by this that I wish to cut your acquaintance. I mean no such thing. What I do wish is that our further acquaintance should depend upon yourself. If such further acquaintance would contribute nothing to your happiness, I am sure it would not to mine. If you feel yourself in any degree bound to me, I am now willing to release you, provided you wish it; while, on the other hand, I am willing and even anxious to bind you faster, if I can be convinced that it will in any degree add to your happiness. This indeed is the whole question with me. Nothing would make me more miserable than to believe you miserable; nothing more happy than to know you were so.

In what I have now said I cannot be misunderstood; and to make myself understood is the only object of this letter. If it suits you best not to answer this, farewell. A long life and a merry one attend you. But if you conclude to write back, speak as plainly as I do. There can be neither harm nor danger in saying to me anything you think just in the manner you think it.

Your friend,
A. Lincoln

THE FROG PRINCE

WILLIAM AND JACOB GRIMM
RETOLD BY P. MOLINERO

*The brothers Grimm have a way of writing fairy tales and fables
with story lines that speak to children and subtleties that cause adults
to ponder. The Frog Prince is one of these thought-provoking stories
of romance and patience.*

In the old times, when it was still of some use to wish for
the thing one wanted, there lived a King whose daughters were
all handsome, but the youngest was so beautiful that the sun
himself, who has seen so much, wondered each time he shone
over her because of her beauty. Near the royal castle there was a
great dark wood, and in the wood under an old linden tree was
a well; and when the day was hot, the King's daughter used to
go forth into the wood and sit by the brink of the cool well, and
if time seemed long, she would take out a golden ball, and
throw it up and catch it again. This was her favorite pastime.

Now it happened one day that the golden ball, instead of
falling back into the maiden's little hand, dropped to the ground
near the edge of the well and rolled in. The King's daughter

followed it with her eyes as it sank, but the well was deep, so deep that the bottom could not be seen. She began to weep, and she wept and wept as if she could never be comforted. In the midst of her weeping she heard a voice saying to her:

"What's wrong, King's daughter? Your tears would melt a heart of stone."

When the girl looked to see where the voice came from, there was nothing but a frog stretching his thick ugly head out of the water.

"Oh, is it you, old waddler?" she said. "I weep because my golden ball has fallen into the well."

"Never mind, do not weep," answered the frog; "I can help you; but what will you give me if I fetch up your ball again?"

"Whatever you like, dear frog," said she; "any of my clothes, my pearls and jewels, or even the golden crown I wear."

Your clothes, your pearls and jewels, and your golden crown are not for me," answered the frog, "but if you would love me, and have me for your companion and playfellow, and let me sit by you at the table, and eat from your plate, and drink from your cup, and sleep in your little bed—if you would promise all this, then I would dive below the water and fetch your golden ball."

"Oh, yes," she answered, "I will promise it all, whatever you want, if you will only get me my ball."

But she thought to herself, "What nonsense he talks! As if he could do anything but sit in the water and croak with the other frogs. How could he possibly be anyone's companion?"

But the frog, as soon as he heard her promise, drew his head under the water and sank down out of sight. After a while he came to the surface again with the ball in his mouth, and he threw it on the grass.

The King's daughter was overjoyed to see her pretty plaything again, so she caught it up and ran off with it.

"Stop, stop!" cried the frog. "Take me up too; I cannot run as fast as you!"

But it was no use, for croak, croak after her as he might, she would not listen to him, but made haste home, and very soon forgot all about the poor frog, who had to go back to his well again.

The next day, when the King's daughter was sitting at the dining table with the King and all the court, and eating from her golden plate, there came something pitter-pattering up the marble palace stairs, and then there came a knocking at the door, and a voice cried out, "Youngest King's daughter, let me in!"

The King's daughter got up and ran to see who it could be, but when she opened the door, there was the frog sitting outside. Then she shut the door hastily and went back to her seat, feeling very uneasy. The King noticed how quickly her heart was beating and said:

"My child, what are you afraid of? Is there a giant standing at the door ready to carry you away?"

"Oh, no," she answered, "no giant, but a horrid frog."

"And what does the frog want?" asked the King.

"O dear father," she answered, "when I was sitting by the well yesterday, and playing with my golden ball, it fell into the water, and while I was crying over its loss, the frog came and got it for me on the condition I would let him be my companion, but I never thought he would leave the water and come after me; but now there he is outside the door, and he wants to come in."

Then everyone in the dining room heard him knocking the second time and crying out:

"Youngest King's daughter,
Open to me!
By the well water
What promised you me?
Youngest King's daughter
Now open to me!"

"What you promised you must perform," said the King; "so now go and let him in."

So she went and opened the door, and the frog hopped in, following at her heels, until she reached her chair. Then he stopped and cried:

"Lift me up to sit by you."

But she hesitated doing so until the King ordered her. When once the frog was on a chair, he wanted to get up on the table; and there he sat and said: "Now push your golden plate a little nearer, so that we may eat together."

And she did; but everyone saw how unwilling she was, and how the frog feasted heartily. But every morsel seemed to stick in her throat.

"I have had enough now" said the frog at last. "I am tired, you must now carry me to your room, and make ready your silken bed. We will lie down together and go to sleep."

Then the King's daughter began to weep; she was afraid that nothing would satisfy the cold frog except he sleep in her pretty clean bed. The King grew angry with her, saying:

"Daughter, what you promised in your time of need, you must now perform."

So she picked up the frog with her finger and thumb, carried him upstairs and put him in a corner of the room. Then she went to her pretty clean bed and lay down. The frog hopped over to the bed saying: "I am tired and want to sleep as much as you do. Pick me up and put me beside you, or I will tell your father."

So the King's youngest daughter picked up the frog and placed him on her pillow. When she laid her head down beside him, something overcame her and she heard the frog whisper, "King's daughter . . . King's daughter . . . give me a kiss."

Just moments before, revulsion would have filled her being, but as the frog whispered into her ear, she seemed unable to do anything but kiss the frog. With that kiss something wonderful happened, the frog hopped to the floor, and all at once became a prince with beautiful, kind eyes.

And it came to pass that, with her father's consent, they became bride and bridegroom. And he told her how a wicked old hag had bound him with one of her spells, with the admonition, "You shall remain a frog until a girl of noble birth kisses you and releases you from my bondage."

"Now," said the Prince, "let us go to my father's kingdom." And there came to the door a carriage drawn by eight white horses, with white plumes on their heads, and with golden harnesses.

The King kissed his daughter on the forehead. Each of her sisters and the members of the court kissed the King's daughter on the forehead. Then her Prince took her by the hand and led her to the coach. He kissed her again, and whispered into her ear, "I will keep my promise to love you forever." And the King's daughter replied, "And so will I. A promise is a promise."

And, I promise you, they all lived happily ever after.

WHY DO I LOVE YOU, SIR?

'Why do I love' You, Sir?
Because—
The Wind does not require the Grass
To answer—Wherefore when He pass
She cannot keep Her place.

Because He knows—and
Do not You—
And We know not—
Enough for Us
The wisdom it be so—

The Lightning—never asked an Eye
Wherefore it struck—when He was by
Because He knows it cannot speak—
And reasons not contained—
—Of Talk—
There be preferred by Daintier Folk—

The Sunrise—Sir—compelleth Me—
Because He's Sunrise—and I see—
Therefore—Then—
I love Thee—34

EMILY DICKINSON

Chapter 5

SPREAD A LITTLE KINDNESS

It was Shakespeare in The Taming of the Shrew
*who has want-to-be husband Petruchio
promising to kill Kate with kindness, and so the
expression has become part of the vernacular.
Like the bumper sticker says, "Spread a little
kindness—Let's start an epidemic."*

*To the Petruchios of this world, kindness
is a weak word. The simple phrase from
1 Corinthians 13:4* (NAS) *"Love is kind,"
reflects a selflessness and a satisfaction with the
uncomplicated things of life. Much like the
attitude expressed in the American folk song,
"Love is where you find it; I've found mine
right here/ Just you and me and the campfire
and the songs we like to hear."*

This also brings to mind a simpler time, when a man's love for a woman could be expressed in terms of the beauty found in nature and the most common things of life. British poet of the First World War, Rupert Brooke, says it best in his image-filled verse, "The Great Lover," and it can be heard in the fragile notes of Beethoven's "Moonlight Sonata."

What does simple imagery have to do with kindness? It is a reminder that the cornerstone of love is selflessness and giving. That's what it's all about.

A Month for Love
Charles R. Swindoll

It is February. Overcast, chilly, bleak-and-barren February. If you're not into skiing the slope, skating on ice, or singin' in the rain, there's not a lot outside to excite you. Sure was gracious of God to make it last only twenty-eight days . . . well, sometimes twenty-nine. No wonder bears hibernate at this time of year—there's not even Monday Night Football!

But wait. There is something extra special about February—Valentine's Day. Hearts 'n Flowers. Sweetheart banquets. A fresh and needed reminder that there is still a heart-shaped vacuum in the human breast that only the three most wonderful words in the English language can fill.

Don't think for a moment that such stuff is mere sentimentality. As a fellow named Smiley Blanton put it in his book many years ago, life really does boil down to Love or Perish:

Without love, hope perishes.

Without love, dreams and creativity perish.

Without love, families and churches perish.

Without love, friendships perish.

Without love, the intimacies of romance perish.

Without love, the desire to go on living can perish.

To love and to be loved is the bedrock of our existence.

But love must also flex and adapt. Rigid love is not true love. It is veiled manipulation, a conditional time bomb that explodes when frustrated. Genuine love willingly waits! It isn't pushy or demanding. While it has its limits, its boundaries are far-reaching. It neither clutches nor clings. Real love is not short-sighted, selfish, or insensitive. It detects needs and does what is best for the other person without being told.

As we read in the greatest treatise ever written on the subject: "Love is patient, love is kind, and is not jealous; love does not brag and is not arrogant, does not act unbecomingly; it does not seek its own, is not provoked, does not take into account a wrong suffered, does not rejoice in unrighteousness, but rejoices in truth; bears . . . believes . . . hopes . . . endures all things" (1 Corinthians 13:4-7 NAS).

Do I write today to a friend? Is love a dominant force in your friendship . . . or has jealousy, arrogance, or perhaps a subtle competitive spirit driven a wedge between the two of you? Love, remember, doesn't seek its own way.

Are my words being read by a husband or a wife? Does your mate know how greatly you treasure her/him? Do you tell her . . . show her? Left him a love note lately? How about a candlelight dinner? Remember when you said, "I do"? This is the month to add two more words: "I do love you."

Those simple little words—we so easily forget to say them. We assume others know how we feel, so we hold back. Strangely, as we grow older and realize more than ever the value of those three powerful words, we say them even less!

"I LOVE YOU." Simple, single syllable words, yet they cannot be improved upon. Nothing even comes close. They are better than "You're great." Much better than "Happy birthday!" or "Congratulations!" or "You're special." And because we don't have any guarantee we'll have each other forever, it's a good idea to say them as often as possible.

It is February. Overcast, chilly, bleak-and-barren February. But when you add love, the whole month gathers a glow about it. So—love!₃₅

FLICKER

The flicker of the campfire, the wind in the pines

The stars in the heavens, the moon that shines

A place where people gather to meet friends of all kinds

A place where old man trouble is always left behind

So give me the light of a campfire, warm and bright

And give me some friends to sing with, I'll be here all night

Love is where you find it; I've found mine right here

Just you and me and the campfire and songs we love to hear

So give me the light of a campfire, warm and bright

And give me some friends to sing with, I'll be here all night

Love is where you find it; I've found mine right here

Just you and me and the campfire and songs we love to hear.

TRADITIONAL, AMERICAN

A LETTER TO HIS WIFE

OBEDIAH HOLMES

SELECTIONS FROM
HIS LAST WILL AND TESTIMONY

It is not surprising if you have not heard of Obediah Holmes
(1607? – 1682), for he was not one of the notables of his century.
He was one of the unsung who left England and made the perilous
journey to the New World, where he and his family settled in Salem,
then moved on to Rhode Island where they became part of
Roger William's free group of Baptists.
Obediah was an uneducated man, but he knew his letters,
"and loved his wife," as his last will and testimony indicates.

My most dear Wife,

My heart has ever cleaved to thee, ever since we came
together, and is knit to thee in death which is the cause of these
lines as a remembrance of God's goodness to us in continuing
us together almost forty years (not diminishing us in our offspring since the first day until now, only our firstborn). God
has made all our conditions comfortable to us, whether in fullness or emptiness, lifted up or thrown down, in honor or disgrace, sickness or health, by giving us contentment and love one

with and to another. But more in a special manner [God has blessed us] in causing His fear to fall upon us and His love to be placed in our hearts and to know His will and to conform up to the obedience of the same—as to be willing to take up the cross and follow the Lord, not fearing what man can do unto us. For the Lord being on our side, who can be against us? For with His rod and His staff He has comforted us. Yea, He has been our present help in a needful time, and we have cause while we live to praise His holy name while we are together. And when death does separate us, may the only one still living praise Him while breath remains.

Wherefore, having some thought that I may go away before thee, having signs or token that my day is but short and it may fall out that I cannot or may not speak to thee at the last, I shall give thee some considerations for thy meditations in a time of trouble or affliction—that they may speak when I cannot (if the Lord is pleased to speak in them and by them). Consider how the Lord carried thee along ever since thou had a being in this world, as by tender parents and since thou came from them, the Lord has provided for thee and preserved thee in many dangers both by sea and land, and has given thee food and raiment with contentment. He has increased our store, sometimes to our admiration, also continuing our health in very great measure. He has given us a great posterity who have increased to a great number and has provided for them in a comfortable manner. And the Lord has kept them from such evils as might have befallen them to our grief, but we have had comfort in them. Also, consider the peace we have enjoyed and love we have obtained from our friends and our neighbors and strangers.

Yet, my dear wife, those things are but common favors that many may have their part in. But consider that the choice particular favor that many receive not which God has given to thee in choosing and calling thee to the knowledge of Himself and His dear Son which is eternal. [So, do] order thy heart to cleave to Him alone, esteeming Him as the chief good, as a pearl of great price, as worthy and causing thy heart to part with all for Him. His love has continued [to help] thee to hearken to His voice, inquiring about His will, so that thou might obey His holy will and commandments, so as to serve Him in thy generation. Oh, consider that great love of the Lord, to cause thy soul to cleave to Him alone and so He to be thy only protection! Having given thee His Son, He has with Him given thee all things thou dost enjoy, and so to be to thee—both in life and in death—thy advantage.

The consideration of this causes me to put thee now in mind, when I am removed, to consider Him as thy husband, as thy father, as thy Lord and Savior who has said that whom He loveth, He loveth to the end. And He will not leave them, nor forsake them, either in the six or seven troubles, but carry thee through all, until he bring thee to glory. Wherefore, lift up thy head and be not discouraged. Say to thy soul, "Why are thou disquieted within me? Hope in God and trust in His name," and thou shall not be disappointed. Let thy love to me end in this: that it is better for me to be out of the body and to be with the Lord at rest with Him and to be freed from that body of sin and death which I was in while I was in this present evil world. [That body] caused much sorrow of heart to me in secret; for, when I would do good, evil was present with me. And consider the fears you had concerning me every day, both for pains and weakness and dangers, of the many troubles that might befall me. But now let thy soul say, He is out of all dangers, freed from sin and Satan and all enemies and doubts; and death is past and he is at rest in a bed of quietness (as to the body) and with the Lord in spirit. And at the resurrection, that weak, corrupt, mortal body shall be raised immortal and glorious and shall see and know as he is known. Therefore, say, Why shall I mourn as one without hope? Rather, rejoice in hope of the glorious resurrection of the just.

And now, my dear wife, do thou live by the faith of the Son of God, exercise patience, and let patience have its perfect work in thee. It will be a little while before thy day will end and thy time come to sleep with me in rest. He that will come will come and will not tarry. Keep close to the Lord in secret, be much with God in prayer, and improve every season for thy soul's advantage, especially in holy meditations. Be cheerful and rejoice in God continually. Care not for the things of this world: say not, What shall I eat or wherewith shall I be clothed, for thy Father knoweth what thou hast need of. And He has given thee much more of these things than ever thou and I could expect or have deserved, and thou hast enough and to spare if His good pleasure be to let thee enjoy the same. If not, He alone is a sufficient portion. Yet, I question not but that He will preserve what thou hast, and bless it to thee. Wherefore, make use of that which He is pleased to let thee enjoy—I say, make use of it for thy present comfort.

Now that thou art weak and aged, cease from thy labor and

great trial, and take a little rest and ease in thy old age. Live on what thou hast, for what the Lord has given us, I freely have given thee for thy life, to make thy life comfortable. Wherefore, see that thou dost [enjoy?] it so long as house, land, or cattle remain. Make much of thyself. At thy death, then, what remains may be disposed of according to my will.

And now, my dear wife whom I love as my own soul, I commit thee to the Lord who has been a gracious, merciful God to us all our days, not once doubting but He will be gracious to thee in life—or death. He will carry thee through the valley of tears with His own supporting hand. Sorrow not at my departure, but rejoice in the Lord, and again I say rejoice in the God of our salvation. In nothing be careful [anxious], but make thy request to Him who only is able to supply thy necessities and to help thee in time of need. Unto Whom I commit thee for counsel, wisdom and strength, and to keep thee blameless to the coming of the Lord Jesus Christ, to Whom be all glory, honor and praise forever and ever, Amen. Fare thee well.[36]

LETTER TO MISS E. B. ON MARRIAGE

MARY SAVAGE

(18TH CENTURY)

Mankind should hope, in wedlock's state,
A friend to find as well as mate:
And ere the charm of person fails,
Enquire what merit there remains,
That may, by help of their wise pate,
Be taught through life to bless the state;
And oft they'd find, by their own fire,
What they in others so admire.
But as 'tis law that each good wife
Should true submission show for life,
What's right at home they often slight,
What's right abroad shines very bright.

Each female would have regal power,
But every male wants something more;
And that same balsam to the mind,
Which both would in compliance find,
Is, to this very time and hour,
Miscalled by them the want of power.
Then right of privilege they claim,
For every fair to vow a flame,
Which we are bound, with partial eye,
To find of true platonic dye;
For they've so fixed the certain rule,
How far with ladies they may fool,
That 'tis impossible they can
Go wrong—though not a man

Among them all would patience find,
If lady-wife should be inclined
To praise each swain, whose face or wit
Might chance her sprightly mind to hit.

Then there's something in the mind
That is not just—but kind;
That's fixed to neither taste nor sense,
Nor to be taught by eloquence;
But yet is that which gives a grace
To every feature of the face;
And is the surest chance for ease:
I mean a strong desire to please.
But own I must (though 'tis with shame)
Both parties are in this to blame;
They take great pains to come together,
Then squabble for a straw or feather;
And oft I fear a spark of pride
Prevails too much on either side.

Then hear, my girl—if 'tis your lot
To marry, be not this forgot:
That neither sex must think to find
Perfection in the human kind;
Each has a fool's cap—and a bell—
And, what is worse, can't always tell
(While they have got it on their head)
How far astray they may be led.
Let it be then your mutual care,
That never both at once may wear
This fatal mark of reason's loss,
That whirlwind-like the soul does toss.
Obtain this point, and friendship's power
Will rise and bless each future hour.

"SHALL I COMPARE THEE TO A SUMMER'S DAY?"

Shall I compare thee to a summer's day?

Thou art more lovely and more temperate:

Rough winds do shake the darling buds of May,

And summer's lease hath all too short a date:

Sometime too hot the eye of heaven shines,

And often is his gold complexion dimmed;

And every fair from fair sometime declines,

By chance, or nature's changing course untrimmed;

But thy eternal summer shall not fade,

Nor lose possession of that fair thou owest,

Nor shall death brag thou wanderest in his shade,

When in eternal lines to time thou growest;

So long as men can breathe, or eyes can see,

So long lives this, and this gives life to thee.

WILLIAM SHAKESPEARE

THE GREAT LOVER

RUPERT BROOKE

*It has been said that before great love can enter a man or woman's
life, there must be a sensitivity to the plain and practical.
One must fall in love with simple things.
This was Rupert Brooke's philosophy. He saw beauty and loveliness
in plain and practical things and events.*

These I have loved:

White plates and cups, clean-gleaming,
Ringed with blue lines; and feathery, faery dust;
Wet roofs, beneath the lamp-light; the strong crust
Of friendly bread; and many tasting food;
Rainbows; and the blue bitter smoke of wood;
And radiant raindrops couching in cool flowers;
And flowers themselves, that sway through sunny hours,
Dreaming of moths that drink them under the moon;
Then, the cool kindliness of sheets, that soon
Smooth away trouble; and the rough male kiss
Of blankets; grainy wood; live hair that is
Shining and free; blue massing clouds; the keen

Unpassioned beauty of a great machine;
The benison of hot water; furs to touch;
The good smell of old clothes; and other such—
The comfortable smell of friendly fingers,
Hair's fragrance, and the musty reek that lingers
About dead leaves and last year's ferns . . .

Dear names,
And thousand other throng to me! Royal flames;
Sweet water's dimpling laugh from tap or spring;
Holes in the ground; and voices that do sing;
Voices in laughter, too; and body's pain,
Soon turned to peace; and the deep-panting train;
Firm sands; the little dulling edge of foam
That browns and dwindles as the wave goes home;
And washen stones, gay for an hour; the cold
Graveness of iron; moist black earthen mold;
Sleep; and high places; footprints in the dew;
And oaks; and brown horse-chestnuts, glossy-new;
And new-peeled sticks; and shining pools on grass;—
All these have been my loves. And these shall pass,
Whatever passes not, in the great hour,
Nor all my passion, all my prayers, have power
To hold them with me through the gate of Death.

O dear my loves, O faithless, once again
This one last gift I give: that after men
Shall know, and later loves, far removed,
Praise you, "All these were lovely"; say, "He loved."[37]

MOONLIGHT SONATA

ANONYMOUS

Of all classical music, perhaps no composition has meant more to lovers than
Beethoven's Moonlight Sonata. *While this is not exactly a love story, it is*
a legendary tale of how the composer came to write the romantic piece.

It happened in Bonn. One moonlit winter's evening I
called upon Ludwig Beethoven, for I wanted him to take a
walk, and afterward sup with me. In passing through some
dark, narrow street, Ludwig paused suddenly. "Hush!" he
said—"what sound is that? It is from my Sonata in F!" he
said eagerly. "Listen how well it is played."

The music poured out of an open window in a mean, little
house. We paused below the window and listened. The player
inside the little house continued to play; but in the midst of the
finale there was a sudden break, then a woman's voice sobbed, "I
cannot play anymore. It is so beautiful, it is utterly beyond my
ability to do it justice. Oh, what would I not give to go to the
concert in Cologne!"

"Oh, my darling," said her companion, "why create regrets,
when there is no remedy? We can scarcely pay our rent."

"You are right; and yet I wish for once in my life to hear
some good music. But I guess it is of no use."

Beethoven looked at me; "Let's go in," he suggested.

"Go in!" I exclaimed. "Why should we go in?"

"I will play to her," he said in an excited voice. "That woman in there has feeling, genius, and understanding. I will play to her, and she will understand it." Before I could prevent him, his hand was upon the door.

A pale young man was standing next to an old-fashioned harpsichord, holding the hand of a seated young girl with a profusion of blond hair falling over her face. Both were poorly but cleanly dressed.

"Pardon me," said Beethoven, "but I heard music and was tempted to enter. I am a musician."

The girl blushed and her companion looked grave—somewhat annoyed.

"I also overheard something of what you said," continued my friend. "You wish to hear someone else play music. Shall I play for you?"

"Thank you," said the slight young man, "but her harpsichord is so wretched, and there is no music."

"No music!" the maestro echoed. "How then does the Fraulein . . . ?"

He paused and his face colored, for the girl looked full at him, and he saw she was blind.

"I beg your pardon," he stammered. "But I did not know. Then you play from ear?"

"Entirely."

"And where do you hear the music, since you frequent no concerts?"

"I used to hear a lady practicing near us, when we lived at Bruhl. During the summer evenings her windows were generally open, and I walked to and fro outside to listen to her."

The young woman seemed shy; so Beethoven said no more, but seated himself quietly before the piano, and began to play. He had no sooner struck the first chord than I knew what would follow—how grand he would be that night. I was not mistaken. Never, during all the years I knew him, did I hear him play as he played to that blind girl and her husband. He was inspired by their love and the unspoken communication that existed between them.

The couple was silent with rapture. The girl's hand reached out for the hand of her lover. I was caught up in the sheer romance of the moment. It was as if we were all bound in a strange dream, and only feared to awake.

Suddenly the flame of the single candle wavered, sank, flickered, and went out. Beethoven paused, and I threw open the shutters admitting a flood of brilliant moonlight. The room was almost as light as before and the illumination fell strongest upon the piano and player. But the chain of his ideas seemed to have been broken by the accident. His head dropped upon his breast; his hands rested upon his knees; he seemed absorbed in meditation. So it was for some time.

At length the young man rose and approached the maestro eagerly, yet reverently. "Wonderful man!" he said in a low tone, "who and what are you?"

"Listen!" the composer said, and he played the opening bars of the Sonata in F.

A cry of delight and recognition burst from them both. "Then you are Herr Beethoven!" They covered his hands with tears and kisses.

The great composer rose to go, but, we held him back with entreaties, "Play for us once more—only once more."

He allowed himself to be led back to the instrument. The moon shone brightly through the window and on his massive figure. "I will improvise a sonata to the moonlight," he promised, looking up thoughtfully to the sky and stars. Then his hands dropped to the keys, and he began a sad and infinitely lovely movement, which crept gently over the instrument like the calm flow of moonlight that spilled over the harpsichord. The notes shimmered and gleamed around the humble little room, while the young man and woman absorbed their radiance as fuel for their love.

"Farewell to you," said Beethoven, pushing back his chair and turning toward the door—"farewell to both of you. Never lose your love or wonder. Remember this night and the heavenly inspiration you have given me."

They followed us in silence more eloquent than words. "You will come again?" the young man finally asked. With an affirmative nod we stepped through the low door.

Out of sight and hearing of our hosts, my friend urged, "Let us make haste back to home, that I may write out that sonata while I can remember it."

We did so, and sat over it till long past day-dawn. And, this was the origin of that sonata held dear by all who are in love.

Did I ever tell you
that I love you
early in the morning
with your toothpaste kisses
and your sleepy eyes?
With your headaches and
grumpiness
that only goes away
if I hold your hand
and whisper the soft things
you like to hear?

Did I ever tell you
that I love you
at mid-afternoon,
during coffee-break time,
when clocks and
crowded cafeterias
make smiles and warm hands
love's best language?
Did I ever tell you
that I love the way
you smell after a bath,
that I love the way
you feel in bed beside me,
that I love the way
you look after I've loved you?

Did I ever tell you
that I love you?
I do,
I do,
I do.[38]

RICHARD EXLEY

Advice to Her Son on Marriage

When you gain her Affection, take care to preserve it;

Lest others persuade her, you do not deserve it.

Still study to heighten the Joys of her Life;

Not treat her the worse, for her being your Wife.

If in Judgment she errs, set her right, without Pride:

'Tis the Province of insolent Fools, to deride.

A Husband's first Praise, is a Friend and Protector.

Then change not these Titles, for Tyrant and Hector.

Let your Person be neat, unaffectedly clean.

Tho' alone with your wife the whole Day you remain.

Chuse Books, for her study, to fashion her Mind,

To emulate those who excell'd of her Kind.

Be Religion the principal Care of your life,

As you hope to be blest in your Children and Wife:

So you, in your Marriage, shall gain its true End;

And find, in your Wife, a Companion and Friend.

Mary Barber

CAN THIS REALLY BE LOVE?

CATHERINE MARSHALL
From *Christy*

If the book Christy *hasn't been part of your reading experience, you have probably seen the short-lived television series about the young college graduate who goes to Cutter Gap in the Great Smokies to teach school. Along with the wonderful mountain people, she becomes friends with Neil McNeil, an arrogant Scottish doctor, and the community's brash young preacher, David Grantland. Both have their hearts set for Christy Huddleston, who tells her own story.*

It began as the golden autumn. Long summer days had melted into shorter autumn days with heavy rains in their wake. Then suddenly, all the stored-up beauty of summer blazed forth in an avalanche of color that tore at the eyeballs and dazzled the senses.

This must be love, I thought. My eyes must be open to beauty because I was in love with David. I was young and he was young and wasn't this what poets sang about? So I went through my days wanting to sing and dance. The trees in their shouting colors were just for us! Only in the mountains had I seen such hues: the dark red of the sourwoods; the brown and bright orange of the red oaks; the luminous gold of hickories; the crimson of sumac and the scarlet oaks—always with the purple-blue Smokies for a backdrop, like the stain of ripe Concord grapes.

Even the nights were lighter and the stars brighter than I had ever seen them. Surely the Little Bear was laughing and the Dipper dripping with wine, and all for me, for me—for us, for us.

And of a morning there would be mists rising from the valley floor. Then day after day the sun would break through to dissolve the frost, to chase away the vapors, and to shine on those golden leaves.

David and I walked and rode horseback through woodland avenues of God and bronze and copper. Sometimes we would rein in our horses to stare, bedazzled by a single tree, looking with the sun shining full on it, as if a fire had been lighted at its heart. And David would lean far over in his saddle to plant a kiss on my lips to seal the moment. Or to tease him, I would go galloping off down one of those woodland avenues with him in full pursuit.

Once I had let David kiss me, a barrier had gone down; each kiss was easier and more natural than the last. So every time we were alone, David would reach out for me.

David was adept at romance and almost too sure of himself, I sometimes thought—and then wondered at myself for thinking it. But surely he was assuming much in our relationship. I still found myself holding back from giving him a final answer, and this did not seem logical even to me. I tried to go back in my mind to exactly what he had said, gesture by gesture, sentence by sentence, on that July night when, in the midst of his sorrow and discouragement after Tom McHone's murder, he had asked me to marry him. His actions now, his kisses, told me that he considered us engaged, a sort of mutual, unspoken agreement. What bothered me most was that though David acted as if he loved me, he never really used the words. If David did not love me enough to say so spontaneously, yes, even to shout it to the world, then could this really be love? If not . . . and then would come a suffocating sensation in my diaphragm, as if I needed air that my lungs could not suck in fast enough. What was wrong?

But then he would appear, gay and vital; and in his presence my doubts would vanish like those morning mists being chased out of our valley by the rising sun. For I enjoyed David's warm lips on mine. I liked being in his arms. Surely, I could not have all that physical feeling for him and not be in love. I must be wrong to be insisting, in my heart, on his saying certain words. Perhaps his actions were all that was necessary. Time would work this out; of course it would.

Then there was Dr. Neil McNeil . . .

"Christy, Christy, you've got to come back to me. Christy, wherever you are, listen to me . . . Christy, I love you, love you, love you. Christy, can you hear me? Down in your spirit, at the depth of you, do you hear what I'm saying to you? I love you! You cannot leave me without knowing this. Christy—"

Then the tone of the words changed. "God, I have fought against You because I have not understood. Not only fought, God, but cursed You. I did not understand why You let Margaret die—and our son. I did not understand anything about You. I still don't understand anything—except that some-how I know You are love. And that in my heart has been born so great a love for Christy as I did not know could exist on this earth. You, God, must be responsible. You have put it there."[39]

RECUERDO

We were very tired, we were very merry—

We had gone back and forth all night on the ferry.

It was bare and bright, and smelled like a stable—

But we looked into a fire, we leaned across a table,

We lay on a hilltop underneath the moon;

And the whistles kept blowing, and the dawn came soon.

We were very tired, we were very merry—

We had gone back and forth all night on the ferry,

And you ate an apple, and I ate a pear,

From a dozen of each we had bought from somewhere;

And the sky went wan, and the wind came cold,

And the sun rose dripping, a bucketful of gold.

We were very tired, we were very merry—

We had gone back and forth all night on the ferry,

We hailed "Good morrow, mother!" to a shawl-covered head,

And bought a morning paper, which neither of us read;

And she wept, "God bless you!" for the apples and the pears,

And we gave her all our money but our subway fares.[40]

EDNA ST. VINCENT MILLAY

THE PRAYER OF
ST. FRANCIS OF ASSISI
FOR THOSE IN LOVE

Based on the *Prayer of St. Francis of Assisi*

*As you lose yourselves in each other's love, keep aware of how easy it
will be to so love and enjoy one another that you shut out those who
need you individually and together.*
Pray this prayer together:

Lord, make us instruments of Thy peace

Where there is hate, may we bring love;

Where offense, may we bring pardon;

May we bring union in place of discord;

Truth, replacing error;

Faith, where once there was doubt;

Hope, for despair;

Light, where there was darkness;

Joy to replace sadness.

Make us not to so crave to be loved as to love.

Help us to learn that in giving we may receive;

In forgetting ourselves, we may find life eternal.

Chapter 6

MAKING LOVE COMPLETE

It was wedding week. There were relatives, friends, in-laws-to-be and school roommates running in and out. For diversion, a card table was set up in the family room, and a 1200-piece jigsaw puzzle of a Victorian garden wedding was scattered all over the tabletop. When anyone had a spare moment, he or she would pause a few moments and rummage for the strategic straight-edged pieces, or contribute to the growing piles of sky blue and fishpond blue pieces. This procedure continued for a few days until the wife and mother of the family finally declared, with a threatening edge to her voice, "Finish that puzzle, or get it out of the family room." That's when the solvers got serious and started working in earnest. Sometimes three or four guests poured over the scrambled nuptial scene. When a new piece was found, a shout went up. Finally, the night before the wedding arrived, and the entourage was about to leave for the wedding rehearsal. The puzzle pro-

*ject was almost complete—1199 pieces were in
place. That's when the Best Man yelled from the
family room, "Hey, there's a piece missing!"*

*What makes the great puzzlement of love complete?
It's the act that places the final piece into the love
relationship, the marriage ceremony.*

*Word artists have reveled in the completing phase
of love. This chapter presents sacred and secular
writers' interpretations of the wedding event and
its celebration. Absorb the magnificent verbiage
of the* Book of Common Prayer *relive the
excitement of the just-married state
as described by O' Henry; read again the description
from* Little Women *of Meg's home-spun family
rite; be present for the courtship and wedding of
notables like Harry and Bess Truman and Ronald
and Nancy Reagan.*

*Invite the Apostle Paul to declare, "We know only
in part . . . but when the complete comes, the
partial will come to an end."*

THE FIRST WEDDING

LOUISA MAY ALCOTT
From *Little Women*

Meg, Jo, Beth, and Amy March are the "Little Women" of this much-loved novel written in 1869. The young ladies live with their mother in a quiet Massachusetts town, while their father serves as an army chaplain during the American Civil War.

The June roses over the porch were awake bright and early on that morning, rejoicing with all their hearts in the cloudless sunshine, like friendly little neighbors, as they were.

Quite flushed with excitement were their ruddy faces, as they swung in the wind, whispering to one another what they had seen, for some peeped in at the dining-room windows where the feast was spread, some climbed up to nod and smile at the sisters as they dressed the bride [Meg], others waved a welcome to those who came and went on various errands in garden, porch, and hall, and all, from the rosiest full-blown flower to the palest baby bud, offered their tribute of beauty and fragrance to the gentle mistress who had loved and tended them so long.

Meg looked very like a rose herself, for all that was best and sweetest in heart and soul seemed to bloom into her face that day, making it fair and tender, with a charm more beautiful than beauty.

Neither silk, lace, nor orange flowers would she have. "I don't want to look strange or fixed up today," she said, "I don't want a fashionable wedding, but only those about me whom I love, and to them I wish to look and be my familiar self."

So she made the wedding gown herself, sewing into it the tender hopes and innocent romances of a girlish heart.

Her sisters braided up her pretty hair, and the only ornaments she wore were the lilies of the valley, which "her John" liked best of all the flowers that grew.

"You do look just like our own dear Meg, only so very sweet and lovely that I should hug you if it wouldn't crumple your dress," cried Amy, surveying her with delight when all was done.

"Then I am satisfied. But please hug and kiss me, everyone, and don't mind my dress. I want a great many crumples of this sort put into it today." And Meg opened her arms to her sisters, who clung about her with April faces for a minute, feeling that the new love had not changed the old.

"Now I'm going to tie John's cravat for him, and then to stay a few minutes with Father quietly in the study." And Meg ran down to perform these little ceremonies, and then to follow her mother wherever she went, conscious that in spite of the smiles on her motherly face, there was a secret sorrow hid in the motherly heart at the flight of the first bird from the nest.

As the younger girls stood together, giving the last touches to their simple toilet.

All three [sisters] wore suits of thin silver gray (their best gowns for the summer), with blush roses in their hair and bosoms; and all three looked just what they were—fresh-faced, happy-hearted girls, pausing a moment in their busy lives to read with wistful eyes the sweetest chapter in the romance of womanhood.

There were to be no ceremonious performances, everything was to be as natural and homelike as possible, so when Aunt March arrived, she was scandalized to see the bride come running to welcome and lead her in, to find the bridegroom fastening up a garland that had fallen down, and to catch a glimpse of the paternal minister marching upstairs with a wine bottle under each arm.

"Upon my word, here's a state of things!" cried the old lady, taking the seat of honor prepared for her, and settling the folds of her lavender moiré with a great rustle. "You oughtn't to be seen till the last minute, child."

"I'm not a show, Aunty, and no one is coming to stare at me, to criticize my dress, or count the cost of my luncheon. I'm too happy to care what anyone says or thinks, and I'm going to have my little wedding just as I like it. John, dear, here's your hammer." And away went Meg to help "that man" in his highly improper employment.

Mr. Brooke didn't even say, "Thank you," but as he stooped for the unromantic tool, he kissed his little bride behind the folding door, with a look that made Aunt March whisk out her pocket handkerchief with a sudden dew in her sharp old eyes.

There was no bridal procession, but a sudden silence fell upon the room as Mr. March and the young pair took their places under the green arch.

Mother and sisters gathered close, as if loath to give Meg up; the fatherly voice broke more than once, which seemed to make the service more beautiful and solemn; the bridegroom's hand trembled visibly, and no one heard his replies; but Meg looked straight up in her husband's eyes, and said, "I will!" with such tender trust in her own face and voice that her mother's heart rejoiced and Aunt March sniffed audibly.

[The family] stood watching [Meg], with faces full of love and hope and tender pride as she walked away, leaning on her husband's arm, with her hands full of flowers and the June sunshine brightening her happy face—and so Meg's married life began.[41]

BELOVED

Beloved, my Beloved, when I think

That thou wast in the world a year ago,

What time I sat alone here in the snow

And saw no footprint, heard the silence sink

No moment at thy voice, but, link by link,

Went counting all my chains as if that so

They never could fall off at any blow

Struck by thy possible hand—why, thus I drink

Of life's great cup of wonder! Wonderful,

Never to feel the thrill the day or night

With personal act or speech—nor ever cull

Some prescience of thee with the blossoms white

Thou sawest growing! Atheists are as dull,

Who cannot guess God's presence out of sight.

ELIZABETH BARRETT
BROWNING
Sonnet XX

Bess and Harry Truman's Courtship and Marriage

DAVID McCULLOUGH

From *Truman*

The love story of Bess Wallace and Harry Truman is the stuff all-American romances are made from. Just as Independence, Missouri, is Heart of America country, so were the families who lived on North Delaware Street in that fair town. Harry Truman knew all about the rather elusive Bess Wallace, or thought he did. "I'm settin' my cap for her," he told his friends the Nolands.

"Well, I saw her," he is said to have exclaimed with a grin to the Noland sisters one summer night in 1910.

Ethel and Nellie Noland, who had both become school-teachers, were still living in the family house on North Delaware Street. According to Ethel, keeper of family history, Harry had stopped for a visit when someone mentioned a cake plate that should be returned to Mrs. Wallace and Harry volunteered "with something approaching the speed of light." He crossed the street, went up the walk to the Gates house, up four steps and onto the porch, cranked the bell of the tall, double-leafed front door, then stood waiting. "And Bess came to the door," remembered Ethel, who must have been watching from her own porch, "and of course nothing could have been a bigger occasion than that, to see her again and talk to her." He didn't return for two hours.

From the [Truman] farm [in Grandview] to North Delaware Street was only sixteen miles, but a long ride by horse and buggy—four hours or more round trip—even assuming John Truman would make the horse and buggy available when Harry wished. Nor was going by train much faster or easier. Harry had to walk into Grandview and catch the Frisco to Kansas City, then change to an Independence train. Relatively few trains stopped at Grandview, however, and connections were poor, with long delays even if everything went right. The one other possibility was to hitch a ride by buggy to a point called Dodson on Blue River, where he could take the interurban, the electric streetcar, into Kansas City, then transfer to another streetcar to Independence. Whichever way he chose seemed designed to make life difficult. Yet he made the trip at every opportunity, often spending the night on a couch at the Nolands'. Old friends and relatives in town were greatly impressed by such ardor. To people in Independence, Grandview was "the sticks."

He was invited to Sunday dinner and sat politely with Bessie and her very formal mother, her brothers, and Grandmother and Grandfather Gates, as a black servant passed dishes. In the parlor afterward he played the piano for them. Bessie also accepted his invitations to concerts and the theater in Kansas City and went with him to meet his former piano teacher, Mrs. White. Harry was sure they would like one another. ("Isn't she a caution?" he said later of Mrs. White.) Yet Bessie, as others noticed, did not go out to the farm to meet his family.

But it was in letter after letter—hundreds of letters as time passed— that he poured himself out to her, saying what he found he never could in her presence, writing more than he ever had in his life and discovering how much satisfaction there was in writing. He also longed desperately for her to write him, which, as he told her, was the main reason he wrote so often and at such length. Phone calls on a party line were out of the question, with the neighbors listening. He didn't like the telephone under any circumstances. "I'm always rattled and can never say what I want to," he explained to her.

What she wrote to him, what tone her correspondence took, can only be imagined, or deduced from what he said in response, since none of her letters from this period have survived.

It was a cheerful, often funny, consistently interesting, extremely alert, straightforward, and irrepressible young man that she came to know in this outpouring of mail from Grandview. And she possessed many of the same qualities. Her vitality and good humor, in particular, had made her quite popular in her own circles. Several young men had found her attractive well before she was rediscovered by Harry Truman. Chrisman Swope, son of one of the wealthiest families in

Independence, had come calling frequently. There was a Mr. Young, a Mr. Harris, and a "romance" apparently with a young man named Julian Harvey from Kansas City. As Harry understood from the start, she was used to attention.

He could not spell very well, as he was aware. ("Say, it sure is a grand thing that I have a high school dictionary handy," he wrote. "I had to look on the back to see how to spell the book itself.") And clearly he delighted in talking about himself. He was his own favorite subject, yet nearly always with a sense of proportion and a sense of humor. She had never received letters anything like them—and very fortunately she saved them.

"It is necessary to sit about half a mile or so from the horses when you drive an old binder [he explained in one] and it's yell or stand still. My whip is just too short. If I make it longer it grinds up in the machinery and causes a disaster not only to the insides of the binder but to my record in the Book of Justice. It's cheaper to cuss the team.

"This morning I was helping to dig a grave," he reported in another letter, attempting to illustrate that farmers "get all kinds of experience in lots of things. . . ."

"It is not nearly such a sad proceeding as you'd think. There were six or seven of us, and we'd take turns digging. Those who weren't digging would sit around and tell lies about the holes they'd dug and the hogs they'd raised. We spent a very pleasant forenoon and then went to the funeral."

They were hardly love letters, no "nonsense or bosh." He told her about Uncle Harry, about the hired men, and while he bragged occasionally of how hard he worked, he in no way romanticized life on the farm for her benefit. If anything, he went to the other extreme. "I have been to the lot and put about a hundred rings in half as many hogs' noses. You really haven't any idea what a soul stirring job it is, especially on a day when the mud is knee deep. . . ." He described being stuck in the eye by a blade of corn, and how his face had burned to the color of raw beef after hauling hay all day.

He had strong opinions and no small share of bigotry, though she never saw it that way, never found his use of expressions like "coon," "nigger," "bohunk," "Dago," or "Chink" objectionable, or she would have let him know and that would have been the end of it, since as he said, "I'm horribly anxious for you to suffer from an excessively good opinion of me!"

In his way he could also become quite philosophical, a word he didn't like.

"You know when people can get excited over the ordinary things in life, they live," he said at one point.

"You've no idea how experience teaches sympathy," he observed in another letter, soon after breaking his leg.

Of his religious convictions, a matter he knew to be of great importance to her mother, he said that while he remembered well their Presbyterian Sunday school days together and though he had since joined the Baptist Church, he was only a reasonably good Baptist as the term was understood in Grandview. "I am by religion like everything else. I think there's more in acting than in talking." Bessie had invited him to attend an Episcopal service in Independence. (The Wallaces, too, had abandoned the Presbyterian Church.) It was his first time at an Episcopal service, he told her. He knew nothing of "Lent and such things." Once, on a Sunday in Kansas City, he confessed, "I made a start for church and landed at the Shubert [theatre]."

They exchanged views on writers. Mark Twain was his patron saint in literature, Harry said. The year before, as he did not tell her, he had spent $25 of his own money for a twenty-five volume set of Twain's works. She urged him to read the longer novels of Dickens and in a letter written in May 1911, after his accident, he told her that to his surprise he was greatly enjoying *David Copperfield:*

I have been reading David Copperfield *and have really found out that I couldn't appreciate Dickens before. I have only read* Oliver Twist *and* Tale of Two Cities. *They didn't make much of an impression on me and I never read anything else. A neighbor sent me* Dombey & Son *and* David C., *and I am glad for it has awakened a new interest. It is almost a reconciliation to having my leg broken to contemplate the amount of reading I am going to do this summer. I am getting better fast and I am afraid I'll get well so soon I won't get to read enough. . . .*

Then, out of the blue, that June, he proposed to her by mail, mixing affection with a little self-deprecation and caution, fearful she might laugh at him.

You know, were I an Italian or a poet I would commence and use all the luscious language of two continents. I am not either but only a kind of good-for-nothing American farmer. I've always had a sneakin' notion that some day maybe I'd amount to something. I doubt it now though like everything. It is a family failing of ours to be poor financiers. I am blest that way. Still that doesn't keep me from having always thought that you were all that a girl could be possibly and impossibly. You may not have guessed it but I've been crazy about you ever since we went to Sunday school together. But I never had the nerve to think you'd even look at me. . . . You said you were tired of these kind of stories in books so I am trying one from real life. I guess it sounds funny to you, but you must bear in mind that this is my first experience in this line and also it is very real to me.

Three weeks passed without a word from her. He waited, agonizing, then wrote to ask if he had said anything to offend her. She responded by turning him down, and apparently over the phone. That same day he wrote as follows:

GRANDVIEW, MO. JULY 12, 1911
Dear Bessie:

You know that you turned me down so easy that I am almost happy anyway. I never was fool enough to think that a girl like you could ever care for a fellow like me but I couldn't help telling you how I felt. I have always wanted you to have some fine, rich-looking man, but I know that if ever I got the chance I'd tell you how I felt even if I didn't even get to say another word to you. What makes me feel good is that you were good enough to answer me seriously and not make fun of me anyway. You know when a fellow tells a girl all his

heart and she makes a joke of it I suppose it would be the awfullest
feeling in the world. You see I never had any desire to say such
things to anyone else. All my girlfriends think I am a cheerful idiot
and a confirmed old bach. They really don't know the reason nor
ever will. I have been so afraid you were not even going to let me be
your good friend. To be even in that class is something.

You may think I'll get over it as all boys do. I guess I am something
of a freak myself. I really never had any desire to make love to a girl
just for the fun of it, and you have always been the reason. I have
never met a girl in my life that you were not the first to be compared
with her, to see wherein she was lacking and she always was.

Please don't think I am talking nonsense or bosh, for if ever I told the
truth I am telling it now and I'll never tell such things to anyone else
or bother you with them again. I have always been more idealist
than practical anyway, so I really never expected any reward for
loving you. I shall always hope though. . . .

Then, promising to put on no hangdog airs when next he
saw her, he changed the subject. Did she know of any way to
make it rain?

They exchanged photographs and Harry had a standing
invitation to Sunday dinner at the Gates house. Week after
week, with no success, he tried to get her to come to Grandview.
In August, he announced he was building a grass tennis court
for her on a level place near the house. She could bring her
friends, make a day of it. At Montgomery Ward in Kansas City
he bought a heavy roller. Since neither he nor anyone else on

the farm, or anyone in Grandview, played tennis or knew the requirements for a court, he had her send directions. He hoped to have everything ready by Labor Day. Mamma would cook a chicken dinner, he promised. "Not town dinner but midday meal, see? So be sure and come. . . . Now be sure and come out on Labor Day."

In the flurry of excitement, seeing how intent on success he was, Matt decided to have several rooms papered. With only three days to go, Harry sent Bessie a map with directions. The Sunday before Labor Day he worked the day through on the court and by nightfall had everything ready, including a supply of watermelons.

But she didn't come. She sent word it was raining in Independence. He wrote at once of his "disappointment" and asked if she could make it another time, adding that Mamma would still like her to come for dinner and that the weather in Grandview on Labor Day had been fine. When she did at last appear, for an impromptu visit some weeks later, the court was found to be insufficiently level for a proper game.

Yet, he would not be discouraged. He kept at courtship as he had kept to his piano lessons, with cheerful, willing determination. He told her of his progress in the Masons, he sent her books, commented on stories in his favorite magazines, *Everybody's, Life,* and *Adventure.* "I was reading Plato's *Republic* this morning," he also informed her at one point, "and Socrates was discoursing on the ideal Republic. . . . You see, I sometimes read something besides *Adventure.*"

He knew he had a gift for conversation. He had found he could get most anything he wanted if he could only talk to people. The letters were his way to talk to her as he never could face to face.

The fact that he had no money and that he craved money came up repeatedly, more often and more obviously than probably he realized. In Grandview circles, financial wealth was something people seldom talked about or judged one another by. "We never rated a person by the amount of money he had," remembered Stephen Slaughter. "Always, first and foremost, it was his character, his integrity." No family, not even the Slaughters, had large bank accounts or costly possessions. Everybody, including the Slaughters, had debts. But Harry wanted more than what sufficed for Grandview; or, in any event, he clearly wanted Bessie Wallace to think he aimed higher.

If only she cared a little, he would double his efforts "to amount to something." Bessie replied saying that she and Mary Paxton had concluded that a woman should think seriously only of a man who could support her in style. Harry said he would take this as a sign of encouragement, whether she meant it that way or not.

She had lately told him Bessie was a name she no longer cared for. So his letters now began "Dear Bess," though they closed as always, "Sincerely, Harry," or sometimes, "Most sincerely, Harry."

Then, at long last, on a Sunday in November 1913, as Harry sat speechless, Bess said that if ever she married anyone it would be him. She wrote a letter to confirm the promise. They agreed they were secretly engaged. Harry was beside himself, "all puffed up and hilarious and happy." She had made a confirmed optimist of him, he said. She called him an enigma. He said that sounded fine to him and especially coming from her, "for I always labored under the impression that it took smart people to be one."

There were no bounds now to his horizons. "How does it feel to be engaged to a clodhopper who has ambitions to be Governor of Montana and Chief Executive of the U.S.?" he inquired, the expansive aspirations intended as humor only. To his surprise, she wrote at once to say how much she cared for him. "I know your last letter word for word and then I read it some forty times a day," he said. "Oh please send me another like it." He thought perhaps he should put it in a safe deposit vault to keep from wearing it out.

"You really didn't know I had so much softness and sentimentality in me, did you? I'm full of it. But I'd die if I had to talk it. I can tell you on paper how much I love you and what one grand woman I think you are, but to tell it to you I can't. I'm always afraid I'd do it so clumsily you'd laugh. . . . I could die happy doing something for you. . . . Since I can't rescue you from any monster or carry you from a burning building or save you from a sinking ship—simply because I'd be afraid of the monsters, couldn't carry you, and can't swim—I'll have to go to work and make money enough to pay my debts and then get you to take me for what I am: just a common everyday man whose instincts are to be ornery, who's anxious to be right. You'll not have any trouble getting along with me for I'm awful good. . . . Do you suppose your mother'll care for me well enough to have me in her family?"

"Mrs. Wallace [Bess's mother] wasn't a bit in favor of Harry," remembered one of the Noland family, all of whom were strongly on Harry's side. "And she says, 'You don't want to marry that farmer boy, he is not going to make it anywhere.' And so she didn't push it at all. She kind of tried to prevent it. . . ."

Every call Harry made at 219 North Delaware Street could only have been a reminder of what distances remained between his world and hers. The etched glass in the front door, the plum-colored Brussels carpets, the good china and heavy lace curtains at the long parlor windows, the accepted use of silver dessert forks, the absence of any sign that survival meant hard physical labor day in, day out, the whole air of privacy, of unruffled comfort and stability, reflected a way of life totally apart from anything in his experience. ("We have moved around quite a bit and always the best people are hardest to know," he once told Bess defensively.) Had he only to overcome the obvious differences in their station, he would have had an uphill haul, as he would have said. But the problem was greatly compounded by how Madge Wallace felt toward anyone or any cause that threatened to take Bess from her.

"Yes, it is true that Mrs. Wallace did not think Harry was good enough for Bess," a member of the Wallace circle would comment with a smile sixty years afterward, her memory of it all quite clear. "But then, don't you see, Mrs. Wallace didn't think *any* man was good enough for Bess."[42]

HARRY AND BESS'S MARRIAGE WAS FURTHER DELAYED WHILE
TRUMAN SERVED HIS COUNTRY IN THE UNITED STATES ARMY.
THOSE DAYS PROVIDED FRIENDS AND A SENSE OF ACHIEVEMENT
THAT WOULD REMAIN WITH HIM THROUGHOUT LIFE.

BESS AND HARRY'S WEDDING

DAVID MCCULLOUGH
From *Truman*

May 6, 1919, at Camp Funston, Kansas, the men [including Harry S. Truman] were given their final discharges, and seven weeks and four days after that Bess and Harry were married. But not before [an] important [event] took place.

On May 8, Harry's birthday and his second day home, he and Bess had their first and apparently their last heated argument. Possibly it was over the wedding plans, or possibly over her mother's insistence that they live with her. Whatever the cause, Harry would remember the day and its misery the rest of his life. In a letter to Bess written thirty years later, he would refer to it as their "final" argument.

The wedding, on Saturday, June 28, 1919, took place at four in the afternoon in tiny Trinity Episcopal Church on North Liberty Street in Independence, and the day was the kind Missouri summers are famous for. The church, full of family and friends, became so stifling hot that all the flowers began to wilt.

The bride wore a simple dress of white georgette crepe, a white picture hat, and carried a bouquet of roses. Her attendants, cousins Helen Wallace and Louise Wells, were dressed in organdy and they too carried roses. The groom had on a fine-checked, gray, three-piece business suit made especially for the occasion, on credit, by his best man, Ted Marks, who had returned to his old trade of gentleman's tailor. The groom also wore a pair of his Army pince-nez spectacles and appeared, as he stood at the front of the church, to have arrived directly from the barbershop.

Frank Wallace, the tall, prematurely balding brother of the bride, escorted her to the altar, where the Reverend J. P. Plunkett read the service.

Present at the reception afterward on the lawn at the Gates house, were Mrs. Wallace and her mother, Mrs. Gates, Mr. and Mrs. Frank Wallace, Mr. and Mrs. George Wallace, and young Fred Wallace, while the "out-of-town" guests, as recorded in the papers, included Mrs. J. A. Truman, her daughter Miss Mary Jane Truman, and Mr. and Mrs. J. Vivian Truman. All the Nolands attended, of course, as did several of Harry's former brothers in arms. One who was unable to be there wrote to him, "I hope you have the same success in this new war as you had in the old."

Punch and ice cream were served. The wedding party posed for pictures, Harry looking extremely serious, Bess a bit bemused. Presently, bride and groom departed for the train in Kansas City, driven by Frank Wallace, with more cars following.

At the station, waiting on the platform, Ted Marks remarked to Harry's mother, "Well, Mrs. Truman, you've lost Harry."

"Indeed, I haven't," she replied.

Recalling the day years later, Mary Jane spoke more of what she had been through before she and Mamma ever reached the church. They had been harvesting wheat at the farm. Mary Jane had cooked noon dinner for twelve farmhands—meat, potatoes, fresh bread, homemade pies, "the usual," she said.

Ethel Noland remembered Harry's expression as he stood watching Bess come down the aisle. "You've just never seen such a radiant, happy look on a man's face."

The honeymoon couple stopped at Chicago, Detroit, and Port Huron, Michigan. In Chicago, they stayed at the Blackstone. At Port Huron, they were at the beaches of Lake Huron, where the weather was as perfect as their time together. So sublime were these days and nights beside the ice-cold lake that for Harry the very words "Port Huron" would forever mean the ultimate in happiness.[43]

TO HUSBAND
AND WIFE

Preserve sacredly the privacies of your own house, your married

state and your heart. Let no father or mother or sister or

brother ever presume to come between you or share the joys or

sorrows that belong to you two alone.

With mutual help build your quiet world, not allowing your

dearest earthly friend to be the confidant of aught that concerns

your domestic peace. Let moments of alienation, if they occur,

be healed at once. Never, no never, speak of it outside; but to

each other confess and all will come out right. Never let the

morrow's sun still find you at variance. Renew and renew your

vow. It will do you good; and thereby your minds will grow

together contented in that love which is stronger

than death, and you will be truly one.

ANONYMOUS

A MARRIAGE BLESSING

From *The Book of Common Prayer*

Most gracious God, we give You thanks for Your tender love in sending Jesus Christ to come among us, to be born of a human mother, and to make the way of the cross to be the way of life. We thank you, also, for consecrating the union of man and woman in His name. By the power of Your Holy Spirit, pour out the abundance of Your blessing upon this man and this woman. Defend them from every enemy. Lead them into all peace. Let their love for each other be a seal upon their hearts, a mantle about their shoulders, and a crown upon their foreheads. Bless them in their work and in their companionship; in their sleeping and in their waking; in their joys and in their sorrows; in their life and in their death. Finally, in Your mercy, bring them to that table where Your saints feast forever in Your heavenly home; through Jesus Christ, who with You and the Holy Spirit, lives and reigns, one God, forever and ever.

Amen.[44]

FOUR MARRIAGE PRAYERS

From *The Book of Common Prayer*

Eternal God, creator and preserver of all life, author of
salvation, and giver of all grace: Look with favor upon the
world You have made, and for which Your Son gave His life,
and especially upon this man and this woman whom You make
one flesh in Holy Matrimony.
Amen.

Give them wisdom and devotion in the ordering of their
common life, that each may be to the other a strength in need,
a counselor in perplexity, a comfort in sorrow, and a
companion in joy.
Amen.

Grant that their wills may be so knit together in Your will, and
their spirits in Your Spirit, that they may grow in love and peace
with You and one another all the days of their life.
Amen.

Give them such fulfillment of their mutual affection that they
may reach out in love and concern for others.
Amen.[45]

THE APACHE
WEDDING PRAYER

Now you will feel no rain,
For each of you will be shelter to the other.
Now you will feel no cold,
For each of you will be warmth to the other.
Now there is no more loneliness,
For each of you will be companion to the other.
Now you are two bodies,
But there is only one life before you.
Go now to your dwelling place
To enter into the days of your togetherness
And may your days be good and long upon the earth.

ANONYMOUS

THIS MARRIAGE

May these vows and this marriage be blessed.
May it be sweet milk,
this marriage, like wine and halvah.
May this marriage offer fruit and shade
like the date palm.
May this marriage be full of laughter,
our every day a day in paradise.
May this marriage be a sign of compassion,
a seal of happiness here and hereafter.
May this marriage have a fair face and a good name,
an omen as welcome as the moon in a clear blue sky.
I am out of words to describe
how spirit mingles in this marriage.[46]

JAL'AL U'DDIN RUMI

THE GIFT OF THE MAGI

O. HENRY

One dollar and eighty-seven cents. That was all. And sixty cents of it was in pennies. Pennies saved one and two at a time by bulldozing the grocer and the vegetable man and the butcher until one's cheeks burned with the silent imputation of parsimony that such close dealing implied. Three times Della counted it. One dollar and eighty-seven cents. And the next day would be Christmas.

There was clearly nothing to do but flop down on the shabby little couch and howl. So Della did it. Which instigates the moral reflection that life is made up of sobs, sniffles, and smiles, with sniffles predominating.

While the mistress of the home is gradually subsiding from the first stage to the second, take a look at the home. A furnished flat at $8 per week. It did not exactly fit beggar description, but it certainly had that word on the lookout for the mendicancy squad.

In the vestibule below was a letter-box into which no letter would go, and an electric button from which no mortal finger could coax a ring. Also appertaining thereunto was a card bearing the name "Mr. James Dillingham Young."

The "Dillingham" had been flung to the breeze during a former period of prosperity when its possessor was being paid $30 per week. Now, when the income was shrunk to $20, the letters of "Dillingham" looked blurred, as though they were thinking seriously of contracting to a modest and unassuming D. But whenever Mr. James Dillingham Young came home and reached his flat above he was called "Jim" and greatly hugged by Mrs. James Dillingham Young, already introduced to you as Della. Which is all very good.

Della finished her cry and attended to her cheeks with the powder rag. She stood by the window and looked out dully at a gray cat walking a gray fence in a gray backyard. Tomorrow would be Christmas Day, and she had only $1.87 with which to buy Jim a present. She had been saving every penny she could for months, with this result. Twenty dollars a week doesn't go far. Expenses had been greater than she had calculated. They always are. Only $1.87 to buy a present for Jim. Her Jim. Many a happy hour she had spent planning for something nice for him. Something fine and rare and sterling— something just a little bit near to being worthy of the honor of being owned by Jim.

There was a pier-glass between the windows of the room. Perhaps you have seen a pier-glass in an $8 flat. A very thin and very agile person may, by observing his reflection in a rapid sequence of longitudinal strips, obtain a fairly accurate conception of his looks. Della, being slender, had mastered the art.

Suddenly she whirled from the window and stood before

the glass. Her eyes were shining brilliantly, but her face had lost its color within twenty seconds. Rapidly she pulled down her hair and let it fall to its full length.

Now, there were two possessions of the James Dillingham Youngs in which they both took a mighty pride. One was Jim's gold watch that had been his father's and his grandfather's. The other was Della's hair. Had the Queen of Sheba lived in the flat across the airshaft, Della would have let her hair hang out the window some day to dry just to depreciate Her Majesty's jewels and gifts. Had King Solomon been the janitor, with all his treasures piled up in the basement, Jim would have pulled out his watch every time he passed, just to see him pluck at his beard from envy.

So now Della's beautiful hair fell about her rippling and shining like a cascade of brown waters. It reached below her knee and made itself almost a garment for her. And then she did it up again nervously and quickly. Once she faltered for a minute and stood still while a tear or two splashed on the worn red carpet.

On went her old brown jacket; on went her old brown hat. With a whirl of skirts and with the brilliant sparkle still in her eyes, she fluttered out the door and down the stairs to the street.

Where she stopped the sign read: "Mme. Sofronie. Hair Goods of All Kinds." One flight up Della ran, and collected herself, panting. Madame, large, too white, chilly, hardly looked the "Sofronie."

"Will you buy my hair?" asked Della.

"I buy hair," said Madame. "Take yer hat off and let's have a sight at the looks of it."

Down rippled the brown cascade.

"Twenty dollars," said Madame, lifting the mass with a practiced hand.

"Give it to me quick," said Della.

Oh, and the next two hours tripped by on rosy wings. Forget the hashed metaphor. She was ransacking the stores for Jim's present.

She found it at last. It surely had been made for Jim and no one else. There was no other like it in any of the stores, and she had turned all of them inside out. It was a platinum fob chain simple and chaste in design, properly proclaiming its value by substance alone and not by meretricious ornamentation—as all good things should do. It was even worthy of The Watch. As soon as she saw it she knew that it must be Jim's. It was like him. Quietness and value—the description applied to both. Twenty-one dollars they took from her for it, and she hurried home with the 87 cents. With that chain on his watch Jim might be properly anxious about the time in any company. Grand as the watch was, he sometimes looked at it on the sly on account of the old leather strap that he used in place of a chain.

When Della reached home her intoxication gave way a little to prudence and reason. She got out her curling irons and lighted the gas and went to work repairing the ravages made by generosity added to love. Which is always a tremendous task, dear friends—a mammoth task.

Within forty minutes her head was covered with tiny, close-lying curls that made her look wonderfully like a truant schoolboy. She looked at her reflection in the mirror long, carefully, and critically.

"If Jim doesn't kill me," she said to herself, "before he takes a second look at me, he'll say I look like a Coney Island chorus girl. But what could I do—oh! what could I do with a dollar and eighty-seven cents?"

At 7 o'clock the coffee was made and the frying-pan was on the back of the stove hot and ready to cook the chops.

Jim was never late. Della doubled the fob chain in her hand and sat on the corner of the table near the door that he always entered. Then she heard his step on the stairway down on the first flight, and she turned white for just a moment. She had a habit of saying little silent prayers about the simplest everyday things, and now she whispered: "Please God, make him think I am still pretty."

The door opened and Jim stepped in and closed it. He looked thin and very serious. Poor fellow, he was only twenty-two—and to be burdened with a family! He needed a new overcoat and he was without gloves.

Jim stopped inside the door, as immovable as a setter at the scent of quail. His eyes were fixed upon Della, and there was an expression in them that she could not read, and it terrified her. It was not anger, nor surprise, nor disapproval, nor horror, nor any of the sentiments that she had been prepared for. He simply stared at her fixedly with that peculiar expression on his face.

Della wriggled off the table and went for him.

"Jim, darling," she cried, "don't look at me that way. I had my hair cut off and sold it because I couldn't have lived through Christmas without giving you a present. It'll grow out again— you won't mind, will you? I just had to do it. My hair grows awfully fast. Say 'Merry Christmas!' Jim, and let's be happy. You don't know what a nice—what a beautiful, nice gift I've got for you."

"You've cut off your hair?" asked Jim, laboriously, as if he had not arrived at that patent fact yet even after the hardest mental labor.

"Cut it off and sold it," said Della. "Don't you like me just as well, anyhow? I'm me without my hair, ain't I?"

Jim looked about the room curiously.

"You say your hair is gone?" he said, with an air almost of idiocy.

"You needn't look for it," said Della. "It's sold, I tell you— sold and gone, too. It's Christmas Eve, boy. Be good to me, for it went for you. Maybe the hairs of my head were numbered," she went on with a sudden serious sweetness, "but nobody could ever count my love for you. Shall I put the chops on, Jim?"

Out of his trance Jim seemed quickly to wake. He enfolded his Della. For ten seconds let us regard with discreet scrutiny some inconsequential object in the other direction. Eight dollars a week or a million a year—what is the difference? A mathematician or a wit would give you the wrong answer. The magi brought valuable gifts, but that was not among them. This dark assertion will be illuminated later on.

Jim drew a package from his overcoat pocket and threw it upon the table.

"Don't make any mistake, Dell," he said, "about me. I don't think there's anything in the way of a haircut or a shave or a shampoo that could make me like my girl any less. But if you'll unwrap that package you may see why you had me going a while at first."

White fingers and nimble tore at the string and paper. And then an ecstatic scream of joy; and then, alas! a quick feminine change to hysterical tears and wails, necessitating the immediate employment of all the comforting powers of the lord of the flat.

For there lay The Combs—the set of combs, side and back, that Della had worshipped for long in a Broadway window. Beautiful combs, pure tortoise shell, with jeweled rims—just the shade to wear in the beautiful vanished hair. They were expensive combs, she knew, and her heart had simply craved and yearned over them without the least hope of possession. And now, they were hers, but the tresses that should have adorned the coveted adornments were gone.

But she hugged them to her bosom, and at length she was able to look up with dim eyes and a smile and say: "My hair grows so fast, Jim!"

And then Della leaped up like a little singed cat and cried, "Oh, oh!"

Jim had not yet seen his beautiful present. She held it out to him eagerly upon her open palm. The dull precious metal seemed to flash with a reflection of her bright and ardent spirit.

"Isn't it a dandy, Jim? I hunted all over town to find it. You'll have to look at the time a hundred times a day now. Give me your watch. I want to see how it looks on it."

Instead of obeying, Jim tumbled down on the couch and put his hands under the back of his head and smiled.

"Dell," said he, "let's put our Christmas presents away and keep 'em a while. They're too nice to use just at present. I sold the watch to get the money to buy your combs. And now suppose you put the chops on."

The magi, as you know, were wise men—wonderfully wise men—who brought gifts to the Babe in the manger. They invented the art of giving Christmas presents. Being wise, their gifts were no doubt wise ones, possibly bearing the privilege of exchange in case of duplication. And here I have lamely related to you the uneventful chronicle of two foolish children in a flat who most unwisely sacrificed for each other the greatest treasures of their house. But in a last word to the wise of these days let it be said that of all who give gifts these two were the wisest. Of all who give and receive gifts, such as they are wisest. Everywhere they are wisest. They are the magi.[47]

GOOD-NIGHT

Good-night. Good-night. Ah, good the night

That wraps thee in its silver light.

Good-night. No night is good for me

That does not hold a thought of thee.

Good-night.

Good-night. Be every night as sweet

As that which made our love complete,

Till that last night when death shall be

One brief "Good-night," for thee and me.

Good-night.

S. WEIR MITCHELL

THE NEWLY WEDDED

Now the rite is duly done,
Now the word is spoken,
And the spell has made us one
Which may ne'er be broken;
Rest we, dearest, in our home,
Roam we o'er the heather:
We shall rest, and we shall roam
Shall we not? together.

From this hour the summer rose
Sweeter breathes to charm us;
From this hour the winter snows
Lighter fall to harm us:
Fair or foul—on land or sea—
Come the wind or weather,
Best and worse, whate'er they be,
We shall share together.

Death, who friend from friend can part,
Brother rend from brother,
Shall but link us, heart and heart,
Closer to each other:
We will call his anger play,
Deem his dart a feather,
When we meet him on our way
Hand in hand together.

WINTHROP MACKWORTH PRAED

A WEDDING HYMN

Jesus, stand beside them
On this day of days,
That in happy wedlock
They may live always.
Join their hands together,
And their hearts make one;
Guard the troth now plighted
And the life begun.
On their pleasant homestead
Let Thy radiance rest;
Making joy and sorrow
By Thy presence blest;
Gild their common duties
With a light divine,
As, in Cana, water
Thou didst change to wine.
Leave them or forsake them;
Ever be their Friend.[48]

THOMAS TIPLADY

MISS MARGARET E. SANGSTER ON LOVE

In 1904 social observer Margaret E. Sangster penned Good Manners for All Occasions. *Her remarks on marriage are notable.*

The sentimental young woman who puts a bit of the wedding cake under her pillow may have a dream that will bring her good fortune.

There is a lovely reason why radiant brides wears white. While ivory satin is quite popular, pure white will always be the more appropriate fabric color.

The giving of wedding gifts has become a cause for concern. In no way should the occasion be an excuse to make a personal impression.

The bride's outfit when she leaves her father's house is very complete, because she will not any longer send her bills to her father or ask him for money to buy clothes.

The bridegroom's family, his mother and sisters, are supposed to see that he discards his old clothes of which the best of men are fond, and starts newly equipped, on his new chapter of life.

Marriage must exemplify friendship's highest ideal, or else it will be a failure.

But granting that a young man and a young woman love one another, have health, have courage, and honor, they need not be deterred from marrying because they have little money. The very smallest income that may be depended upon will do as a beginning.

More liberty is allowed than was formerly the case, but in fashionable circles it is generally considered that a young lady should not be seen without a chaperon in any place of public amusement.[49]

MISS EMILY POST ON THE BRIDE

From *Etiquette*, 1922

The bride, above all, must not reach up and wig-wag signals while she is receiving, any more than she must wave to people as she goes up and down the aisle of the church.

She must not cling to her husband, stand pigeon-toed, or lean against him or the wall, or any person or thing.

She must not run her arm through his and let her hand flop on the other side;

She must not swing her arms as though they were dangling ropes;

She must not switch herself this way and that, nor must she "hello" or shout.[50]

THE WORD

My friend, my bonny friend, when we are old,

And hand and hand go tottering down the hill,

May we be rich in love's refined gold,

May love's gold

coin be current with us still.

May love be sweeter for the vanished days,

And your most perfect beauty still as dear

As when your troubled singer stood at gaze

In the dear March of a most sacred year.

May what we are be all we might have been,

And that potential, perfect, O my friend,

And may there still be many shears to glean

In our love's acre, comrade, till the end.

And may we find, when ended is the page,

Death but a tavern on our pilgrimage.[51]

JOHN MASEFIELD

MARRIAGE

As much as we love our country, most people would perhaps agree that something needs to be done about certain problems. Marriage, for example. I think it was an old Roman who said, "The empire begins at the fireside." Certainly the strength of a nation is derived from the home. Family statistics in 1979 showed the divorce rate up 69 percent in ten years, with the average lasting 6.6 years; and 40 percent of the children born in the seventies spent some of their youth in a one-parent family. I was fortunate to be born in the closing years of the 19th century when the home was secure and marriage was for life.[52]

NORMAN VINCENT
PEALE
From *This Incredible Century*

LOVE SONG

There is a strong wall about me to protect me:
It is built of the words you have said to me.

There are swords about me to keep me safe:
They are the kisses of your lips.

Before me goes a shield to guard me
from harm:
It is the shadow of your arms between me
and danger.

All the wishes of my mind know your name,
And the white desires of my heart
They are acquainted with you.
The cry of my body for completeness,
That is a cry to you.
My blood beats out your name to me,
unceasing, pitiless
Your name, your name.

MARY CAROLYN DAVIES

NANCY & RONALD REAGAN

RONALD REAGAN
From *An American Life*

The telephone call was from director Mervyn Leroy, who told me an actress working on one of his pictures needed my help. The young woman, Nancy Davis, was extremely upset because the name of another actress identified as Nancy Davis had appeared on the membership rosters of several Communist front groups and she was receiving notices of their meetings in her mail.

Mervyn said he was sure the young woman had absolutely no interest in left-wing causes, and knowing of the work we had done to clear movie people unfairly accused as Communists, he asked me if I would look into it.

As president of the Screen Actors Guild, I did a little research and found out that there was more than one Nancy Davis connected with show business—in fact there were several—and it took me only a few minutes to establish that Mervyn's Nancy Davis was not the one who belonged to several Communist front groups. I told him to tell her we had cleared her, that she had nothing to worry about.

Pretty soon, Mervyn called back and said his assurances hadn't been enough to satisfy the young lady.

"She's a worrier," he said. "She's still worried that people are going to think she's a Communist. Why don't you give her a call? I think she will take it better from you than from me. Just take her out to dinner and tell her the whole story yourself."

I agreed, and, besides, taking out a young actress under contract to MGM, even sight unseen, didn't seem like a bad idea to me—and I could call it part of my duties as president of the Guild.

To be on the safe side, however, when I called her, I said: "I have an early call in the morning, so I'm afraid we'll have to make it an early evening."

"Fine," Nancy said, "I've got an early call, too. I can't stay out too late either."

She had her pride, too.

We were both lying.

When I picked her up that evening at her apartment, I was standing on two canes a la Pete MacArthur: several months earlier I'd shattered my right thighbone during a charity softball game and was still hobbling around because of it.

I took her to a restaurant on the Sunset Strip and soon realized that Mervyn hadn't been exaggerating when he'd said she was really steamed up over having been confused with someone else.

Well, I suggested, one solution would be to change her name—actresses did it all the time, I said.

When I said that, Nancy looked at me with her hazel eyes and a sense of logic that made me feel a little ridiculous: "But Nancy Davis is my name," she said.

Pretty soon, we weren't talking any more about her problem, but about her mother, who had been a Broadway actress, and her father, a prominent surgeon, and our lives in general. Although we'd agreed to call it an early night, I didn't want the evening to end, so I said: "Have you ever seen Sophie Tucker? She's singing at Ciro's just down the street. Why don't we go see the first show?"

Well, she'd never heard Sophie Tucker before so we went to Ciro's to catch the first show. Then we stayed for the second show and we got home about three o'clock in the morning. No mention was made of early calls. I invited her to dinner the following night and we went to the Malibu Inn.

After that, we dated occasionally, sometimes with our good friends, Bill and Ardis Holden, but both of us continued to date other people, and now and then our paths would cross while we were out with someone else.

This had been going on for several months when I found myself booked for a speech to the Junior League Convention at the Del Coronado Hotel in San Diego. I had always looked forward to that trip down the Coast Highway: In those days before freeways, it was my favorite drive, with the blue Pacific on my right and the rolling green hills of California on my left.

I wanted to share the ride with someone and wondered who I should ask to join me. Then it suddenly occurred to me there was really only one person I wanted to share it with—Nancy Davis. I called her and she accepted and said she was a member of the Junior League in Chicago.

Pretty soon, Nancy was the only one I was calling for dates. And one night over dinner as we sat at a table for two, I said, "Let's get married."

She deserved a more romantic proposal than that, but—bless her—she put her hand on mine, looked into my eyes, and said, "Let's." Right after that, I had pictures coming up, so we had to wait two or three months before we could marry.

If the Hollywood press had gotten wind of our plans, they would have stormed the church, so, apologizing to Nancy, I suggested we have a quiet, secret wedding. She agreed and we were married in a touching ceremony in the Little Brown Church in the Valley on March 4, 1952. There were just five of us in an empty church: Nancy and me; Bill Holden, my best man; Ardis, Nancy's matron of honor; and the minister.

After we said "I do," Bill and Ardis took us to their house for dinner where they had a photographer who took our wedding photos. After dinner, we drove to Riverside about seventy miles southeast of Los Angeles, where we stayed overnight before driving on to Phoenix, where Nancy's parents were vacationing.

If ever God gave me evidence that He had a plan for me, it was the night He brought Nancy into my life.

I have spent many hours of my life giving speeches and expressing my opinions. But it is almost impossible for me to express fully how deeply I love Nancy and how much she has filled my life.

Sometimes, I think my life really began when I met Nancy.

From the start, our marriage was like an adolescent's dream of what a marriage should be. It was rich and full from the beginning, and it has gotten more so with each passing day.

Nancy moved into my heart and replaced an emptiness that I'd been trying to ignore for a long time. Coming home to her is like coming out of the cold into a warm, firelit room. I miss her if she just steps out of the room.

After we were married, Nancy asked to be released from her seven-year contract at MGM: Maybe some women can handle a career and a marriage, she said, but she wasn't going to try. She was going to be my wife.

I can sum up our marriage in a line I spoke when I played the great pitcher Grover Cleveland Alexander, a line spoken by him in life to his wife, Aimee: "God must think a lot of me to have given me you."

I thank Him every day for giving me Nancy.[53]

LOVE GIVES
BIRTH TO LIFE

A HYMN

One God, one life, one love;
One heart and mind and hand;
From love He brought a world to birth,
And from himself, a man.

Two lives, one love, a child;
Two tiny, helpless hands;
And parents gladly spend themselves
To pay all love demands.

REFRAIN:

For love gives birth to life,
Through joy and sacrifice.
Our Father freely gives Himself
To pay its precious price.

If love gives birth to life,
O Lord, let love arise
And fill our days with faith and praise
And joyful sacrifice.
Let love give birth to life.

Our sin, His Son, the cross;
The jeers, the nails, the pain;
His dying love released a life
That death cannot contain.

Yet still they groan and die
And never know You care.
Through us express in tenderness
The love You long to share.

KEN BIBLE

WHO GAVE US THIS LOVE?

*Poet and hymn writer Ken Bible wrote the following for
the marriage ceremony of his son and daughter-in-law.*

Who brought our lives together?
Whose finger lit the flame?
Whose heart has made this miracle—
That we should feel the same?

Who changed me so completely,
That I should give myself,
That I should gladly risk it all
And think of no one else
But you . . .
Just you . . .
Who gives us this love?

You weren't in my plans.
I didn't choose the day
When something happened in my heart
And you were there to stay.

You took me by surprise.
Now all the plans we've made
Will take us where we cannot see,
But I am not afraid.

The One who planned this moment,
Whose finger lit the flame,
Whose heart has made this miracle,
Who let us feel the same—

He'll be there for a lifetime
He'll help me care enough
To set aside each lesser thing
And always, only love
Just you . . .
Just you . . .
I thank Him for you.

KEN BIBLE

How to Predict a Happy Marriage

Les Parrott, III and Leslie Parrott

From *Saving Your Marriage Before It Starts*

Over the last two decades, marriage specialists have researched the ingredients of a happy marriage. As a result, we know more about building a successful marriage today than ever before. For example, happily married couples will have:

- healthy expectations of marriage

- a realistic concept of love

- a positive attitude and outlook toward life

- the ability to communicate their feelings

- an understanding and acceptance of their gender differences

- the ability to make decisions and settle arguments

- a common spiritual foundation and goal[54]

FROM A DAD TO A DAUGHTER

CHARLES SWINDOLL

Well, Colleen, my now grown-up daughter, Saturday is the big day. The Big Day. It's the one we have talked about, planned on, and pictured in our minds since you were just a tot, playing make-believe. Remember? I sure do. Those moments of imaginary ecstasy have spilled over into our conversation dozens (maybe even hundreds) of times during your twenty three years under our roof. Wonderful dreamlike moments, which today seem terribly significant to this proud father of the bride. They are moments your mother and I will forever cherish. But come Saturday, you will trade the make-believe for the real thing. And knowing your love for reality, I have the feeling you'll never look back and wish for the way you were. The Big Day will begin, for you and Mark, the best there is.

And why not? You entered our world bubbling over with excitement and enthusiasm. With a healthy set of lungs and a little round face we couldn't help but cover with kisses, you reminded us that you wouldn't be ignored and that life was to be enjoyed, not endured. Your tiny, warm frame in our arms took the chill out of our New England existence and didn't stop doing its magic through Texas and on out to California. That voice, those eyes, the touch of your hand, your burst of laughter. . . .

Forgive me, sweetheart, but memories of yesteryear flood my mind. Take camping, for example. Listening to the rain from inside our tent, sitting around the campfire roasting marshmallows, and shooting the rapids on inner tubes. Wow! I even remember that dreadful day up at Jedediah Smith State Park when you got lost and the Swindoll search party went to work to find you. I acted cool, but deep inside I was dangerously near panic . . . couldn't bear the thought of losing you. Suddenly, after about an hour's time, you came rumbling toward us, riding shotgun in the state park pickup, sitting next to some bewildered park ranger who had been listening to you ramble and jabber. He seemed more relieved than I when he deposited you in our arms! I never told you, but that night I asked God to keep a safety net about you and never let you lose your way again. How good of Him to answer my request.

Then there were your famous parties: birthday parties, slumber parties, swimming-pool parties, school parties, cheer-leader parties, graduation parties, New Year parties, all of which were incomplete without the same strange ritual of our entire front yard being covered with toilet paper. I'll never forget the time I slipped out the front door early in the morning to get the paper, following one of your crazy parties. Standing on the front porch without my glasses, I really thought it had snowed. No such luck . . . just another T.P. job.

Hasn't it been fun washing cars together? And picking out Mother's Day cards together? And getting yogurt together? And jogging together? And doing dishes together? And speak-ing of together, your mom and I will long remember our early-morning, coffee-sipping times where the three of us laughed and cried, probed and prayed, read to each other, listened to each other, struggled through issues, and sort of hammered out life together back on the sun porch.

Such meaningful memories. Twenty-three years of them. Seems only last week that seasoned nurse at Boston Hospital handed you to me and I welcomed you to our family. It's hard to believe that you are now a mature woman, excited about life, hopelessly in love, and deeply committed to this man who has stolen your heart. His life, his love, his ministry, his future are now your most cherished hopes and plans . . . and that is as it should be. The one I once held ever so closely I willingly release to him to enjoy and nurture and adore.

You're ready, he's ready . . . it's right.

You are a spiritually sensitive young woman. By bringing that quality to your marriage, your presence can only enhance your husband's devotion to Christ. You are also an encourager. Mark's years in seminary will take on new dimensions and those tough days of study won't seem nearly so hard, thanks to your affirmation and confidence. Your sense of humor will give light to otherwise dark and dismal tunnels through which the two of you must travel . . . so, whatever else you do, laugh often and prompt your man to do the same.

Both of you have a lifetime together before you, by God's grace. Enjoy every bit of it. As your Aunt Luci would say, "Savor each moment."

In only a matter of hours, The Big Day will arrive. We shall celebrate and sing. We shall embrace one another. The Swindolls and the Danes will become one . . . and I don't think it's an exaggeration to say the angels of heaven will sing, smile, and celebrate with us.

When the two of you slip away on Saturday evening your mother and I will step aside, arm-in-arm, and smile through tears of joy as we happily let you go to enjoy the best years of your life. At long last, your make-believe dream will be transformed from the distant sunset of childhood fantasy to the delightful sunrise of husband and wife reality.

It's okay if I miss you from time to time, isn't it?

With all my love,
Dad[55]

WHERE THERE IS HOPE: C. S. LEWIS AND JOY DAVIDSON

LES PARROTT III AND LESLIE PARROTT
From *Saving Your Marriage Before It Starts*

One of the most compelling love stories of our time involves a couple who, in the beginning, lived an ocean apart. He was a scruffy old Oxford bachelor, a Christian apologist and an author of best-selling books for children. She, an American, was much younger and divorced with two sons.

After first meeting during her visit to England in 1952, C. S. Lewis and Joy Davidson fed their relationship by mail. Intellectual sparks from the minds of each ignited their appreciation and respect for each other. When Joy moved to England with her boys, the relationship enjoyed the benefits of proximity. And when her departure from England seemed imminent because of a lack of funds and an expiring visitor's visa, C. S. Lewis made a decision: if Joy would agree they would be married.

Early in the marriage Joy's body revealed a secret it had kept hidden. She had cancer—and it was irreversible. The well-ordered life of C. S. Lewis suffered a meltdown. But in the process, the English man of letters realized how deep his love for Joy really was.

Moving on with their lives, the Lewises sought and got the added blessing of the church on their marriage, which had originally been formalized in a registration office. They gave Joy the best treatment available. Then he brought her home, committed to her care. It is not surprising that Joy's body responded. However, her remission was short lived.

Near death, Joy told him, "You have made me happy." Then a little while after, "I am at peace with God." Joy died at 10:15 that evening in 1960. "She smiled," Lewis later recalled, "but not at me."[56]

Remembering Joy

We feasted on love; every mode of it, solemn

and merry, romantic and realistic, sometimes

as dramatic as a thunder- storm, sometimes

comfortable and unemphatic as putting on

your soft slippers. She was my pupil and

my teacher, my subject and my sovereign,

my trusty comrade, friend, shipmate, fellow-

soldier. My mistress, but at the same time all

that any man friend has ever been to me.[57]

C. S. Lewis

ALL I EVER WANTED

All I ever wanted,—
A little, little house
With sunlight in the kitchen
And chambers deep in boughs;
To get up in the morning,
Crisp bacon, shape a theme
From outline of new silver,
Blue cups and yellow cream;
To whisk the rooms to neatness,
Dispatch the work along,
And all the time be humming
Gay snatches of a song;
To run out on the doorstep
For one look at the lake,
And pull a spray of lilacs
To cool me while I bake;
Perhaps in middle morning
Sit where the breeze draws through,
And write some singing verses
Out of my love for you;
To press my newest muslin

And start to pay a call,

—The joy of being a landlord,

And locking doors, and all!—

Sit with the other women,

Gossip a bit, and sew,

But all the time be conscious

Of that deep inner glow;

To hurry home from calling

Because it's after four,

And make your favorite shortcake

From fruit the garden bore,

Then comb my hair out softly

The way you like it most,

And listen for your footsteps

While garnishing the roast.

—Swift days, shot through with loving,

With laughter gay as light,

And walks of courtship glamour

When moons are high and white.—

And then before the fire,

From close against your chest,

To whisper you that secret

Which glorifies the rest.

FLORENCE JACOBS

FROM *ALL FOR LOVE*

Witness, ye days and nights, and all ye hours,

That danced away with down upon your feet,

As all your business were to count my passion!

One day passed by, and nothing saw but love;

Another came, and still 'twas only love:

The suns were wearied out with looking on,

And I untired with loving.

I saw you every day, and all the day;

And every day was still but as the first,

So eager was I still to see you more....

JOHN DRYDEN

Chapter 7

How beautifully the Apostle Paul stated

it in his treatise on love; "[Love] bears all

things, believes all things, hopes all

things." And because love is hope,

"it endures all things."

In Resurrection *Margie is Miss Cather's*

middle-aged spinster schoolteacher into whose

life reappears a love from other years: "She felt

as though some great force had been unlocked

within her, great and terrible enough to rend her asunder . . . It is not an easy thing, after a woman has shut the great natural hope out of her life, to open the floodgates and let the riotous, aching current come throbbing through again through the shrunken channels, waking a thousand undreamed-of possibilities of pleasure and pain."

Oh, celebrate hope, which along with faith, is the handmaiden of love.

THE KINGDOM OF THE ABSURD

MAX LUCADO

To a couple about to celebrate their diamond wedding anniversary,
the Spirit of God brings a message that renews hope.

The kingdom of heaven. Its citizens are drunk on wonder. Consider the case of Sarai. She is in her golden years, but God promises her a son. She gets excited. She visits the maternity shop and buys a few dresses. She plans her shower and remodels her tent . . . but no son. She eats a few birthday cakes and blows out a lot of candles . . . still no son. She goes through a decade of wall calendars . . . still no son.

So Sarai decides to take matters into her own hands. ("Maybe God needs me to take care of this one.")

She convinces Abram that time is running out. ("Face it, Abe, you ain't getting any younger, either.") She commands her maid Hagar, to go into Abram's tent and see if he needs anything. ("And I mean 'anything'!") Hagar goes in a maid. She comes out a mom. And the problems begin.

Hagar is haughty. Sarai is jealous. Abram is dizzy from the dilemma. And God calls the baby boy a "wild donkey"—an appropriate name for one born out of stubbornness and destined to kick his way into history.

It isn't the cozy family Sarai expected. And it isn't a topic Abram and Sarai bring up very often at dinner.

Finally, fourteen years later, when Abram is pushing a century of years and Sarai ninety . . . when Abram has stopped listening to Sarai's advice, and Sarai has stopped giving it . . . when the wallpaper in the nursery is faded and the baby furniture is several seasons out of date . . . when the topic of the promised son brings sighs and tears and long looks into a silent sky . . . God pays them a visit and tells them that they'd better select a name for their new son.

Abram and Sarai have the same response: laughter. They laugh partly because it is too good to happen and partly because it might. They laugh because they have given up hope, and hope born anew is always funny before it is real.

They laugh at the lunacy of it all.

Abram looks over at Sarai—toothless and snoring in her rocker, head back and mouth wide open, as fruitful as a pitted prune and just as wrinkled. And he cracks up. He tries to contain it, but he can't. He has always been a sucker for a good joke.

Sarai is just as amused. When she hears the news, a cackle escapes before she can contain it. She mumbles something about her husband's needing a lot more than what he's got and then laughs again.

They laugh because that is what you do when someone says he can do the impossible. They laugh a little *at* God, and a lot *with* God—for God is laughing, too. Then with a smile still on his face, he gets busy doing what he does best—the unbelievable.

He changes a few things—beginning with their names. Abram, the father of one, will now be Abraham, the father of a multitude. Sarai, the barren one, will now be Sarah, the mother.

But their names aren't the only things God changes. He changes their minds. He changes their faith. He changes the number of their tax deductions. He changes the way they define the word *impossible*.

But most of all He changes Sarah's attitude about trusting God. Were she to hear Jesus' statement about being poor in spirit, she could give a testimony: "He's right. I do things my way, I get a headache. I let God take over, I get a son. You try to figure that out. All I know is I am the first lady in town to pay her pediatrician with a Social Security check."[58]

A RESURRECTION

WILLA CATHER

"I contend that you ought to have set them house plants different, Margie, closer around the pulpit rail." Mrs. Skimmons retreated to the back of the church to take in the full effect of the decorations and give further directions to Margie. Mrs. Skimmons had a way of confining her services as chairman of the decorative committee to giving directions, and the benefit of her artistic eye.

Miss Margie good-naturedly readjusted the "house plants" and asked, "How is that?"

"Well, it's some better," admitted Mrs. Skimmons, critically, "but I contend we ought to have had some evergreens, even if they do look like Christmas. And now that you've used them hy'cinths for the lamp brackets, what are you goin' to put on the little stand before the pulpit?"

"Martin Dempster promised to bring some Easter lilies up from Kansas City. I thought we'd put them there. He ought to be here pretty soon. I heard the train whistle in a bit ago." "That's three times he's been to Kansas City this month. I don't see how he can afford it. Everybody knows the old ferry boat can't pay him very well, and he wasn't never much of a business-man. It beats me how some people can fly high on nothing. There's his railroad fare and his expenses while he is there. I can't make out what he's doin' down there so much. More'n likely it's some girl or other he's goin' down the river after again.

Now that you and your mother have brought up his baby for him, it would be just like Mart Dempster to go trapesin' off and marry some giddy thing and maybe fetch her up here for you to bring up, too. I can't never think he's acted right by you, Margie."

"So long as I'm satisfied, I can't see why it should trouble other people, Mrs. Skimmons."

"O, certainly not, if you are goin' to take offense. I meant well."

Margie turned her face away to avoid Mrs. Skimmons' scrutinizing gaze, and went on quietly with the decorations.

Miss Margie was no longer a girl. Most of the girls of her set who had frolicked and gone to school with her had married and moved away. Yet, though she had passed that dread meridian of thirty, and was the village schoolmistress to boot, she was not openly spoken of as an old maid. When a woman retains much of her beauty and youthful vigor the world, even the petty provincial world, feels a delicacy about applying to her that condemning title that when once adopted is so irrevocable. Then Miss Marjorie Pierson had belonged to one of the best families in the old days, before Brownville was shorn of its glory and importance by the railroad maneuvers that had left everybody poor. She had not always taught towheaded urchins for a living, but had once lived in a big house on the hill and gone to boarding school and driven her own phaeton, and entertained company from Omaha. These facts protected her somewhat.

She was a tall woman, finely, almost powerfully built and admirably developed. She carried herself with an erect pride that ill accorded with the humble position as the village schoolmistress. Her features were regular and well cut, but her face was comely chiefly because of her vivid coloring and her deeply set gray eyes, that were serious and frank like a man's.

She was one of those women one sometimes sees, designed by nature in her more artistic moments, especially fashioned for all the fullness of life; for large experiences and the great world where a commanding personality is felt and valued, but condemned by circumstances to poverty, obscurity, and all manner of pettiness. There are plenty of such women, who were made to ride in carriages and wear jewels and grace first nights at the opera, who, through some unaccountable blunder of stage management in this little *comedic humaine,* have the wrong parts assigned them, and cook for farm hands, or teach a country school like this one, or make gowns for ugly women and pad them into some semblance of shapeliness, while they themselves, who need no such artificial treatment, wear cast-offs; women who were made to rule, but who are doomed to serve. There are plenty of living masterpieces that are as completely lost to the world as the lost nine books of Sappho, or as the (Grecian marbles that were broken under the barbarians' battle axes. The world is full of waste of this sort.

While Margie was arranging the "house plants" about the pulpit platform, and the other member of the committee was giving her the benefit of her advice, a man strode lazily into the church carrying a small traveling bag and a large pasteboard box.

"There you are, Miss Margie," he cried, throwing the box on the platform; and sitting down in the front pew he proceeded to fan himself with his soft felt hat.

"O, Martin, they are beautiful! They are the first things that have made me feel a bit like Easter."

"One of 'em is for you, Miss Margie, to wear tomorrow," said Martin bashfully. Then he hastened to add, "I feel more like it's Fourth of July than Easter. I'm right afraid of this weather, Mrs. Skimmons. It'll coax all the buds out on the fruit trees and then turn cold and nip 'em. And the buds'll just be silly enough to come out when they are asked. You've done well with your decorations, Mrs. Skimmons."

Mrs. Skimmons looked quizzically at Martin, puzzled by this unusual loquaciousness.

"Well, yes," she admitted, in a satisfied tone, "I think we've done right well considerin' this tryin' weather. I'm about prostrated with the heat myself. How are things goin' down in Kansas City? You must know a good deal about everything there, seein' you go down so much lately."

"'Bout the same," replied Martin, in an uncommunicative tone which evidently offended Mrs. Skimmons.

"Well," remarked that lady briskly, "I guess I can't help you no more now, Margie. I've got to run home and see to them boys of mine. Mr. Dempster can probably help you finish." With this contemptuous use of his surname as a final thrust, Mrs. Skimmons departed.

Martin leaned back in the pew and watched Margie arranging the lilies. He was a big broad-chested fellow, who wore his broad shoulders carelessly and whose full muscular throat betrayed unusual physical strength. His face was simple and honest, bronzed by the weather, and with deep lines about the mild eyes that told that his simple life had not been altogether negative, and that he had not sojourned in this world for forty years without leaving a good deal of himself by the wayside.

"I didn't thank you for the lilies, Martin. It was very kind of you," said Margie, breaking the silence.

"O, that's all right. I just thought you'd like 'em," and he again relapsed into silence, his eyes following the sunny path of the first venturesome flies of the season that buzzed in and out of the open windows. Then his gaze strayed back to where the sunlight fell on Miss Margie and her lilies.

"The fact is, Miss Margie, I've got something to tell you. You know for a long time I've thought I'd like to quit the ferry and get somewhere where I'd have a chance to get ahead. There's no use trying to get ahead in Brownville, for there's nothing to get ahead of. Of late years I wanted to get a job on the lower Mississippi again, on a boat, you know. I've been going down to Kansas City lately to see some gentlemen who own boats down the river, and I've got a place at last, a first rate one that will pay well, and it looks like I could hold it as long as I want it."

Miss Margie looked up from the lilies she was holding and asked sharply, "Then you are going away, Martin?"

"Yes, and I'm going away this time so you won't never have to be ashamed of me for it."

"I ought to be glad on your account. You're right, there's nothing here for you, nor anybody else. But we'll miss you very much, Martin. There are so few of the old crowd left. Will you sell the ferry?"

"I don't just know about that. I'd kind of hate to sell the old ferry. You see I haven't got things planned out very clear yet. After all it's just the going away that matters most."

"Yes, it's just the going away that matters most," repeated Miss Margie slowly, while she watched something out of the window. "But of course you'll have to come back often to see Bobbie."

"Well, you see I was counting on taking Bobbie with me. He's about old enough now, and I don't think I could bear to be apart from him."

"You are not going to take Bobbie away from us, Martin?" cried Miss Margie in a tone of alarm.

"Why yes, Miss Margie. Of course I'll take him, and if you say so—"

"But I don't say so," cried Miss Margie in a tone of tremulous excitement. "He is not old enough, it would be cruel to take a bit of a child knocking around the world like that."

"I can't go without Bobbie. But, Miss Margie—"

"Martin," cried Miss Margie—she had risen to her feet now and stood facing him, her eyes full of gathering anger and her breast rising and falling perceptibly with her quick-drawn breathing—"Martin, you shall not take Bobbie away from me. He's more my child than yours, anyway. I've been through everything for him. When he was sick I walked the floor with him all night many a time and went with a headache to my work next morning. I've lived and worked and hoped just for him. And I've done it in the face of everything. Not a day passes but some old woman throws it in my face that I'm staying here drivelling my life out to take care of the child of the man who jilted me. I've borne all this because I loved him, because he is all my niggardly life has given me to love. My God! a woman must have something. Every woman's got to have. And I've given him everything, all that I'd starved and beat down and crucified in me. You brought him to me when he was a little wee baby, the only thing of your life you've ever given to mine. From the first time I felt his little cheek on mine I knew that a new life had come into me, and through another woman's weakness and selfishness I had at least one of the things which was mine by right. He was a helpless little baby, dependent on me for everything, and I loved him for just that. He needed my youth and strength and blood, and the very warmth of my body, and he was the only creature on earth who did. In spite of yourself you've given me half my womanhood and you shall not take it from me now. You shall not take it from me now!"

Martin heard her going, he heard the sob that broke as she reached the door but he did not stir from his seat or lift his bowed head. He sat staring at the sunlit spot in front of the pulpit where she had stood with the lilies in her hand, looking to him, somehow, despite her anger, like the pictures of the Holy woman who is always painted with lilies.

When the twilight began to fall and the shadows in the church grew dim he got up and went slowly down to the river toward the ferry boat. Back over the horseshoe-shaped gulch in which the town is built the sky was glorious with red splotches of sunset cloud just above the horizon. The big trees on the bluffs were tossing their arms restlessly in the breeze that blew up the river, and across on the level plains of the Missouri side the lights of the farm houses began to glow through the soft humid atmosphere of the April night. The smell of burning grass was everywhere, and the very air tasted of spring.

The boat hands had all gone to supper, and Martin sat down on the empty deck and lit his pipe. When he was perplexed or troubled he always went to the river. For the river means everything to Brownville folk; it has been at once their making and their undoing.

Brownville was not always the sleepy, deserted town that it is today, full of empty buildings and idle men and of boys growing up without aim or purpose. No, the town has had a history, a brief, sad little history which recalls the scathing epigram that Herr Heine once applied to M. Alfred de Musset; it is a young town with a brilliant past. It was the first town built on the Nebraska side of the river, and there, sheltered by the rugged bluffs and washed by the restless Missouri, a new state struggled into existence and proclaimed its right to be. Martin Dempster was the first child born on the Nebraska side, and he had seen the earth broken for the first grave. There, in Senator Tipton's big house on the hillside, when he was a very little boy, he had heard the first telegraph wire ever stretched across the Missouri click its first message that made the blood leap in all his boyish veins, "Westward the course of Empire takes it way."

In the days of his boyhood Brownville was the head of river navigation and the old steamboat trade. He had seen the time when a dozen river steamers used to tie up at the wharves at one time, and unload supplies for the wagon trains that went overland to Pikes Peak and Cherry Creek, that is Denver now. He had sat on the upper veranda of the old Marsh House and listened to the strange talk of the foreign potentates that the Montana and Silver Heels used to bring up the river and who stopped there on their way into the big game country. He had listened with them to the distant throbbing of the engines that once stirred the lonely sand-split waters of the old river, and watched the steamers swing around the bend at night, glittering with lights, with bands of music playing on their decks and the sparks from the smokestacks blowing back into the darkness. He had sat under the gigantic oak before the Lone Tree Saloon and heard the teamsters of the wagon trains and the boat hands exchange stories of the mountains and alkali deserts for stories of the busy world and its doings, filling up the pauses in conversation with old frontier songs and the strumming of banjos. And he could remember only too well when the old Hannibal brought up the steel rails for the Union Pacific Railroad, the road that was to kill Brownville.

Brownville had happened because of the steamboat trade, and when the channel of the river had become so uncertain and capricious that navigation was impossible, Brownville became impossible too, and all the prosperity that the river had given it took back in its muddy arms again and swept away. And ever since, overcome by shame and remorse, it had been trying to commit suicide by burying itself in the sand. Every year the channel grows narrower and more treacherous and its waters more turbid. Perhaps it does not even remember anymore how it used to hurry along into the great aorta of the continent, or the throb of the wheels of commerce that used to beat up the white foam on its dark waters, or how a certain old Indian chief desired to be buried sitting bolt upright upon the bluff that he might always watch the steamers go up and down the river.

So it was that the tide went out at Brownville, and the village became a little Pompcii buried in bonded indebtedness. The sturdy pioneers moved away and the "river rats" drifted in, a nondescript people who came up the river from nowhere, and bought up the big houses for a song, cut down the tall oaks and cedars in the yards for firewood, and plowed up the terraces for potato patches, and were content after the manner of their kind. The river gypsies are a peculiar people; like the Egyptians of old their lives are for and of the river. They each have their skill and burn driftwood and subsist on catfish and play their banjos, and forget that the world moves—if they ever knew it. The river is the school and religion of these people.

And Martin Dempster was one of them. When most of the better people of the town moved away Martin remained loyal to the river. The feeling of near kinship with the river had always been in him, he was born with it. When he was a little boy he had continually run away from school, and when his father hunted for him he always found him about the river. River boys never take kindly to education; they are always hankering for the water. In summer its muddy coolness is irresistibly alluring, and in winter its frozen surface is equally so. The continual danger which attends its treacherous currents only adds to its enticing charm. They know the river in all its changes and fluctuations as a stock broker knows the markets.

When Martin was a boy his father owned a great deal of Brownville real estate and was considered a wealthy man. Town property was a marketable article in those days, though now no real estate ever sells in Brownville—except cemetery lots. But

Martin never cared for business. The first ambition he was ever guilty of was that vague yearning which stirs in the breasts of all river boys, to go down the river sometime, clear down, as far as the river goes. Then, a little later, when he heard an old stump speaker who used to end all his oratorical flights with a figure about "rearing here in the Missouri Valley a monument as high as the thought of man," he had determined to be a great navigator and to bring glory and honor to the town of Brownville. And here he was, running the old ferry boat that was the last and meanest of all the flock of mighty river crafts. So it goes. When we are very little we all dream of driving a street car or wearing a policeman's star or keeping a peanut stand; and generally, after catching at the clouds a few times, we live to accomplish our juvenile ambitions more nearly than we ever realize.

When he was sixteen Martin had run away as cabin boy on the Silver Heels. Gradually he had risen to the pilot house on the same boat. People wondered why Marjorie Pierson should care for a fellow of that stamp, but the fact that she did care was no secret. Perhaps it was just because he was simple and unworldly and lived for what he liked best that she cared.

Martin's downfall dated back to the death of the steamboat trade at Brownville. His fate was curiously linked with that of his river. When the channel became so choked with sand that the steamers quit going up to Brownville, Martin went lower down the river, making his headquarters at St. Louis. And there the misfortune of his life befell him. There was a girl of French extraction, an Aimée de Mar, who lived down in the shipping district. She lived by her wits principally. She was just a wee mite of a thing, with brown hair that fluffed about her face and eyes that were large and soft like those of Guido's penitent Magdalen, and which utterly belied her. You would wonder how so small a person could make so much harm and trouble in the world. Not that she was naturally malignant or evil at all. She simply wanted the nice things of this world and was determined to have them, no matter who paid for them, and she enjoyed life with a frank sort of hedonism, quite regardless of what her pleasure might cost others. Martin was a young man who stood high in favor with the captains and boat owners and who seemed destined to rise. So Aimee concentrated all her energies to one end, and her project was not difficult of accomplishment under the circumstances. A wiser or worse man would have met her on her own ground and managed her easily enough. But Martin was slow at life as he had been at books, heady and loyal and foolish, the kind of man who pays for his follies right here in this world and who keeps his word if he walks alive into hell for it. The upshot of it was that, after writing to Margie the hardest letter he ever wrote in his life, he married Aimee de Mar.

Then followed those three years that had left deep lines in Martin's face and gray hairs over his temples. Once married Aimee did not sing "Toujours j'aimais!" anymore. She attired herself gorgeously in satins and laces and perfumed herself heavily with violettes de Parme and spent her days visiting her old friends of the milliners' and hairdressers' shops and impressing them with her elegance. The evenings she would pass in a box at some second-rate theatre, ordering ices brought to her between the acts. When Martin was in town he was dragged willy-nilly through all these absurdly vulgar performances, and when he was away matters went even worse. This would continue until Martin's salary was exhausted, after which Aimee would languish at home in bitter resentment against the way the world is run, and consoling herself with innumerable cigarettes de Caporale until payday. Then she would blossom forth in a new outfit and the same program would be repeated. After running him heavily into debt, by some foolish attempt at a flirtation with a man on board his own boat, she drove Martin into a quarrel which resulted in a fierce hand-to-hand scrimmage on board ship and was the cause of his immediate discharge. In December, while he was hunting work, living from hand to mouth and hiding from his creditors, his baby was born. "As if," Aimee remarked, "the weather were not disagreeable enough without that!"

In the spring, at Mardi Gras time, Martin happened to be out of town. Aimee was thoroughly weary of domesticity and poverty and of being shut up in the house. She strained her credit for all it was worth for one last time, and on the first night of the fete, though it was bitterly cold, she donned an airy domino and ran away from her baby, and went down the river in a steam launch, hung with colored lights and manned by some gentlemen who were neither sober nor good boatmen. The launch was overturned a mile below the Point, and three of the party went to the bottom. Two days later poor little Aimee was picked up in the river, the yellow and black velvet of her butterfly dress covered with mud and slime, and her gay gauze wings frozen fast to her pretty shoulders.

So Martin spoke the truth when he said that everything that had ever affected his life one way or the other was of the river. To him the river stood for Providence, for fate.

Some of the saddest fables of ancient myth are of the fates of the devotees of the River gods. And the worship of the River gods is by no means dead. Martin had been a constant worshipper and a most faithful one, and here he was at forty, not so well off as when he began the world for himself at sixteen. But let no one dream that because the wages of the River god cannot be counted in coin or numbered in herds of cattle, that they are never paid. Its real wages are of the soul alone, and not visible to any man. To all who follow it faithfully, and not for gain but from inclination, the river gives a certain simpleness of life and freshness of feeling and receptiveness of mind not to be found among the money changers of the marketplace. It feeds his imagination and trains his eye, and gives him strength and courage. And it gives him something better than these, if aught can be better. It gives him, no matter how unlettered he may be, something of that intimate sympathy with inanimate nature that is the base of all poetry, something of that which the high-faced rocks of the gleaming Sicilian shore gave Theocritus.

Martin had come back to Brownville to live down the memory of his disgrace. He might have found a much easier task without going so far. Every day for six years he had met the reproachful eyes of his neighbors unflinchingly, and he knew that his mistake was neither condoned nor forgotten. Brownville people have nothing to do but to keep such memories perennially green. If he had been a coward he would have run away from this perpetual condemnation. But he had the quiet courage of all men who have wrestled hand to hand with the elements, and who have found out how big and terrible nature is. So he stayed.

Miss Margie left the church with a stinging sense of shame at what she had said, and wondered if she were losing her mind. For the women who are cast in that tragic mold are always trying to be like their milder sisters, and are always flattering themselves that they have succeeded. And when some fine day the fire flames out they are more astonished and confounded than anyone else can be. Miss Margie walked rapidly through the dusty road, called by courtesy a street, and crossed the vacant building lots unmindful that her skirts were switching among the stalks of last year's goldenrods and sunflowers. As she reached the door a little boy in much abbreviated trousers ran around the house from the back yard and threw his arms about her. She kissed him passionately and felt better. The child seemed to justify her in her own eyes. Then she led him in and began to get supper.

"Don't make my tea as strong as you did last night, Margie. It seems like you ought to know how to make it by this time," said the querulous invalid from the corner.

"All right, Mother. Why Mother, you worked my buttonholes in black silk instead of blue!"

"How was I to tell, with my eyes so bad? You ought to have laid it out for me. But there is always something wrong about everything I do," complained the old lady in an injured tone.

"No, there isn't, it was all my fault. You can work a better button hole than I can, any day."

"Well, in my time they used to say so," said Mrs. Pierson somewhat mollified.

Margie was practically burdened with the care of two children. Her mother was crippled with rheumatism, and only at rare intervals could "help about the house." She insisted on doing a little sewing for her daughter, but usually it had to come out and be done over again after she went to bed. With the housework and the monotonous grind of her work at school, Miss Margie had little time to think about her misfortunes, and so perhaps did not feel them as keenly as she would otherwise have done. It was a perplexing matter, too, to meet even the modest expenses of their small household with the salary paid a country teacher. She had never touched a penny of the money Martin paid for the child's board, but put it regularly in the bank for the boy's own use when he should need it.

After supper she put her mother to bed and then put on the red wrapper that she always wore in the evening hour that she had alone with Bobbie. The woman in one dies hard, and after she had ceased to dress for men the old persistent instinct made her wish to be attractive to the boy. She heard him say his "piece" that he was to recite at the Easter service tomorrow, and then sat down in the big rocking chair before the fire and Bobbie climbed up into her lap.

"Bobbie, I want to tell you a secret that we mustn't tell grandma yet. Your father is talking about taking you away."

"Away on the ferry boat?" his eyes glistened with excitement.

"No dear, away down the river; away from grandma and me for good."

"But I won't go away from you and grandma, Miss Margie. Don't you remember how I cried all night the time you were away?"

"Yes, Bobbie, I know, but you must always do what your father says. But you wouldn't like to go, would you?"

"Of course I wouldn't. There wouldn't be anybody to pick up chips, or go to the store, or take care of you and grandma, 'cause I'm the only boy you've got."

"Yes, Bobbie, that's just it, dear heart, you're the only boy I've got!"

And Miss Margie gathered him up in her arms and laid her hot cheek on his and fell to sobbing, holding him closer and closer.

Bobbie lay very still, not even complaining about the tears that wetted his face. But he wondered very much why anyone should cry who had not cut a finger or been stung by a wasp or trodden on a sand-burr. Poor little Bobbie, he had so much to learn! And while he was wondering he fell asleep, and Miss Margie undressed him and put him to bed.

During the five years since that night when Marjorie Pierson and her mother, in the very face of the village gossips, had gone to the train to meet Martin Dempster when he came back to Brownville, worn and weak with fever, and had taken his wailing little baby from his arms, giving it the first touch of womanly tenderness it had ever known, the two lonely women had grown to love it better than anything else in the world, better even than they loved each other. Marjorie had felt every ambition of her girlhood die out before the strength of the vital instinct which this child awakened and satisfied within her. She had told Martin in the church that afternoon that "a woman must have something." Of women of her kind this is certainly true. You can find them everywhere slaving for and loving other women's children. In this sorry haphazard world such women are often cut off from the natural outlet of what is within them; but they always make one. Sometimes it is an aged relative, sometimes an invalid sister, sometimes a waif from the streets no one else wants, sometimes it is only a dog. But there is something, always.

When the child was in his bed Miss Margie took up a bunch of examination papers and began looking through them. As she worked she heard a slow rapping at the door, a rap she knew well indeed, that had sent the blood to her cheeks one day. Now it only left them white.

She started and hesitated, but as the rap was repeated she rose and went to the door, setting her lips firmly.

"Good evening, Martin, come in," she said quietly. "Bobbie is in bed. I'm sorry."

Martin stood by the door and shook his head at the proffered chair. "I didn't come to see Bobbie, Margie. I came to finish what I began to say this afternoon when you cut me off. I know I'm slow spoken. It's always been like it was at school, when the teacher asked a question I knew as well as I knew my own name, but some other fellow'd get the answer out before me. I started to say this afternoon that if I took Bobbie to St. Louis I couldn't take him alone. There is somebody else I couldn't bear to be apart from, and I guess you've known who that is this many a year."

A painful blush overspread Miss Margie's face and she turned away and rested her arm on the mantel. "It is not like you to take advantage of what I said this afternoon when I was angry. I wouldn't have believed it of you. You have given me pain enough in years gone by without this—this that makes me sick and ashamed."

"Sick and ashamed? Why Margie, you must have known what I've been waiting in Brownville for all these years. Don't tell me I've waited too long. I've done my best to live it down. I haven't bothered you nor pestered you so folks could talk. I've just stayed and stuck it out till I could feel I was worthy. Not that I think I'm worthy now, Margie, but the time has come for me to go and I can't go alone."

He paused, but there was no answer. He took a step nearer. "Why Margie, you don't mean that you haven't known I've been loving you all the time till my heart's near burst in me? Many a night down on the old ferry I've told it over and over again to the river till even it seemed to understand. Why Margie, I've"—the note of fear caught in his throat and his voice broke and he stood looking helplessly at his boots.

Miss Margie still stood leaning on her elbow, her face from him. "You'd better have been telling it to me, Martin," she said bitterly.

"Why Margie, I couldn't till I got my place. I couldn't have married you here and had folks always throwing that other woman in your face."

"But if you had loved me you would have told me, Martin, you couldn't have helped that."

He caught her hand and bent over it, lifting it tenderly to his lips. "O Margie, I was ashamed, bitter ashamed! I couldn't forget that letter I had to write you once. And you might have had a hundred better men than me. I never was good enough for you to think of one minute. I wasn't clever nor ready spoken like you, just a tramp of a river rat who could somehow believe better in God because of you."

Margie felt herself going and made one last desperate stand. "Perhaps you've forgotten all you said in that letter, perhaps you've forgotten the shame it would bring to any woman. Would you like to see it? I have always kept it."

He dropped her hand.

"No, I don't want to see it and I've not forgot. I only know I'd rather have signed my soul away than written it. Maybe you're right and there are things a man can't live down—not in this world. Of course you can keep the boy. As you say he is more yours than mine, a thousand times more. I've never had anything I could call my own. It's always been like this and I ought to be used to it by this time. Some men are made that way. Good night, dear."

"O Martin, don't talk like that, you could have had me any day for the asking. But why didn't you speak before? I'm too old now!" Margie leaned closer to the mantel and the sobs shook her.

He looked at her for a moment in wonder, and, just as she turned to look for him, caught her in his arms. "I've always been slow spoken, Margie—I was ashamed—you were too good for me," he muttered between his kisses.

"Don't Martin, don't! That's all asleep in me and it must not come, it shan't come back! Let me go!" cried Margie breathlessly.

"O I'm not near through yet! I'm just showing you how young you are—it's the quickest way," came Martin's answer muffled by the trimmings of her gown.

"O Martin, you may be slow spoken, but you're quick enough at some things," laughed Margie as she retreated to the window, struggling hard against the throb of reckless elation that arose in her. She felt as though some great force had been unlocked within her, great and terrible enough to rend her asunder, as when a brake snaps or a band slips and some ponderous machine grinds itself in pieces. It is not an easy thing, after a woman has shut the great natural hope out of her life, to open the floodgates and let the riotous, aching current come throbbing again through the shrunken channels, waking a thousand undreamed-of possibilities of pleasure and pain.

Martin followed her to the window and they stood together leaning against the deep casing while the spring wind blew in their faces, bearing with it the yearning groans of the river.

"We can kind of say good-bye to the old place tonight. We'll be going in a week or two now," he said nervously.

"I've wanted to get away from Brownville all my life, but now I'm someway afraid to think of going."

"How did that piece end we used to read at school, 'My chains and I—' Go on, you always remember such things."

"My very chains and I grew friends,
So much a long communion tends
To make us what we are. Even I
Regained my freedom with a sigh,"

quoted Margie softly.

"Yes, that's it. I'm counting on you taking some singing lessons again when we get down to St. Louis."

"Why I'm too old to take singing lessons now. I'm too old

for everything. O Martin, I don't believe we've done right. I'm afraid of all this! It hurts me."

He put his arm about her tenderly and whispered: "Of course it does, darling. Don't you suppose it hurts the old river down there tonight when the spring floods are stirring up the old bottom and tearing a new channel through the sand? Don't you suppose it hurts the trees tonight when the sap is climbing up and up till it breaks through the bark and runs down their sides like blood? Of course it hurts."

"Oh Martin, when you talk like that it don't hurt anymore."

Truly the service of the river has its wages and its recompense, though they are not seen of men. Just then the door opened and Bobby came stumbling sleepily across the floor, trailing his little night gown after him.

"It was so dark in there, and I'm scared of the river when it sounds so loud," he said, hiding his face in Margie's skirts.

Martin lifted him gently in his arms and said, "The water won't hurt you, my lad. My boy must never be afraid of the river."

And as he stood there listening to the angry grumble of the swollen waters, Martin asked their benediction on his happiness. For he knew that a river man may be happy only as the river wills.[59]

LONESOME DOVE

So far away from friends and home
There's one so dear to me
There's one forever in my mind
And that fair one is she
Come back, come back, my own true love
And stay awhile with me
For if ever I had a friend on this earth
You have been a friend to me
Hush up, hush up, my own true love
For I hate to hear you cry
For the best of friends on earth must part
And so must you and I

Don't you see that lonesome dove
That flies from pine to pine
She's mourning for her own true love
Just like I mourn for mine
O don't you see the crow fly high
She turns both black and white
If ever I prove false to you
The day will turn to night
O take this ring I will to thee
And wear it on your right hand
And think of my poor aching heart
When I'm in a foreign land

TRADITIONAL, AMERICAN

WHEN YOU ARE OLD

When you are old and gray and full of sleep

And nodding by the fire, take down this book,

And slowly read, and dream of the soft look

Your eyes had once, and of their shadows deep;

How many loved your moments of glad grace,

And loved your beauty with love false or true;

But one man loved the pilgrim soul in you,

And loved the sorrows of your changing face.

And bending down beside the glowing bars,

Murmur, a little sadly, how love fled

And paced upon the mountains overhead,

*And his face amid a crowd of stars.*₆₁

WILLIAM BUTLER YEATS

ANTONY AND
CLEOPATRA

WILLIAM SHAKESPEARE

ENOBARUS: . . . The barge she sat in, like a burnish'd throne,

Burn'd on the water. The poop was beaten gold;

Purple the sails, and so perfumed that

The winds were love-sick with them; the oars were silver,

Which to the tune of flutes kept stroke, and made

The water which they beat to follow faster,

As amorous of their strokes. For her own person,

It beggar'd all description. She did lie

In her pavilion, cloth of gold, of tissue,

O'er picturing that Venus where we see

The fancy out-work nature. On each side her

Stood pretty dimpled boys, like smiling Cupids,

With divers colour'd fans, whose wind did seem

To glow the delicate cheeks which they did cool,

And what they undid did.

AGRIPA: O, rare for Antony!

ENOBARBUS: Her gentlewomen, like Nereides,

So many mermaids, tended her i' th' eyes,

And made their bends adornings. At the helm

A seeming mermaid steers. The silken tackle
Swell with the touches of those flower-soft hands
That yarely frame the office. From the barge
A strange invisible perfume hits the sense
Of the adjacent wharfs. The city cast
Her people out upon her; and Antony,
Enthron'd i' th' marketplace did sit alone,
Whistling to th' air; which, but for vacancy,
Had gone to gaze on Cleopatra too,
And made a gap in nature.

AGRIPPA: Rare Egyptian!

ENOBARBUS: Upon her landing, Antony sent to her,
Invited her to supper. She replied
It should be better he became her guest;
Which she entreated. Our courteous Antony,
Whom ne'er the word of 'No' woman heard speak,
Being barber'd ten times o'er, goes to the feast,
And for his ordinary pays his heart
For what his eyes eat only.

The success of a marriage comes not in finding the "right"

person, but in the ability of both partners to adjust to the real

person they inevitably realize they married.

JOHN FISHER

There are as many minds as there are heads, so there are as

many kinds of love as there are hearts.

LEO TOLSTOY

THE HAPPY PRINCE

OSCAR WILDE

It is probably debatable whether this is a love story or not. It may be difficult for some readers to find much romantic about a princely gilded statue and a little swallow. Nonetheless, the underlying virtue this fable demonstrates, is the basis of all meaningful relationships of heart-abiding sacrifice. Read it with someone you love.

High above the city, on a tall column, stood the statue of the Happy Prince. He was gilded all over with thin leaves of fine gold, for eyes he had two bright sapphires, and a large red ruby glowed on his sword-hilt.

He was very much admired indeed. "He is as beautiful as a weathercock," remarked one of the Town Councilors who wished to gain a reputation for having artistic tastes, "only not quite so useful," he added, fearing lest people should think him unpractical, which he really was not.

"Why can't you be like the Happy Prince?" asked a sensible mother of her little boy who was crying for the Moon. "The Happy Prince never dreams of crying for anything."

"I am glad there is someone in the world who is quite happy," muttered a disappointed man as he gazed at the wonderful statue.

"He looks just like an angel," said the Charity Children as they came out of the cathedral in their bright scarlet cloaks and their clean white pinafores.

"How do you know?" said the Mathematical Master, "you have never seen one."

"Ah, but we have, in our dreams," answered the children; and the Mathematical Master frowned and looked very severe, for he did not approve of children dreaming.

One night there flew over the city a little Swallow. His friends had gone away to Egypt six weeks before, but he had stayed behind, for he was in love with the most beautiful Reed. He had met her early in the spring as he was flying down the river after a big yellow moth, and had been so attracted by her slender waist that he had stopped to talk to her.

"Shall I love you?" said the Swallow, who liked to come to the point at once, and the Reed made him a low bow. So he flew round and round her, touching the water with his wings, and making silver ripples. This was his courtship, and it lasted all through the summer.

"It is a ridiculous attachment," twittered the other Swallows; "she has no money, and far too many relations"; and indeed the river was quite full of Reeds. Then, when the autumn came, they all flew away.

After they had gone he felt lonely, and began to tire of his ladylove. "She has no conversation," he said, "and I am afraid that she is a coquette, for she is always flirting with the wind." And certainly, whenever the wind blew, the Reed made the most graceful curtseys. "I admit that she is domestic," he continued, "but I love traveling, and my wife, consequently, should love traveling also."

"Will you come away with me?" he said finally to her; but the Reed shook her head, she was so attached to her home.

"You have been trifling with me," he cried. "I am off to the Pyramids. Good-bye!" and he flew away.

All day long he flew, and at nighttime he arrived at the city. "Where shall I put up?" he said; "I hope the town has made preparations."

Then he saw the statue on the tall column.

"I will put up there," he cried; "it is a position with plenty of fresh air." So he alighted just between the feet of the Happy Prince.

"I have a golden bedroom," he said softly to himself as he looked around, and he prepared to go to sleep; but just as he was putting his head under his wing a large drop of water fell on him. "What a curious thing!" he cried; "there is not a single cloud in the sky, the stars are quite clear and bright, and yet it is raining. The climate in the north of Europe is really dreadful. The Reed used to like the rain, but that was merely her selfishness."

Then another drop fell.

"What is the use of a statue if it cannot keep the rain off?" he said, "I must look for a good chimney-pot," and he determined to fly away.

But before he had opened his wings, a third drop fell, and he looked up, and saw—Ah! what did he see?

The eyes of the Happy Prince were filled with tears, and tears were running down his golden cheeks. His face was so beautiful in the moonlight that the little Swallow was filled with pity.

"Who are you?" he said.

"I am the Happy Prince."

"Why are you weeping then?" asked the Swallow; "you have quite drenched me."

"When I was alive and had a human heart," answered the statue, "I did not know what tears were, for I lived in the Palace of Sans-Souci, where sorrow is not allowed to enter. In the daytime I played with my companions in the garden, and in the evening I led the dance in the Great Hall. Round the garden ran a very lofty wall, but I never cared to ask what lay beyond it, everything about me was so beautiful. My courtiers called me the Happy Prince, and happy indeed I was, if pleasure be happiness. So I lived, and so I died. And now that I'm dead they have set me up here so high that I can see all the ugliness and all the misery of my city, and though my heart is made of lead yet I cannot choose but weep."

"What! is he not solid gold?" said the Swallow to himself. He was too polite to make any personal remarks out loud.

"Far away," continued the statue in a low musical voice, "far away in a little street there is a poor house. One of the windows is open, and through it I can see a woman seated at a table. Her face is thin and worn, and she has coarse, red hands, all pricked by the needle, for she is a seamstress. She is embroidering passionflowers on a satin gown for the loveliest of the Queen's maids-of-honor to wear at the next Court-ball. In a bed in the corner of the room her little boy is lying ill. He has a fever, and is asking for oranges. His mother has nothing to give him but river water, so he is crying. Swallow, Swallow, little Swallow, will you not bring her the ruby out of my sword-hilt? My feet are fastened to this pedestal and I cannot move."

"I am waited for in Egypt," said the Swallow. "My friends are flying up and down the Nile, and talking to the large lotus-flowers. Soon they will go to sleep in the tomb of the great King. The King is there himself in his painted coffin. He is wrapped in yellow linen, and embalmed with spices. Round his neck is a chain of pale green jade, and his hands are like withered leaves."

"Swallow, Swallow, little Swallow," said the Prince, "will you not stay with me for one night, and be my messenger? The boy is so thirsty, and the mother is so sad."

"I don't think I like boys," answered the Swallow. "Last summer, when I was staying on the river, there were two rude boys, the miller's sons, who were always throwing stones at me. They never hit me, of course; we swallows fly far too well for that, and besides, I come of a family famous for its agility; but still, it was a mark of disrespect."

But the Happy Prince looked so sad that the little Swallow was sorry. "It is very cold here," he said; "but I will stay with you for one night, and be your messenger."

"Thank you, little Swallow," said the Prince.

So the Swallow picked out the great ruby from the Prince's sword, and flew away with it in his beak over the roofs of the town.

He passed by the cathedral tower, where the white marble angels were sculptured. He passed by the palace and heard the sound of dancing. A beautiful girl came out on the balcony with her lover. "How wonderful the stars are," he said to her, "and how wonderful is the power of love!"

"I hope my dress will be ready in time for the State-ball," she answered; "I have ordered passion flowers to be embroidered on it, but the seamstresses are so lazy.

He passed over the river, and saw the lanterns hanging to the masts of the ships. He passed over the Ghetto, and at last came to the poor house and looked in. The boy was tossing feverishly on his bed, and the mother had fallen asleep, she was so tired. In he hopped, and laid the great ruby on the table beside the woman's thimble. Then he flew gently around the bed, fanning the boy's forehead with his wings. "How cool I feel," said the boy, "I must be getting better;" and he sank into a delicious slumber.

Then the Swallow flew back to the Happy Prince, and told

him what he had done. "It is curious," he remarked, "but I feel quite warm now, although it is so cold."

"That is because you have done a good action," said the Prince. And the little Swallow began to think, and then he fell asleep. Thinking always made him sleepy.

When day broke he flew down to the river and had a bath. "What a remarkable phenomenon," said the Professor of Ornithology as he was passing over the bridge, "A Swallow in winter!"

"Tonight I go to Egypt," said the Swallow, and he was in high spirits at the prospect. He visited all the public monuments and sat a long time on top of the church steeple. Wherever he went the sparrows chirruped, and said to each other: "What a distinguished stranger!" so he enjoyed himself very much.

When the moon rose he flew back to the Happy Prince. "Have you any commissions for Egypt?" he cried; "I am just starting."

"Swallow, Swallow, little Swallow," said the Prince, "will you not stay with me one night longer?"

"I am waited for in Egypt," answered the Swallow. "Tomorrow my friends will fly up the Second Cataract. The river-horse couches there among the bulrushes, and on a great granite throne sits the god Memnon. All night long he watches the stars, and when the morning star shines he utters one cry of joy, and then he is silent. At noon the yellow lions come down to the water's edge to drink. They have eyes like green beryls, and their roar is louder than the roar of the cataract."

"Swallow, Swallow, little Swallow," said the Prince, "far away across the city I see a young man in a garret. He is leaning over a desk covered with papers, and in a tumbler by his side there is a bunch of withered violets. His hair is brown and crisp, and his lips are red as a pomegranate, and he has large and dreamy eyes. He is trying to finish a play for the Director of the Theatre, but he was too cold to write anymore. There is no fire in the grate, and hunger has made him faint."

"I will wait with you one night longer," said the Swallow, who really had a good heart. "Shall I take him another ruby?"

"Alas! I have no ruby now," said the Prince; "my eyes are all that I have left. They are made of rare sapphires, which were brought out of India a thousand years ago. Pluck out one of them and take it to him. He will sell it to the jeweler, and buy food and firewood, and finish his play."

"Dear Prince," said the Swallow, "I cannot do that"; and he began to weep.

"Swallow, Swallow, little Swallow," said the Prince, "do as I command you."

So the Swallow plucked out the Prince's eye, and flew away to the student's garret. It was easy enough to get in, as there was a hole in the roof. Through this he darted, and came into the room. The young man had his head buried in his hands, so he did not hear the flutter of the bird's wings, and when he looked up he found the beautiful sapphire lying on the withered violets.

"I am beginning to be appreciated," he cried; "this is from some great admirer. Now I can finish my play," and he looked quite happy.

The next day the Swallow flew down to the harbor. He sat on the mast of a large vessel and watched the sailors hauling big chests out of the hold with ropes. "Heave a-hoy!" they shouted as each chest came up. "I am going to Egypt," cried the Swallow, but nobody minded, and when the Moon rose he flew back to the Prince. "I am come to bid you good-bye," he cried.

"Swallow, Swallow, little Swallow," said the Prince, "will you not stay with me one night longer?"

"It is winter," answered the Swallow, "and the chill snow will soon be here. In Egypt the sun is warm on the green palm trees, and the crocodiles lie in the mud and look lazily about them. My companions are building a nest in the Temple of Baalbec, and the pink and white doves are watching them and cooing to each other. Dear Prince, I must leave you, but I will never forget you, and next spring I will bring you back two beautiful jewels in place of those you have given away. The ruby shall be redder than a red rose, and the sapphire shall be as blue as the great sea."

"In the square below," said the Happy Prince, "there stands a little match girl. She has let her matches fall in the gutter, and they are all spoiled. Her father will beat her if she does not bring home some money, and she is crying. She has no shoes or stockings, and her little head is bare. Pluck out my other eye, and give it to her, and her father will not beat her."

"I will stay with you one night longer," said the Swallow,

"but I cannot pluck out your eye. You would be quite blind then."

"Swallow, Swallow, little Swallow," said the Prince, "do as I command you."

So he plucked out the Prince's other eye, and darted down with it. He swooped past the match girl, and slipped the jewel into the palm of her hand. "What a lovely piece of glass," cried the little girl; and she ran home, laughing.

Then the Swallow came back to the Prince. "You are blind now," he said, "so I will stay with you always."

"No, little Swallow," said the poor Prince, "you must go away to Egypt."

"I will stay with you always," said the Swallow, and he slept at the Prince's feet.

All the next day he sat on the Prince's shoulder, and told him stories of what he had seen in strange lands. He told him of the red Ibises, who stand in long rows on the banks of the Nile, and catch goldfish in their beaks; of the Sphinx, who is as old as the world itself, and lives in the desert, and knows everything; of the merchants, who walk slowly by the side of their camels, and carry amber beads in their hands; of the King of the Mountains of the Moon, who is as black as ebony, and worships a large crystal; of the great green snake that sleeps in a palm tree, and has twenty priests to feed it with honeycakes; and of pygmies who sail over a big lake on large flat leaves, and are always at war with the butterflies.

"Dear little Swallow," said the Prince, you tell me of marvelous things, but more marvelous than anything is the suffering of men and women. There is no Mystery so great as Misery. Fly over my city, little Swallow, and tell me what you see there."

So the Swallow flew over the great city, and saw the rich making merry in their beautiful homes, while the homeless were sitting at the gates. He flew into dark lanes, and saw the faces of starving children looking out listlessly at the black streets. Under the archway of a bridge two little boys were lying in one another's arms to try and keep themselves warm. "How hungry we are!" they said. "You must not lie here," shouted the Watchman, and they wandered out into the rain.

Then he flew back and told the Prince what he had seen.

"I am covered with fine gold," said the Prince, "you must take it off leaf by leaf, and give it to my poor; the living always think that gold can make them happy."

Leaf after leaf of the fine gold the Swallow picked off, till the Happy Prince looked quite dull and gray. Leaf after leaf of the fine gold he brought to the poor, and the children's faces grew rosier, and they laughed and played games in the street. "We have bread now!" they cried.

Then the snow came, and after snow came the frost. The streets looked as if they were made of silver, they were so bright and glistening; long icicles like crystal daggers hung down from the eaves of the houses, everybody went about in furs, and the little boys wore scarlet caps and skated on the ice.

The poor little Swallow grew colder and colder, but he would not leave the Prince, he loved him too well. He picked up crumbs outside the baker's door when the baker was not looking, and tried to keep himself warm by flapping his wings.

But at last he knew that he was going to die. He had just strength to fly up to the Prince's shoulder once more. "Good-bye, dear Prince!" he murmured, "will you let me kiss your hand?"

"I am glad that you are going to Egypt at last, little Swallow," said the Prince, "you have stayed too long here; but you must kiss me on the lips, for I love you."

"It is not to Egypt that I am going," said the Swallow, "I am going to the House of Death. Death is the brother of sleep, is he not?"

And he kissed the Happy Prince on the lips, and fell down dead at his feet.

At that moment a curious crack sounded inside the statue, as if something had broken. The fact is that the leaden heart had snapped right in two. It certainly was a dreadfully hard frost.

Early the next morning the Mayor was walking in the square below in company with the Town Councilors. As they passed the column he looked up at the statue: "Dear me! how shabby the Happy Prince looks!" he said.

"How shabby indeed!" cried the Town Councilors, who always agreed with the Mayor; and they went up to look at it.

"The ruby has fallen out of his sword, his eyes are gone, and he is golden no longer," said the Mayor; "in fact, he is little better than a beggar!"

"Little better than a beggar," said the Town Councilors.

"And there is actually a dead bird at his feet!" continued the Mayor. "We must issue a proclamation that birds are not allowed to die here." And the Town Clerk made a note of the suggestion.

So they pulled down the statue of the Happy Prince. "As he is no longer beautiful he is no longer useful," said the Art Professor at the University.

Then they melted the statue in a furnace, and the Mayor held a meeting of the Corporation to decide what was to be done with the metal. "We must have another statue, of course," he said, "and it shall be a statue of myself."

"Of myself," said each of the Town Councilors, and they quarreled. When I last heard of them they were quarreling still.

"What a strange thing!" said the overseer of the workmen at the foundry. "This broken lead heart will not melt in the furnace. We must throw it away." So they threw it on a dust heap where the dead Swallow was also lying.

"Bring me the two most precious things in the city," said God to one of His Angels; and the Angel brought Him the leaden heart and the dead bird.

"You have rightly chosen," said God, "for in My garden of Paradise this little bird shall sing forevermore, and in My city of gold the Happy Prince shall praise Me." 62

O NIGHTINGALE THAT ON YON BLOOMY SPRAY

O nightingale, that on yon bloomy spray

Warblest at eve, when all the woods are still,

Thou with fresh hope the lover's heart dost fill,

While the jolly hours lead on propitious May.

Thy liquid notes that close the eye of day,

First heard before the swallow cuckoo's bill,

Portend success in love—oh, if Jove's will

Have linked that amorous power to thy soft lay,

Now timely sing, ere the rude bird of hate

Foretell my hopeless doom in some grove nigh:

As thou from year to year has sung too late

For my relief, yet hadst no reason why,

Whether the Muse or Love call thee his mate,

Both them I serve, and of their train am I.

JOHN MILTON

LOVE IN THE VALLEY

GEORGE MEREDITH

Under yonder beech-tree single on the green-sward,
Couched with her arms behind her golden head,
Knees and tresses folded to slip and ripple idly,
Lies my young love sleeping in the shade.
Had I the heart to slide an arm beneath her,
Press her parting lips as her waist I gather slow,
Waking in amazement she could not but embrace me:
Then would she hold me and never let me go?
Shy as the squirrel and wayward as the swallow
Swift as the swallow along the river's light
Circleing the surface to meet his mirrored winglets,
Fleeter she seems in her stay than in her flight.
Shy as the squirrel that leaps among the pine-tops,
Wayward as the swallow overhead at set of sun,
She whom I love is hard to catch and conquer,
Hard, but O the glory of the winning were she won!
When her mother tends her before the laughing mirror,
Tying up her laces, looping up her hair,
Often she thinks, were this wild thing wedded,
More love should I have, and much less care.
When her mother tends her before the lighted mirror,
Loosening her laces, combing down her curls,
Often she thinks, were this wild thing wedded,

I should miss but one for many boys and girls.
Heartless she is as the shadow in the meadows
Flying to the hills on a blue and breezy noon.
No, she is athirst and drinking up her wonder:
Earth to her is young as the slip of the new moon.
Deals she an unkindness, 'tis but her rapid measure,
Even as in a dance; and her smile can heal no less:
Like the swinging May-cloud that pelts the flowers with
hailstones
Off a sunny border, she was made to bruise and bless.
Lovely are the curves of the white owl sweeping
Wavy in the dusk lit by one large star.
Lone on the fir-branch, his rattle-note unvaried,
Brooding o'er the gloom, spins the brown eve-jar.
Darker grows the valley, more and more forgetting:
So were it with me if forgetting could be willed.
Tell the grassy hollow that holds the bubbling wellspring,
Tell it to forget the source that keeps it filled.
Stepping down the hill with her fair companions,
Arm in arm, all against the raying West
Boldly she sings, to the merry tune she marches,
Brave in her shape, and sweeter unpossessed.
Sweeter, for she is what my heart first awaking
Whispered the world was; morning light is she.
Love that so desires would fain keep her changeless;
Fain would fling the net, and fain have her free.
Happy happy time, when the white star hovers
Low over dim fields fresh with bloomy dew,
Near the face of dawn, that draws athwart the darkness,
Threading it with colour, as yewberries the yew.
Thicker crowd the shades while the grave East deepens

Glowing, and with crimson a long cloud swells.
Maiden still the morn is; and strange she is, and secret;
Strange her eyes; her cheeks are cold as cold sea shells.
Sunrays, leaning on our southern hills and lighting
Wild cloud-mountains that drag the hills along,
Oft ends the day of your shifting brilliant laughter
Chill as a dull face frowning on a song.
Ay, but shows the South-West a ripple-feathered bosom
Blown to silver while the clouds are shaken and ascend
Scaling the mid-heavens as they stream, there comes a sunset
Rich, deep like love in beauty without end.
When at dawn she sighs, and like an infant to the window
Turns grave eyes craving light, released from dreams,
Beautiful she looks, like a white water-lily
Bursting out of bud in havens of the streams.
When from bed she rises clothed from neck to ankle
In her long nightgown sweet as boughs of May,
Beautiful she looks, like a tall garden lily
Pure from the night, and splendid for the day.
Mother of the dews, dark eye-lashed twilight,
Low-lidded twilight, o'er the valley's brim,
Rounding on thy breast sings the dew-delighted skylark,
Clear as though the dewdrops had their voice in him.
Hidden where the rose-flush drinks the rayless planet,
Fountain-full he pours the spraying fountain-showers.
Let me hear her laughter, I would have her ever
Cool as dew in twilight, the lark above the flowers.
All the girls are out with their baskets for the primrose;
Up lanes, woods through, they troop in joyful bands.
My sweet leads: she knows not why, but now she totters,
Eyes the bent anemones, and hangs her hands.

Such a look will tell that the violets are peeping,
Coming the rose: and unaware a cry
Springs in her bosom for odours and for colour,
Covert and the nightingale; she knows not why.
Kerchiefed head and chin she darts between her tulips,
Streaming like a willow grey in arrowy rain:
Some bend beaten cheek to gravel, and their angel
She will be; she lifts them, and on she speeds again.
Black the driving raincloud breasts the iron gateway:
She is forth to cheer a neighbour lacking mirth.
So when sky and grass met rolling dumb for thunder
Saw I once a white dove, sole light of earth.
Prim little scholars are the flowers of her garden,
Trained to stand in rows, and asking if they please.
I might love them well but for loving more the wild ones:
O my wild ones! they tell me more than these.
You, my wild one, you tell of honied field-rose,
Violet, blushing eglantine in life; and even as they,
They by the wayside are earnest of your goodness,
You are of life's, on the banks that line the way.
Peering at her chamber the white crowns the red rose,
Jasmine winds the porch with stars two and three.
  Parted is the window; she sleeps; the starry jasmine
Breathes a falling breath that carries thoughts of me.
Sweeter unpossessed, have I said of her my sweetest?
Not while she sleeps: while she sleeps the jasmine breathes,
Luring her to love; she sleeps; the starry jasmine
Bears me to her pillow under white rose-wreaths.
Yellow with birdfoot-trefoil are the grass-glades;
Yellow with cinquefoil of the dew-grey leaf;
Yellow with stonecrop; the moss-mounds are yellow;

[283]

Blue-necked the wheat sways, yellowing to the sheaf:
Green-yellow bursts from the copse the laughing yaffle;
Sharp as a sickle is the edge of shade and shine:
Earth in her heart laughs looking at the heavens,
Thinking of the harvest: I look and think of mine.
This I may know: her dressing and undressing
Such a change of light shows as when the skies in sport
Shift from cloud to moonlight; or edging over thunder
Slips a ray of sun; or sweeping into port
White sails furl; or on the ocean borders
White sails lean along the waves leaping green.
Visions of her shower before me, but from eyesight
Guarded she would be like the sun were she seen.
Front door and back of the mossed old farmhouse
Open with the morn, and in a breezy link
Freshly sparkles garden to stripe-shadowed orchard,
Green across a rill where on sand the minnows wink.
Busy in the grass the early sun of summer
Swarms, and the blackbird's mellow fluting notes
Call my darling up with round and roguish challenge:
Quaintest, richest carol of all the singing throats!
Cool was the woodside; cool as her white dairy
Keeping sweet the cream-pan; and there the boys from school,
Cricketing below, rushed brown and red with sunshine;
O the dark translucence of the deep-eyed cool!
Spying from the farm, herself she fetched a pitcher
Full of milk, and tilted for each in turn the beak.
Then a little fellow, mouth up and on tiptoe,
Said, "I will kiss you": she laughed and leaned her cheek.
Doves of the fir-wood walling high our red roof
Through the long noon coo, crooning through the coo.

Loose droop the leaves, and down the sleepy roadway
Sometimes pipes a chaffinch; loose droops the blue.
Cows flap a slow tail knee-deep in the river,
Breathless, given up to sun and gnat and fly.
Nowhere is she seen; and if I see her nowhere,
Lightning may come, straight rains and tiger sky.
O the golden sheaf, the rustling treasure-armful!
O the nutbrown tresses nodding interlaced!
O the treasure-tresses one another over
Nodding! O the girdle slack about the waist!
Slain are the poppies that shot their random scarlet
Quick amid the wheatears: wound about the waist,
Gathered, see these brides of Earth one blush of ripeness!
O the nutbrown tresses nodding interlaced!
Large and smoky red the sun's cold disk drops,
Clipped by naked hills, on violet shaded snow:
Eastward large and still lights up a bower of moonrise,
Whence at her leisure steps the moon aglow.
Nightlong on black print-branches our beech-tree
Gazes in this whiteness: nightlong could I.
Here may life on death or death on life be painted.
Let me clasp her soul to know she cannot die!
Gossips count her faults; they scour a narrow chamber
Where there is no window, read not heaven or her.
"When she was tiny," one aged woman quavers,
Plucks at my heart and leads me by the ear.
Faults she had once as she learnt to run and tumbled:
Faults of feature some see, beauty not complete.
Yet, good gossips, beauty that makes holy
Earth and air, may have faults from head to feet.
Hither she comes; she comes to me; she lingers,

Deepens her brown eyebrows, while in new surprise
High rise the lashes in wonder of a stranger;
Yet am I the light and living of her eyes.
Something friends have told her fills her heart to brimming,
Nets her in her blushes, and wounds her, and tames.—
Sure of her haven, O like a dove alighting,
Arms up, she dropped: our souls were in our names.
Soon will she lie like a white-frost sunrise.
Yellow oats and brown wheat, barley pale as rye,
Long since your sheaves have yielded to the thresher,
Felt the girdle loosened, seen the tresses fly.
Soon will she lie like a blood-red sunset.
Swift with the to-morrow, green-winged
Spring! Sing from the South-West, bring her back the truants,
Nightingale and swallow, song and dipping wing.
Soft new beech-leaves, up to beamy April
Spreading bough on bough a primrose mountain, you,
Lucid in the moon, raise lilies to the skyfields,
Youngest green transfused in silver shining through:
Fairer than the lily, than the wild white cherry:
Fair as in image my seraph love appears
Borne to me by dreams when dawn is at my eyelids:
Fair as in the flesh she swims to me on tears.
Could I find a place to be alone with heaven,
I would speak my heart out: heaven is my need.
Every woodland tree is flushing like the dog-wood,
Flashing like the whitebeam, swaying like the reed.
Flushing like the dog-wood crimson in October;
Streaming like the flag-reed South-West blown;
Flashing as in gusts the sudden-lighted white beam:
All seem to know what is for heaven alone.63

LOVE REFINES

Love refines
The thoughts, and heart enlarges, hath his seat
In reason, and is judicious, is the scale
By which to heavenly love thou mayest ascend.

JOHN MILTON
From *Paradise Lost*

ULYSSES RETURNS TO PENELOPE

HOMER
From *The Odyssey*
TRANSLATED BY SAMUEL BUTLER

"I will say what I think will be best," answered Ulysses. "First wash and put your shirts on; tell the maids also to go to their own room and dress; Phemius shall then strike up a dance tune on his lyre, so that if people outside hear, or any of the neighbors, or someone going along the street, happens to notice it, they may think there is a wedding in the house, and no rumors about the death of the suitors will get about in the town, before we can escape to the woods upon my own land. Once there, we will settle which of the courses heaven vouchsafes us shall seem wisest."

Thus did he speak, and they did even as he had said. First they washed and put their shirts on, while the women got ready. Then Phemius took his lyre and set them all longing for sweet song and stately dance. The house reechoed with the sound of men and women dancing, and the people outside said, "I suppose the queen has been getting married at last. She ought to be ashamed of herself for not continuing to protect her husband's property until he comes home."

This was what they said, but they did not know what it was that had been happening. The upper servant Eurynome washed and anointed Ulysses in his own house and gave him a shirt and cloak, while Minerva made him look taller and stronger than before; she also made the hair grow thick on the top of his head, and flow down in curls like hyacinth blossoms; she glorified him about the head and shoulders just as a skillful workman who has studied art of all kinds under Vulcan or Minerva—and his work is full of beauty—enriches a piece of silver plate by gilding it. He came from the bath looking like one of the immortals, and sat down opposite his wife on the seat he had left. "My dear," said he, "heaven has endowed you with a heart more unyielding than woman ever yet had. No other woman could bear to keep away from her husband when he had come back to her after twenty years of absence, and after having gone through so much. But come, nurse, get a bed ready for me; I will sleep alone, for this woman has a heart as hard as iron."

"My dear," answered Penelope, "I have no wish to set myself up, nor to depreciate you; but I am not struck by your appearance, for I very well remember what kind of a man you were when you set sail from Ithaca. Nevertheless, Euryclea, take his bed outside the bed chamber that he himself built. Bring the bed outside this room, and put bedding upon it with fleeces, good coverlets, and blankets."

She said this to try him, but Ulysses was very angry and said, "Wife, I am much displeased at what you have just been saying. Who has been taking my bed from the place in which I left it? He must have found it a hard task, no matter how skilled a workman he was, unless some god came and helped him to shift it. There is no man living, however strong and in his prime, who could move it from its place, for it is a marvelous curiosity which I made with my very own hands. There was a young olive growing within the precincts of the house, in full vigor, and about as thick as a bearing-post. I built my room round this with strong walls of stone and a roof to cover them, and I made the doors strong and well-fitting. Then I cut off the top boughs of the olive tree and left the stump standing. This I dressed roughly from the root upwards and then worked with carpenter's tools well and skillfully, straightening my work by drawing a line on the wood, and making it into a bed-prop. I then bored a hole down the middle, and made it the center-post of my bed, at which I worked till I had finished it, inlaying it with gold and silver; after this I stretched a hide of crimson leather from one side of it to the other. So you see I know all about it, and I desire to learn whether it is still there, or whether anyone has been removing it by cutting down the olive tree at its roots."

When she heard the sure proofs Ulysses now gave her, she fairly broke down. She flew weeping to his side, flung her arms about his neck, and kissed him, "Do not be angry with me, Ulysses," she cried, "you, who are the wisest of mankind. We have suffered, both of us. Heaven has denied us the happiness of spending our youth, and of growing old, together; do not then be aggrieved or take it amiss that I did not embrace you thus as soon as I saw you. I have been shuddering all the time through fear that someone might come here and deceive me with a lying story; for there are many very wicked people going about. Jove's daughter Helen would never have yielded herself to a man from a foreign country, if she had known that the sons of Achaeans would come after her and bring her back. Heaven put it in her heart to do wrong, and she gave no thought to that sin, which has been the source of all our sorrows. Now, however, that you have convinced me by showing that you know all about our bed (which no human being has ever seen but you and I and a single maidservant, the daughter of Actor, who was given me by my father on my marriage, and who keeps the doors of our room), hard of belief though I have been I can mistrust no longer."

Then Ulysses in his turn melted, and wept as he clasped his dear and faithful wife to his bosom. As the sight of land is welcome to men who are swimming towards the shore, when Neptune has wrecked their ship with the fury of his winds and waves; a few alone reach the land, and these, covered with brine, are thankful when they find themselves on firm ground and out of danger—even so was her husband welcome to her as she looked upon him, and she could not tear her two fair arms from about his neck. Indeed they would have gone on indulging their sorrow till rosy-fingered morn appeared, had not Minerva determined otherwise, and held night back in the far west, while she would not suffer Dawn to leave Oceanus, nor to yoke the two steeds Lampus and Phaethon that bear her onward to break the day upon mankind.

At last, however, Ulysses said, "Wife, we have not yet reached the end of our troubles. I have an unknown amount of toil still to undergo. It is long and difficult, but I must go through with it, for thus the shade of Teiresias prophesied concerning me, on the day when I went down into Hades to ask about my return and that of my companions. But now let us go to bed, that we may lie down and enjoy the blessed boon of sleep."[64]

DAPHNE

From *The Metamorphoses of Ovid*

Apollo, while rejoicing over slaying the Python, saw Cupid armed with his bow and arrow, and began to tease him saying: "What have you to do with the arrow? That is my weapon, for I have proved it by killing a terrible monster. You must be content to light the hidden fires of love and not claim my honors."

Cupid, a quick-tempered little god, replied, "Thy dart may pierce all other things, but mine shall pierce you." Then he flew off and alighted on a shady peak of Parnassus, and began to think of some way by which he might make Apollo feel his marksmanship.

By and by he saw a beautiful nymph, Daphne, wandering about in the grove, and he took from his quiver two darts of opposite effects. The one inducing love was sharp pointed and made of gold; the other was blunt and made of dull lead. He pierced Daphne with a leaden arrow and then planted a golden arrow in Apollo's heart. Away he flew satisfied.

No sooner had the sun god caught a glimpse of the beautiful nymph than he fell deeply in love with her; and just as quickly, Daphne began to hate Apollo and flee from his approach. Marveling at her beautiful form, Apollo cried: "Stay!

Do not run from me. I will do you no harm. Stop and see who your lover is. I am no mountain-dweller nor shepherd boy but the great sun god Apollo."

But terrified she fled at full speed, while Apollo on wings of love ran more swiftly. He had almost reached her side when she stretched out her arms to her father, Peneus, the god of the river along whose banks she was fleeing. "Oh, Father," she cried, "help me! help me! Either let the earth swallow me or change this form of mine so that Apollo will not love me."

Scarcely had she thus prayed when her limbs grew heavy and a thin bark began to cover her skin. Her hair was changed into leaves, her arms to slender branches, her feet, which had carried her along so swiftly, grew fast in sluggish roots, and her head was now a tree's top. Peneus had answered her prayer, and had changed her into a laurel tree.

When Apollo saw her, he wept and threw his arms around the newly formed bark and said: "Since you cannot be my bride, you shall be my tree, my laurel. My hair, my lyre, and my quiver shall always be entwined with thee. Your foliage shall be used to crown other brides, and victors and shall be green alike in summer and in winter." And so it came to be, the laurel, Apollo's emblem, became from that day the sign of honor and triumph.[65]

THE LETTER

I take my pen in hand
there was a meadow
Besides a field of oats, beside a wood,
Beside a road, beside a day spread out
Green at the edges, yellow at the heart.
The dust lifted a little, a finger's breadth,
The word of the wood pigeon traveled slow,
A slow half pace behind the tick of time.

To tell you I am well and thinking of you
And of the walk through the meadow, and of another walk
Along the neat piled ruin of the town
Under a pale heaven, empty of all but death
And rain beginning. The river ran beside.

It has been a long time since I wrote. I have no news.
I put my head between my hands and hope
My heart will choke me. I put out my hand
To touch you and touch air. I turn to sleep
And find a nightmare, hollowness, and fear.

And by the way, I have had no letter now
For eight weeks, it must be
a long eight weeks,
Because you have nothing to say, nothing at all,
Not even to record your emptiness
Or guess what's to become of you without love.

I know that you have cares,
Ashes to shovel, broken glass to mend
And many a cloth to patch before the sunset.

Write to me soon, and tell me how you are.
If you still tremble, sweat and glower, still stretch
A hand for me at dusk, play me the tune,
Show me the leaves and towers, the lamb, the rose.

Because I always wish to hear of you
And feel my heart swell, and the blood run out
At the ungraceful syllable of your name
Said through the scent of stocks, the little snore of fire,
The shoreless waves of symphony, the murmuring night.

I will end this letter now. I am yours with love.
Always with love, with love.

ELIZABETH RIDDELL

TEAM BUILDING GOD'S WAY

BOB AND YVONNE TURNBULL

Love does not consist in gazing at each other,
but in looking outward together in the same direction.
—ANTOINE DESAINT-EXUPERY

When people ask us where we met, Bob always answers with "I met Yvonne when she was working a hotel in Waikiki."

Eyebrows go up, so Yvonne quickly adds, "That sounds great, Dear. Now are you going to tell them what you mean by that?"

BOB: *I was walking down the hallway of the Reef Towers Hotel in Hawaii, en route to my office at the Waikiki Beach chaplaincy. I always passed by a travel agency office and would automatically look in and wave to the staff. The owner, a friend of mine, was a man, but his staff were all local Hawaii-born females, each with beautiful long black hair, just like you'd see on "Hawaii 5-0" and "Magnum, P.I." But one day as I walked and waved, out of the corner of my eye I noticed there was this blond in the midst of the black-haired girls. So I said to my thongs, "Halt. Back up." They reversed themselves until I was able to take that famous second look. Sure enough, there she was, standing in the middle of the room, very animated and looking mighty good. Little did I know that someday this bubbly blond would become my wife. Since my eyes noticed this* new talent in town, I quickly seized the moment to snake—I mean ease—my way into the room to extend the friendly aloha spirit.

YVONNE: *After graduating from Washington State University and then doing some post-graduate work at the University of Washington, I needed some rest and relaxation. So I went to Hawaii for a few weeks, which stretched into a few months. Being a new Christian, I heard about a worship service on the beach at the Hilton Hawaiian Village every Sunday morning. It was well known on Oahu as "Sun and Soul Talk." That sounded like my style of worship, so I went one Sunday morning to hear the Waikiki Beach chaplain speak. I had heard so much about him, but on the Sunday I attended he was speaking on the mainland. The service was nice, but I didn't return. When I noticed this hunk walk into my office that day, and when he introduced himself to me, I realized this was the man I had gone to hear at the beach, and after looking at him, I thought, "All right—I'm definitely going back to the beach service!"*

BOB: *I wanted to get to know her but didn't want to get too pushy by asking for a date since I had known her for only 30 seconds. So I did the safe thing. I invited her to come to the beach service the next Sunday. She agreed.*

YVONNE: *I was hoping I would get to see him again, so when he invited me to the beach service I was happy to accept. I wasn't even thinking that I was a "cheap date"—only that I would get to know him better. The next Sunday I showed up with a beach towel, bathing suit, and sunglasses, and that was the start of many cheap dates to the beach services and Bible studies for the next three years.*

We got married a full three years after that first meeting. The long wait was mainly because neither of us was quite sure we were ready for that big step of marriage. Second, half of each year Bob traveled the mainland speaking, so it took us longer to build our relationship than if he had remained in Hawaii day in and day out.

The special day finally arrived, and we were both eager to say our "I dos." Our wedding took place in a garden setting in beautiful Manoa Valley, against the mountains, complete with a mist falling upon the small gathering of family and friends.

Yvonne was a nervous bride for more than the usual reasons. Bob had to fly into Hawaii in time for the wedding, and he was starting his journey to the wedding from Israel. With international flights, there can be many delays for a variety of reasons. Bob had to fly from Israel to Rome to New York to Los Angeles to Honolulu and get there by 3:00 for a 5:00 wedding. That would make any bride pretty nervous!

Fortunately, Bob's plane arrived in Honolulu at 3:15. The wedding started on time, and Mr. and Mrs. Bob Turnbull IV were united in Christ and ready to start an adventure they never would have dreamed of or imagined. A "happily ever after" marriage!

YVONNE: *My first thought when awaking the morning of our wedding day was "This is a dream come true." I had found a man who would fulfill all my needs for love and attention. He would be so eager to rush home to me every night and spend all his time just talking to and listening to me. He would surprise me with little gifts and things he had done for me. We would keep the romance fires flaming for the rest of our married life.*

BOB: *Wow—I'm getting a wife. A wife created by God to meet my needs. I'll be the head of the home. She'll be the heart. I'll be the leader, and she'll be the submissive "little woman." What more could I want? This'll be great—just great!*

YVONNE: *I read all the fairy tales as a young girl, and evidently I believed the one about Prince Charming carrying his princess off to his castle. The problem was that no one told me that besides picking up after him I was going to have to clean up after his horse. The reality check for me came as soon as our honeymoon. It began with my husband going back to work Sunday morning, after a Friday wedding, to speak at the beach service. It wasn't just that the length of the honeymoon was so short. It was that I hardly spent any time with him. He slept most of the honeymoon because he was so exhausted from having just returned from his lengthy trip to Israel. Then he spent most of the hours he was awake working on his Sunday message.*

BOB: *I assumed Yvonne knew I would be tired from my lengthy trip and that I had only a short time to get my Sunday message prepared. I realized this was a quickie honeymoon and not the ideal circumstances, but I assumed she would understand and would overlook it.*

YVONNE: *That weekend I was already asking, "Hey—what happened to the long hours of talking, cuddling, and romancing?" I found this reality was the beginning of a pattern for many years in our marriage. I discovered early that work was what seemed to capture most of his time and effort. I always felt as if I got the leftovers. So to get his attention, guess what I started doing? That's right— nagging, by saying things like "How come it seems you don't want to talk to me?" "How come everyone else's needs seem so much more important than mine?"*

BOB: *I would shrug her off with inane comments like "Honey, just hang in there. I'm really involved doing God's work, and you know that. I'll spend time with you on my day off."*

YVONNE: *Guess what usually happened on his day off? Ministry emergencies that he just had to attend to, of course. Other married members of the Waikiki Beach chaplaincy spent time together on their days off, but not my Bob. It was then that I began to feel that he was married to the ministry more than to me. But he was doing God's work, so who was I to speak against that? Thus, in order not to feel the pain of loneliness and rejection, I decided to become very busy. I would definitely stay married, because neither of us would consider divorce as an option, but I started living a double life. By that I mean that Bob and I remained a married couple, but I also started a life for myself apart from Bob. I put my energies into many activities, either alone or with my girlfriends. I figured that since he was busy I would be busy too.*

Both of us desired to be close to each other. We just didn't know how. It seemed everything we tried either just didn't click or completely backfired. We were agonizingly and slowly drifting farther apart. This went on for years. No one told us that it's not easy to live happily ever after.

As with many other couples, numerous circumstances entered in that put more stress on an already-stressed marriage. We were moving nearly every two years of our married life. Some of the moves took us completely across the country. Others were just a matter of blocks away. Most were related to job opportunities, while others were because the rental houses we were in were either sold or foreclosed on. We looked forward to some of the moves. Some we did not—like the two cross-country ones we did at Christmastime.

In the midst of all of this, our finances were stretched to the edge. Matters worsened once when we were in California and we both lost our jobs on the same day. We were co-hosting a Monday-through-Friday radio show, and when the new management took over they fired everyone working at the station. In radio parlance, that's called

"The Friday Massacre." Instead of working together as a team during those stress-filled times, we battled each other. It seemed that every time we tried to talk to each other, the result would be an argument. Our marriage started as an ideal but then became an ordeal that bottomed out as a raw deal. What we needed was a new deal.

The God of Hope Intervened

YVONNE: *We were at our lowest point. I remember one afternoon when I was, as usual, home alone. I sat on the couch and burst into tears. Deep tears. I was so lonely and hurt. I cried out, "Dear God, we need Your intervention. We need Your help. We need hope that our marriage can and will be different."*

BOB: *As Yvonne was crying and praying, I was just a few blocks away from home, just moments from pulling into the driveway. I was depressed and frustrated and echoed a similar prayer to God. I remember almost shouting, "God, please give us a verse of hope that we can cling to so we can start rebuilding our marriage!" It was then the Lord pulled up a verse from my memory that I hadn't used in years. Rom. 15:13 - "May the God of hope fill you with all joy and peace as you trust in him, so that you may overflow with hope by the power of the Holy Spirit."*

YVONNE: *Bob rushed into the room, looked at me, dropped to his knees in front of me, and said, "Honey, Romans 15:13. We need to believe it, claim it, and apply it." He quoted it to me and added, "We have little hope, joy, or peace in our marriage, because, though we're Christians, we're trying to make this marriage work in our own strength. We're not trusting—really trusting—in God. Our marriage needs to overflow with hope by the power of the Holy Spirit, who lives in us. That can happen. Let's do it!*[66]

Chapter 8

LOVE'S CLANGING NOISE

Even in the best of loving relationships there come those times that St. Paul compares to "clanging cymbals." Sometimes they're funny—at least by the silver anniversary.

Poets and humorists often have the ability of looking at all loving situations (or lack of loving) through their funny bones.

William Shakespeare—the bard himself— enjoyed humorously clanging the romance- cymbals in some of his best loved plays.

And then, there are the limerick writers and the Scottish balladeers to whom love was worth a laugh or two.

Just remember, even if you can say, "I love you," so convincingly that the angel in your life believes you, but you don't have self-giving love, you are a noisy clanger. Of course, even angels like a good laugh! So enjoy the following pages!

SYMPTOMS OF LOVE

Love is a universal migraine,
A bright stain on the vision
Blotting out reason.

Symptoms of true love
Are leanness, jealousy,
Laggard dawns;

Are omens and nightmares—
Listening for a knock,
Waiting for a song:
For a touch of her fingers
In a darkened room,
For a searching look.

Take courage, lover!
Can you endure such grief
At any hand but hers?[67]

ROBERT GRAVES

THE OLD BACHELORS' SALE

I dreamed a dream in the midst of my slumbers,
And as fast as I dreamed it was coined into numbers,
My thoughts ran along in such beautiful meter,
I'm sure I ne'er saw any poetry sweeter.

It seemed that a law had been recently made
That a tax on old bachelors' pates should be laid.
And in order to make them all willing to marry,
The tax was as large as a man could well carry.

The bachelors grumbled and said 'twas no use,
'Twas horrid injustice and horrid abuse,
And declared that to save their own hearts' blood from spilling,
Of such a vile tax they would not pay a shilling.

But the rulers determined them still to pursue,
So they set all the old bachelors up at vendue;
A crier was sent through the town to and fro,
To rattle his bell and his trumpet to blow.
And to call out to all he might meet in his way:
"Ho! forty old bachelors sold here today!"

And presently all the old maids in the town
Each in her very best bonnet and gown,
From thirty to sixty, fair, plain, red and pale,
Of every description, all flocked to the sale.

The auctioneer then to his labor began,
And called out aloud, as he held up a man,
"How much for a bachelor? Who wants to buy?"
In a twinkle every lady responded, "I! I!"
In short, at a highly extravagant price,
The bachelors were all sold off in a trice.
And forty old maids—some younger, some older—
Each lugged an old bachelor home on her shoulder.[68]

ANONYMOUS
From *More Heart Throbs*

TO THE VIRGINS, TO MAKE MUCH OF TIME

Gather ye rosebuds while ye may,

Old Time is still a-flying:

And this same flower that smiles today

Tomorrow will be dying.

The glorious lamp of heaven, the sun,

The higher he's a-getting,

The sooner will his race be run,

And nearer he's to setting.

That age is best which is the first,

When youth and blood are warmer;

But being spent, the worse, and worse

Times still succeed the former.

Then be not coy, but use your time,

And while ye may, go marry:

For having lost but once your prime,

You may forever tarry.

ROBERT HERRICK

SALLY IN OUR ALLEY

Of all the girls that are so smart
There's none like pretty Sally;
She is the darling of my heart,
And she lives in our alley.
There is no lady in the land
Is half so sweet as Sally;
She is the darling of my heart,
And she lives in our alley.

Her father he makes cabbage-nets,
And through the streets does cry 'em;
Her mother she sells laces long
To such as pleases as buy 'em;
But sure such folks could ne'er beget
So sweet a girl as Sally!
She is the darling of my heart,
And she lives in our alley.

When she is by, I leave my work,
I love her so sincerely;
My master comes like any Turk,
And bangs me most severely;
But let him bang his bellyful,
I'll bear it all for Sally,
She is the darling of my heart,
And she lives in my alley.

Of all the days that's in the week
I dearly love but one day—
And that's the day that comes betwixt
A Saturday and Monday;
For then I'm dressed all in my best
To walk abroad with Sally;
She is the darling of my heart,
And she lives in our alley.

When Christmas comes about again,
O, then I shall have money;
I'll hoard it up, and box it all,
I'll give it to my honey:
I would it were ten thousand pound,
I'd give it all to Sally;
She is the darling of my heart
And she lives in our alley.

My master and the neighbors all
Make game of me and Sally,
And, but for her, I'd better be
A slave and row a galley;
But when my seven long years are out,
O, then I'll marry Sally;
O, then we'll wed, and then we'll bed
But not in our alley![69]

HENRY CAREY

WHEN WE FIGHT

milk curdle in coffee

toast burn

hot water run out

shampoo empty

tire flat

bus late

rain come

umbrella break

shoelace snap

stocking run

button fall off coat

glove disappear

pocketbook vanish

earring break

nail polish chip

typewriter key stuck

white out spill

xerox machine jam

envelope don't seal

stamps stuck together

check bounce

pizza burn mouth

tomato sauce on white blouse

heel break off left shoe

key fall down sewer

mail box empty

answering machine silent

cat misses litter box

dog vomit

toilet overflow

lettuce rot in crisper

finger cut instead of onion

meat spoil

bread green

soda flat

newspaper don't come

TV fuzzy

plant on window sill die

pages fall out of book

pen run dry

light bulb burn out

heart stop[70]

LESLEA NEWMAN

LOVE QUOTES

Love is as much of an object as an obsession, everybody wants it, everybody seeks it, but few ever achieve it, those who will cherish it, be lost in it, and among all, never . . . never forget it.

CURTIS JUDALET

It is best to love wisely, no doubt; but to love foolishly is better than not to have loved at all.

THACKERAY

A man snatches the first kiss, pleads for the second, demands the third, takes the fourth, accepts the fifth—and endures all the rest.

HELEN ROWLANDS

A SONG FROM MUCH ADO ABOUT NOTHING

Sigh no more, ladies, sigh no more
Men were deceivers ever;
One foot in sea, and one on shore,
To one thing constant never.

Then sigh not so
But let them go.

And be you blith and bonny,
Converting all your sounds of woe
Into Hey nonny, nonny.
Sing no more ditties, sing no more
Of dumps so dull and heavy;
The fraud of men was ever so,
Since summer first was leavy.

Then sigh not so,
But let them go,

And be you blith and bonny,
Converting all your sounds of woe
Into Hey nonny, nonny.

WILLIAM SHAKESPEARE

THE LONG WAIT

Bill Nye, when a young man, once made an engagement with a lady friend of his to take a horse and carriage ride around the park. The appointed day came, but at the livery stable all the horses were taken out save one old, shaky, exceedingly bony animal.

Mr. Nye hired the nag and drove to his friend's residence. The lady let him wait nearly an hour before she was ready, and then on viewing the disreputable gray mare, flatly refused to accompany Mr. Nye.

"Why," she exclaimed sneeringly, "that horse may die of old age at any minute."

"Madame," Mr. Nye replied, "when I arrived that horse was a prancing young steed."

AUTHOR UNKNOWN

LOVE LIMERICKS

There was a young fellow of Lyme,
Who lived with three wives at a time.
When asked, "Why the third?"
He replied, "One's absurd,
And bigamy, sir, is a crime."

ANONYMOUS

A certain young chap named Bill Beebee,
Was in love with a lady named Phoebe;
"But," he said, "I must see
What the clerical fee
Be before Phoebe be Phoebe Beebee."

ANONYMOUS

Concerning the bees and the flowers,
In the fields and the gardens and bowers;
You will tell at a glance
That their ways of romance
Haven't any resemblance to ours.

ANONYMOUS

A bottle of perfume that Willie sent,
Was highly displeasing to Millicent;
Her thanks were so cold,
That they quarrelled, I'm told,
Over the silly scent Willie sent Millicent.

ANONYMOUS

There was an old lady of Harrow,
Whose views were exceedingly narrow;
At the end of her paths,
She built two bird baths—
For the different sexes of sparrows.

ANONYMOUS

There was a young lady of Florence,
Who for kissing professed great abhorrence;
But when she'd been kissed,
And found what she missed,
She cried till her tears came in torrents.

ANONYMOUS

GREENSLEEVES

Alas, my love, you do me wrong,

To cast me off discourteously.

For I have loved you well and long,

Delighting in your company.

Greensleeves was all my joy

Greensleeves was my delight,

Greensleeves was my heart of gold,

And who but my Lady Greensleeves?

Your vows you've broken, like my heart,

Oh, why did you so enrapture me?

Now I remain in a world apart

But my heart remains in captivity.

I have been ready at your hand,

To grant whatever you would crave,

I have both wagered life and land,

Your love and goodwill for to have.

If you intend thus to disdain,

It does the more enrapture me,

And even so, I still remain

A lover in captivity.

My men were clothed all in green,

And they did ever wait on thee;

All this was gallant to be seen,

And yet thou wouldst not love me.

Thou couldest desire no earthly thing,

but still thou hadst it readily.

Thy music still to play and sing;

And yet thou wouldst not love me.

Well, I will pray to God on high,

That thou my constancy mayst see,

And that yet once before I die,

Thou wilt vouchsafe to love me.

Ah, Greensleeves, now farewell, adieu,

To God I pray to prosper thee,

For I am still thy lover true,

Come once again and love me.

KING HENRY VIII

KISSIN'

Some say kissin's a sin,
But I say, not at a';
For it's been in the world
Ever since there were twa [two].
If it were not lawful,
Lawyers wouldn't allow it;
If it were not holy,
Ministers wouldn't do it;
If it were not modest,
Maidens wouldn't taste it;
If it were not plenty,
Poor folks couldn't have it.[71]

A SCOTTISH SAYING

THE WORLD'S SHORTEST ROMANTIC SHORT STORIES

Steve Moss has brought together a collection of stories that contain no more than 55 words. Here are a few selections.

A SECOND CHANCE
JAY BONESTELL

His love had gone. In despair he flung himself off the Golden Gate Bridge.

Coincidentally, a few yards away, a girl made her own suicide plunge. The two passed in midair.

Their eyes met.

Their chemistry clicked.

It was true love.

They realized it.

Three feet above the water.

RITES OF PASSAGE
MARK TURNER

He'd known her since she was very young. She was the most beautiful girl in the world, and he loved her deeply. At one time, he had been her idol. Now he was losing her to another man.

Eyes glistening, he kissed her cheek softly, then smiled as he gave her away to the groom.

THE DANCE
JOY JOLISSAINT

He shuffles to my locker. Skinny Steve with the zits. Yuck! Probably wants to ask me to the dance. My last chance. Oh, well. Better than being a wallflower, like Jenny.

Deep breath. "Hi, Steve."

"Hi, Sue."

"You wanted to ask me something?"

Even his zits blushed.

"I wondered . . . do you have Jenny's phone number?"

YOU CAN NEVER GO BACK
JAY BONESTELL

Five years ago she plucked a dandelion and a bindweed blossom from the grass at the mobile home park. Now they're pressed between the pages of an old Moffatt's Bible marking the 23rd Psalm.

She never thinks about that day she handed him the tiny flowers. He can never forget.[72]

ROBERT G. LEE
Christian media personality

Explain weddings to me. A bride will make her best friends in
the whole world wear the ugliest dresses known to mankind.
And she will lie to them by saying "I'm sure you can wear it
again!" To which every bridesmaid is thinking, *Sure I will, if the
Polka Festival ever comes to town.*

A primer for any couple should be the book *Men Are from Mars,
Women Are from Venus.* It explains that men and women are
from different planets. For example, women like to verbalize
their feelings on relationships. It's difficult for a man to even
admit he's in a relationship.

After fifteen years of marriage, my wife wants us to recommit
our vows. As a man, I don't understand her need to get married
again. We've got our toaster, let's move on.

I've been married to the same woman for fourteen years.
Which is like eighty-something in L.A. years.

My wife and I went on a three-day cruise. Actually, it was more
like a three-day meal. They tell you to bring just one outfit, but
in three different sizes: large, extra large, and blimp.[73]

ADIVCE TO YOUNG LADIES

WILLIAM MAKEPEACE THACKERAY
From *Vanity Fair*

The title of this ninteenth century novel, Vanity Fair, *comes from the allegorical* Pilgrim's Progress, *by John Bunyan, where it is the place designated as the center of human corruption. The Thackeray work is a multi-layered metaphor for the human condition. While tongue-in-cheek, the following advice does reflect what it meant to be virtuous.*

Be cautious then, young ladies; be wary how you engage. Be shy of loving frankly; never tell all you feel, or (a better way still) feel very little. See the consequences of being prematurely honest and confiding, and mistrust yourselves and everybody. Get yourselves married as they do in France, where the lawyers are the bridesmaids and confidants. At any rate, never have any feelings which may make you uncomfortable, or make any promises which you cannot at any required moment command and withdraw. That is the way to get on, and be respected, and have a virtuous character in Vanity Fair.

THE ART OF COQUETRY

First form your artful looks with studious care,
From mild to grave, from tender to severe.
Oft on the careless youth your glances dart,
A tender meaning, let each glance impart.
Whene'er he meet your looks, with modest pride
And soft confusion turn your eyes aside,
Let a soft sigh steal out, as if by chance,
Then cautious turn, and steal another glance.
Caught by these arts, with pride and hope elate,
The destined victim rushes on his fate:
Pleased, his imagined victory pursues,
And the kind maid with soft attention views,
Contemplates now her shape, her air, her face,
And thinks each feature wears an added grace;
Till gratitude, which first his bosom proves,
By slow degrees sublimed, at length he loves.
'Tis harder still to fix than gain a heart;
What's won by beauty must be kept by art.

Too kind a treatment the blest lover cloys,
And oft despair the growing flame destroys:
Sometimes with smiles receive him, sometimes tears,
And wisely balance his hopes and fears.
Perhaps he mourns his ill-requited pains,
Condemns your sway, and strives to break his chains;
Behaves as if he now your scorn defied,
And thinks at last he shall alarm your pride:
But with indifference view the seeming change,
And let your eyes to seek new conquests range;
While his torn breast with jealous fury burns,
He hopes, despairs, adores, and hates by turns;
With anguish now repents the weak deceit,
And powerful passion bears him to your feet.

CHARLOTTE LENNOX
eighteenth century

MR. PICKWICK'S ROMANTIC ADVENTURE

CHARLES DICKENS

"It is the best idea," said Mr. Pickwick to himself, smiling till he almost broke his nightcap strings—"it is the best idea, my losing myself in this place, and wandering about. Droll, droll, very droll." Here Mr. Pickwick smiled again, a broader smile than before, and was about to continue the process of undressing, in the best possible humor, when he was suddenly stopped by the most unexpected interruption; to wit, the entrance into the room of some person with a candle, who, after locking the door, advanced to the dressing table, and set down the light upon it.

The smile that played on Mr. Pickwick's features was instantaneously lost in a look of the most unbounded and wonder-stricken surprise. The person, whoever it was, had come in so suddenly and with so little noise, that Mr. Pickwick had no time to call out, or oppose their entrance. Who could it be? A robber? Some evil-minded person who had seen him come upstairs with a handsome watch in his hand, perhaps. What was he to do?

The only way in which Mr. Pickwick could catch a glimpse of his mysterious visitor with the least danger of being seen himself was by creeping on to the bed, and peeping out from between the bed curtains on the opposite side. To this maneuver he accordingly resorted. Keeping the curtains carefully closed with his hand, so that nothing more of him could be seen than his face and nightcap, and putting on his spectacles, he mustered up courage, and looked out.

Mr. Pickwick almost fainted with horror and dismay. Standing before the dressing glass was a middle-aged lady in yellow curl-papers, busily engaged in brushing what ladies call their "back hair." However the unconscious middle-aged lady came into that room, it was quite clear that she contemplated remaining there for the night; for she had brought a rushlight and shade with her, which, with praiseworthy precaution against fire, she had stationed in a basin on the floor, where it was glimmering away like a gigantic lighthouse, in a particularly small piece of water.

"Bless my soul!" thought Mr. Pickwick, "what a dreadful thing!"

"Hem!" said the lady; and back into the curtains went Mr. Pickwick's head with automaton-like rapidity.

"I never met with anything so awful as this," thought poor Mr. Pickwick, the cold perspiration starting in drops upon his nightcap—"never. This is fearful."

It was quite impossible to resist the urgent desire to see what was going on. So out went Mr. Pickwick's head again. The prospect was worse than before. The middle-aged lady had finished arranging her hair, and carefully enveloped it in a muslin nightcap with a small plaited border, and was gazing pensively on the fire.

"This matter is growing alarming," reasoned Mr. Pickwick with himself. "I can't allow things to go on in this way. By the self-possession of that lady, it's clear to me that I must have come into the wrong room. If I call out, she'll alarm the house; but if I remain here the consequence will be still more frightful!"

Mr. Pickwick, it is quite unnecessary to say, was one of the most modest and delicate-minded of mortals. The very idea of exhibiting his nightcap to a lady overpowered him, but he had those confounded cap strings in a knot, and do what he would, he couldn't get it off. The disclosure must be made. There was only one other way of doing it. He shrunk behind the curtains, and called out very loudly—

"Ha—hum."

That the lady started at this unexpected sound was evident by her falling up against the dressing table; that she persuaded herself it must have been the effect of imagination was equally clear, for when Mr. Pickwick, under the impression that she had fainted away, stone-dead from fright, ventured to peep out again, and there she was, gazing pensively on the fire as before.

Most extraordinary female this, thought Mr. Pickwick, popping his head in again. "Ha—hum."

"Gracious Heaven!" said the middle-aged lady, "what's that?"

"It's—it's—only a gentleman, ma'am," said Mr. Pickwick from behind the bed curtains.

"A gentleman!" said the lady, with a terrific scream.

It's all over, thought Mr. Pickwick.

"A strange man," shrieked the lady. Another instant and the house would be alarmed. Her garments rustled as she rushed toward the door.

"Ma'am," said Mr. Pickwick, thrusting out his head, in extremity of his desperation—"ma'am."

Now although Mr. Pickwick was not actuated by any definite object in putting out his head, it was instantaneously productive of a good effect. The lady, as we have already stated, was near the door. She must pass it in order to reach the staircase, and she would most undoubtedly have done so by this time, had not the sudden apparition of Mr. Pickwick's nightcap driven her back into the remotest corner of the apartment, where she stood staring wildly at Mr. Pickwick, while Mr. Pickwick in his turn stared wildly at her.

"Wretch," said the lady, covering her eyes with her hands,

"what do you want here?"

"Nothing, ma'am—nothing whatever, ma'am," said Mr. Pickwick earnestly.

"Nothing!" said the lady, looking up.

"Nothing, ma'am, upon my honor," said Mr. Pickwick, nodding his head so energetically that the tassel of his nightcap danced again. "I am almost ready to sink, ma'am, beneath the confusion of addressing a lady in my nightcap" (here the lady hastily snatched off hers), "but I can't get it off, ma'am" (here Mr. Pickwick gave it a tremendous tug to prove his statement). "It is evident to me, ma'am, now, that I have mistaken this bedroom for my own. I had not been here five minutes, ma'am, when you suddenly entered it."

"If this improbable story be really true, sir," said the lady, sobbing violently, "you will leave instantly."

"I will, ma'am, with the greatest of pleasure," replied Mr. Pickwick.

"Instantly, sir," said the lady.

"Certainly, ma'am," interposed Mr. Pickwick, very quickly— "certainly, ma'am. I—I—am very sorry, ma'am," said Mr. Pickwick, making his appearance at the bottom of the bed, "to have been the innocent occasion of this alarm and emotion— deeply sorry, ma'am."

The lady pointed to the door. One excellent quality of Mr. Pickwick's character was beautifully displayed at this moment under the most trying circumstances. Although he had hastily put on his hat over his nightcap, although he carried his shoes and gaiters in his hand, and his coat and waistcoat over his arm, nothing could subdue his native politeness.

"I am exceedingly sorry, ma'am," said Mr. Pickwick, bowing very low.

"If you are, sir, you will at once leave the room," said the lady.

"Immediately, ma'am; this instant, ma'am," said Mr. Pickwick, opening the door, and dropping both his shoes with a loud crash in doing so.

"I trust, ma'am," resumed Mr. Pickwick, gathering up his shoes, and turning round to bow again—"I trust, ma'am, that my unblemished character, and the devoted respect I entertain for your sex, will plead as some slight excuse for this"—But before Mr. Pickwick could conclude the sentence the lady had thrust him into the hall, and locked and bolted the door behind him.

"Sam," said Mr. Pickwick, suddenly appearing before him, "where's my bedroom?"

The Valet stared at Mr. Pickwick with the most emphatic surprise; and it was not until the question had been repeated several times, that he turned round, and led the way to the long-sought bedroom.

"Sam," said Mr. Pickwick, as he got into bed, "I have made one of the most extraordinary mistakes tonight."

"Very likely, sir," replied the valet.

"But of this I am determined, Sam," said Mr. Pickwick; "that if I were to stop in this house for six months, I would never trust myself alone again."

"That's the very prudentest resolution as you could come to, sir," replied the servant. "Good night, Mr. Pickwick."

"Good night, Sam."

THE IMPORTANCE OF BEING EARNEST

OSCAR WILDE

*Hope falls somewhere in the engagement process;
either before or during. Oscar Wilde has much fun
with engagement hope in this brief excerpt . . .*

ALGERNON [speaking very rapidly]: Cecily, ever since I first looked upon your wonderful and incomparable beauty, I have dared to love you wildly, passionately, devotedly, hopelessly.

CECILY: I don't think that you should tell me that you love me wildly, passionately, devotedly, hopelessly. Hopelessly doesn't seem to make much sense, does it?

ALGERNON: Cecily! . . . I don't care for anyone in the whole world but you. I love you, Cecily. You will marry me, won't you?

CECILY: You silly boy! Of course. Why we have been engaged for the last three months.

ALGERNON: For the last three months?

CECILY: Yes, it will be exactly three months on Thursday.

ALGERNON: But how did we become engaged?

CECILY: Well, ever since dear Uncle Jack first confessed to us that he had a younger brother who was very wicked and bad, you, of course, have formed the chief topic of conversation between myself and Miss Prism. And, of course, a man who is much talked about is always very attractive. One feels there must be something in him, after all. I dare say it was foolish of me, but I fell in love with you, Ernest.

ALGERNON: Darling. And when was the engagement actually settled?

CECILY: On the 14th of February last. Worn out by your entire ignorance of my existence, I determined to end the matter one way or another, and after a long struggle with myself I accepted you under this dear old tree here. The next day I bought this little ring in your name, and this is the little bangle with the true lovers' knot I promised you always to wear.

ALGERNON: Did I give you this? It's very pretty, isn't it?

CECILY: Yes, you've wonderfully good taste, Ernest. It's the excuse I've always given for your leading such a bad life. And this is the box in which I keep all your dear letters. *[Kneels at table, opens box, and produces letters tied up with blue ribbon.]*

ALGERNON: My letters! But my own sweet Cecily, I have never written you any letters.

CECILY: You need hardly remind me of that, Ernest. I remember only too well that I was forced to write your letters for you. I wrote always three times a week, and sometime oftener.

ALGERNON: Oh, do let me read them, Cecily?

CECILY: Oh, I couldn't possibly. They would make you far too conceited. *[Replaces box.]* The three you wrote after I had broken off the engagement are so beautiful, and so badly spelled, that even now I can hardly read them without crying a little.
Algernon: But was our engagement ever broken off?

CECILY: Of course it was. On the 22nd of last March. You can see the entry if you like. *[Shows diary.]* "Today I broke off my engagement with Ernest. I feel it is better to do so. The weather still continues to be charming."

ALGERNON: But why on earth did you break it off? What had I done? I had done nothing at all. Cecily, I am very much hurt indeed to hear you broke it off. Particularly when the weather was so charming.

CECILY: It would hardly have been a really serious engagement if it hadn't been broken off at least once. But I forgave you before the week was out.

RIPEST APPLES

Madam, I am come to court you
If so be you'd let me in
Sit you down, you're kindly welcome
Then perhaps you'll call again

Madam I've got gold and silver
Madam, I've got house and land
Madam, I've got a world of pleasure
All to be at your command

I don't value your gold and silver
I don't value your house and land
I don't value your worlds of pleasure
All I want is a handsome man

Why do you dive so deep in beauty
It's a flower will soon decay
You pick it on a summer's morning
Before evening it fades away

Ripest apples are soonest rotten
Hottest love is soonest cold
Young men's words are soon forgotten
Pretty maid, don't be so bold.

After cowslips there come roses
After night there comes day
After false love there comes a true love
So our time will pass away.

TRADITIONAL, IRISH

Love is like a tennis match;
you'll never
win consistently until you
learn to serve well.

Dan P. Herod

THE BEWITCHED CLOCK

A FOLK TALE

From *More Heart Throbs*

About half-past eleven o'clock on Sunday night a human leg, enveloped in blue broadcloth, might have been seen entering Cephas Barberry's kitchen window. The leg was followed finally by the entire person of a lively Yankee, attired in his Sunday go-to-meetin' clothes. It was, in short, Joe Mayweed, who thus burglariously, in the dead of night, won his way into the deacon's kitchen.

"Wonder how much the old deacon made by orderin' me not to darken his door again?" soliloquized the young man. "Promised him I wouldn't, but didn't say nothin' about winders. Winders is just as good as doors, if there ain't no nails to tear your trousers onto. Wonder if Sal'll come down? The critter promised me. I'm afraid to move here, 'cause I might break my shins over sumthin' or 'nother, and wake the old folks. Cold enough to freeze a polar bear here. Oh, here comes Sally!" The beautiful maiden descended with a pleasant smile, a tallow candle, and a box of matches.

After receiving a rapturous greeting, she made up a roaring fire in the cooking-stove, and the happy couple sat down to enjoy the sweet interchange of views and hopes. But the course of true love ran no smoother in old Barberry's kitchen than it did elsewhere, and Joe, who was making up his mind to treat himself to a kiss, was startled by the voice of the deacon, her father, shouting from her chamber door:

"Sally, what are you getting up in the middle of the night for?"

"Tell him it's most morning," whispered Joe.

"I can't tell a fib," said Sally.

"I'll make it a truth, then," said Joe, and running to the huge old-fashioned clock that stood in the corner, he set it at five.

"Look at the clock and tell me what time it is," cried the old gentleman upstairs.

"It's five by the clock," answered Sally, and, corroborating the words, the clock struck five.

The lovers sat down again, and resumed the conversation. Suddenly the staircase began to creak.

"Good gracious! It's father."

"The deacon, by thunder!" cried Joe. "Hide me, Sal!"

"Where can I hide you?" cried the distracted girl.

"Oh, I know," said he; "I'll squeeze into the clockcase."

And without another word he concealed himself in the case, and drew to the door behind him.

The deacon was dressed, and, sitting himself down by the cooking stove, pulled out his pipe, lighted it, and commenced smoking very deliberately and calmly.

"Five o'clock, eh?" said he. "Well, I shall have time to smoke three or four pipes; then I'll go and feed the critters."

"Hadn't you better go and feed the critters first, sir, and then smoke afterward?" suggested the ever dutiful Sally.

"No; smokin' clears my head and wakes me up," answered the deacon, who seemed not a whit disposed to hurry his enjoyment.

Bur-r-r-r—whiz—z—ding—ding! went the clock.

"Tormented lightning!" cried the deacon, starting up, and dropping his pipe on the stove. "What in creation is that?"

Whiz! ding! ding! ding! went the old clock furiously.

"It's only the clock striking five," said Sally, tremulously.

"Powers of mercy!" cried the deacon, "striking five! It's struck a hundred already."

"Deacon Barberry!" cried the deacon's better half, who had hastily robed herself, and now came plunging down the staircase in the wildest state of alarm, "what is the matter of the clock?"

"Goodness only knows," replied the old man.

"It's been in the family these hundred years, and never did I know it to carry on so before."

Whiz! bang! bang! bang! went the clock.

"It's burst itself!" cried the old lady, shedding a flood of tears, "and there won't be nothing left of it."

"It's bewitched," said the deacon, who retained a leaven of New England superstition in his nature. "Anyhow," he said, after a pause, advancing resolutely toward the clock, "I'll see what's got into it."

"Oh, don't!" cried the daughter, affectionately seizing one of his coattails, while his faithful wife hung to the other.

"Don't," chorused both the women together.

"Let go my raiment!" shouted the deacon; "I ain't afraid of the powers of darkness."

But the women would not let go; so the deacon slipped off his coat, and while, from the sudden cessation of resistance, they fell heavily on the floor, he darted forward and laid his hand on the door of the clock-case. But no human power could open it. Joe was holding it inside with a death-grasp. The deacon began to be dreadfully frightened. He gave one more tug. An unearthly yell, as of a fiend in distress, came from the inside, and then the clock-case pitched headforemost on the floor, smashed its face, and wrecked its proportions.

The current of air extinguished the light; the deacon, the old lady and Sally fled upstairs, and Joe Mayweed, extricating himself from the clock, effected his retreat in the same way that he had entered. The next day all Appleton was alive with the story of how Deacon Barberry's clock had been bewitched; and though many believed its version, some, and especially Joe Mayweed, affected to discredit the whole affair, hinting that the deacon had been trying the experiment of tasting frozen cider, and that the vagaries of the clock-case existed only in a distempered imagination.[74]

"Tell me," Counselor asked, looking directly at Him and Her, "how do you two respond to the concept that truth is the very foundation of a loving relationship?"

Him reached over for Her's hand. "I've never lied to Her yet."

Her smiled demurely. "Nor I to Him."

"Good," Counselor responded, reaching for 1 Corinthians 13. "How do you two react to this statement about love from St. Paul? 'Love is patient, kind, not envious or rude. It does not insist on its own way; it isn't

irritable or resentful; it does not rejoice in wrongdoing, but rejoices in the truth.'"

"I think we're up to it," Him replied, letting go of Her's hand. "Just so she remembers that I'm only human."

"Only human" is the understatement of all time. There is nothing "only" about the human experience of love. Humankind has been blessed by the Creator with the capacity of experiencing this emotion. In fact, the Creator thought so much of it that He filled His Word with countless examples. Beginning with the Genesis creation of Adam and Eve, the divine record is filled with pure and not-so-pure human love.

According to the Apostle Paul love run amok is not love founded in truth. Now, discover love based upon the Book of God.

I Quiet Myself
in Your Love

I am Your child,
And You are my Father.
I quiet myself in Your love.
You are the Lord
Above every other.
I quiet myself in Your love.
You are the greatest, and I am the least.
You are the joy that will never cease.
Here in Your presence is perfect peace,
And I quiet myself in your love.
When I'm in pain,
You feel what I'm feeling.
I quiet myself in Your love.
When I am weak,
You're power and healing.
I quiet myself in Your love.
You are the greatest, and I am the least.
You are the joy that will never cease.
Here in Your presence is perfect peace,
And I quiet myself in Your love.
You are my hope, My glory and treasure.
I quiet myself in Your love.
Praise to You, God!
I'll sing it forever!
I quiet myself in Your love.
You are the greatest, and I am the least.
You are the joy that will never cease.
Here in Your presence is perfect peace,
And I quiet myself in Your love.

KEN BIBLE

From *Praying in His Presence*

THE SENSITIVE MAN AND ROMANCE

CHARLES STANLEY

The sensitive man knows there is a distinct difference between sex and love. Sex should include love, but often it does not. Many popular songs portray love as being little more than a kind of animal lust, beneath the dignity of personalities made in the image of God. Far from being love, illicit sex is a sin by which a man "destroyeth his own soul" (Proverbs 6:32 KJV).

Not only single people are ignorant of true love. Married couples can express hostility or contempt in the sex act. Sex is the expression of many things—but not according to God's plan. Because it is the deepest intimacy between committed husband and wife, its perversion becomes the highest travesty against love.

A woman would like to live her whole life experiencing romantic love because God made women to be loved. If you have lost all traces of your romantic days of courtship, you are a big loser. Sex, love, and romance are not always synonymous but they can be, and they are for the complete man.

Romantic love reaches out in little ways, showing attention and admiration. Romantic love remembers what pleases a woman, what excites her and what surprises her. Its action whispers: you are the most special person in my life.

Someone said in infancy a woman needs love and care, in childhood she needs fun, in her twenties she needs romance, in her thirties she needs admiration, in her forties she needs sympathy, and in her fifties she needs cash! The needs of a whole woman would more likely be the same in her fifties as in her infancy; love and care. This never changes.[75]

FROM TWO LYRICS

Let my voice ring out and over the earth,
Through all the grief and strife,
With a golden joy in a silver mirth
Thank God for Life!

Let my voice swell out through the great abyss
To the azure dome above,
With a chord of faith in the harp of bliss:
Thank God for Love!

Let my voice thrill out beneath and above,
The whole world through:
O my Love and Life, O my Life and Love,
Thank God for you!

JAMES THOMPSON

THE SONG OF SOLOMON

*The voice of my beloved! behold, he cometh leaping upon
the mountains, skipping upon the hills.*

*My beloved is like a roe or a young hart: behold, he standeth
behind our wall, he looketh forth at the windows, showing
himself through the lattice.*

*My beloved spake, and said unto me, Rise up, my love,
my fair one, and come away.*

For, lo, the winter is past, the rain is over and gone;

*The flowers appear on the earth; the time of the singing of birds is
come, and the voice of the turtle is heard in our land;*

*The fig tree putteth forth her green figs,
and the vines with the tender grape give a good smell.
Arise, my love, my fair one, and come away.*

*O my dove, that art in the clefts of the rock, in the secret places of
the stairs, let me see thy countenance, let me hear thy voice; for
sweet is thy voice, and thy countenance is comely.*

*Take us the foxes, the little foxes, that spoil the vines:
for our vines have tender grapes.*

*My beloved is mine, and I am his: he feedeth among the lilies.
Until the day break, and the shadows flee away,
turn, my beloved, and be thou like a roe
or a young hart upon the mountains of Bether.*

THE SONG OF SOLOMON 2:8-17 KJV

LOVE WISDOM

Set me as a seal upon your heart,
As a seal upon your arm;
For love is strong as death,
Passion fierce as the grave.
Its flashes are flashes of fire,
A raging flame.
Many waters cannot quench love,
Neither can floods drown it.
If one offered for love
All the wealth of his house,
It would be utterly scorned.

SONG OF SOLOMON 8:6-7 NRSV

SONG OF SONGS

I opened for my lover,
But my lover had left;
He was gone.
My heart sank at his
Departure.
SONG OF SOLOMON 5:6 NIV

FULFILLMENT

The husband should fulfill his marital

duty to his wife, and likewise the wife

to her husband. The wife's body does

not belong to her alone but also to her

husband. . . . Do not deprive each

other except by mutual consent and

for a time, so that you may devote

yourselves to prayer. Then come

together again so that Satan

will not tempt you because of

your lack of self-control.

1 CORINTHIANS 7:3-5 NIV

ST AUGUSTINE

From *The Confessions*

St. Augustine wasn't always a stained glass saint.
In his devotional classic The Confessions *he recalls an earlier time*
when the Lord taught him about true love.
Look beneath the Shakespearean language
and discover this truth, too.

And what was it that I delighted in, but to love and to be loved? But love kept not that moderation of one's mind loving another mind, as the lightsome bounder of true friendship; but out of that puddly concupiscence of my flesh, certain mists and bubblings of youth fumed up, which beclouded and so overcast my heart that I could not discern the beauty of a chaste affection from a fog of impure lustfulness. Both did confusedly boil in me, and ravished away my unstayed youth over the downfalls of unchaste desires, and drenched me over head and ears in the very whirlpool of most heinous impurities. . . .

There is comeliness now in all beautiful bodies, both in gold and silver, and all things; and in the touch of flesh, sympathy pleases much. Each other sense hath his proper object answerably tempered. Worldly honour hath also its grace, in commanding and overcoming by its own power; whence spring also the thirst of revenge. But yet, might a man obtain all these, he were not to depart from thee, O Lord, nor to decline from Thy Law. The life also which here we live hath its proper enticement, and that by reason of a certain proportion of comeliness of its own, and a correspondency with all the inferior beauties. That friendship also which is amongst society, we see endeared with a sweet tie, even by reason of the union of many hearts . . . for these low things have their delights, but nothing like my Lord God, who hath made these all. . . .

An impure love inflames the mind and summons the soul destined to perish to lust after earthly things, and to follow what is perishable, and precipitates it into the lowest places, and sinks it in the abyss; so holy love raiseth us, and inflames us to what is eternal, and excites the soul to those things which do not pass away and die, and from the depths of hell raiseth it to heaven. Yet all love hath a power of its own, nor can love in the soul of the lover be idle; it must needs draw it on. But dost thou wish to know of what sort love is? See whither it leadeth. We do not therefore warn you to love nothing; but that you love not the world, that you may freely love Him who made the world. For the soul when bound by the love of the earth, hath as it were birdlime on its wings; it cannot fly. But when purged from the sordid affections of the world, extending as it were its pair of wings, and freeing them from every impediment, flyeth upon them, that is to say, upon the commandments of love unto God and our neighbour. Whither will it fly, but by rising in its flight to God? For it riseth by loving. Before it can do this, it groaneth on earth, if it hath already in it the desire for flight; and saith "who will give me wings like a dove, and I will fly and be at rest." . . . From the midst of offences, then, from the medley of evil men, from the chaff mingled with the grain, it longeth to fly, where it may not suffer the society of any wicked one, but may live in the holy company of angels, the citizens of the eternal Jerusalem.

TRANSLATED BY WILLIAM WATTS

THE WIFE OF
NOBLE CHARACTER

These verses from Proverbs have been held up to young women
for thousands of years. Do they need to be contemporized?
How do they relate to today's wife and mother?

A wife of noble character who can find?
She is worth far more than rubies.
Her husband has full confidence in her
and lacks nothing of value.
She brings him good, not harm.
all the days of her life.
She selects wool and flax
and works with eager hands.
She is like the merchant ships,
bringing her food from afar.
She gets up while it is still dark;
she provides food for her family
and portions for her servant girls.
She considers a field and buys it;
out of her earnings she plants a vineyard.
She sets about her work vigorously;
her arms are strong for her tasks.
She sees that her trading is profitable,
and her lamp does not go out at night.
In her hand she holds the distaff
and grasps the spindle with her fingers.
She opens her arms to the poor
and extends her hands to the needy.

When it snows, she has no fear for her household;
for all of them are clothed in scarlet.
She makes coverings for her bed;
she is clothed in fine linen and purple.
Her husband is respected at the city gate,
where he takes his seat among the elders of the land.
She makes linen garments and sells them,
and supplies the merchants with sashes.
She is clothed with strength and dignity;
she can laugh at the days to come.
She speaks with wisdom,
and faithful instruction is on her tongue.
She watches over the affairs of her household
and does not eat the bread of idleness.
Her children arise and call her blessed;
her husband also, and he praises her:
"Many women do noble things,
but you surpass them all."
Charm is deceptive, and beauty is fleeting;
but a woman who fears the Lord is to be praised.
Give her the reward she has earned,
and let her works bring her praise at the city gate.

PROVERBS 31:10-31 NIV

A Man with a Maiden

There are three things that are

too amazing for me,

four that I do not understand:

the way of an eagle in the sky,

the way of a snake on a rock,

the way of a ship on the high seas,

and the way of a man with a maiden.

Proverbs 30:18 NIV

THE GLORY OF GOD AT A WEDDING

P. MOLINERO

John 2:1-11

"Son, did you get an invitation to Salema and Joel's wedding?"

"I got one, but haven't thought too much about it."

"I think you ought to go, son. Joel's parents were friends of Joseph and me. Do you remember how much fun you and Joel used to have playing in the shop?"

"Joel was a good friend."

"So, will you go to his wedding?"

"The timing isn't good. I am still trying to pull my team together. I have asked a young fisherman named Andrew to join me in our cause. His brother, Simon Peter, a fine fellow named John, and some others have already come on board. I think I'll need a total of twelve or so."

"You haven't answered my question, son."

"Since we're going to stay here in Galilee for a while, I think we can get over to Cana. It will be good to meet Joel's fiancée. The Disciples will enjoy the food, too."

"If you go, would you mind if I went along with you? I really dislike to go to social events like this by myself."

"Sure, mother. I want you to meet my new friends, too. We're going to have to get an early start."

"I'll make a nice lunch. I have some wonderful figs that we'll enjoy."

Father, I have been baptized by John and am now beginning my ministry. Tomorrow I will travel to Cana and will celebrate a wedding. Is it time to let the world know that I am your Son? What shall I say when neighbors ask, "Well, when will we come to your wedding, Jesus?" Shall I tell them that I am the world's Bridegroom?

"Welcome to my home, Mary. And Jesus, I am glad you are able to be here, too. Have you talked with Joel, yet?"

"No, where is he?"

"I'll find him. . . ."

"I'm glad we could come here together, Son. I'm so proud of you."

"Here he is, Jesus. Here's Joel!"

"Congratulations, Joel. Where is the fortunate girl?"

"Thanks, Jesus. Salema is with her mother and sisters. So, when is it your turn?"

"My turn for what?"

"For marriage!"

"Oh, I don't think . . ."

"How old are you, Jesus? Thirty yet?"

"I'm thirty-three. . . ."

"Joel, will you come with me for just a minute, please?"

"Sure, father. Excuse me."

Father, has the time come to reveal my Sonship? May I give Your blessing to Joel and Selema? Shall I tell these happy feasting guests that I have come to give abundant life that is greater than any food or drink?

"Friends, family, guests, I'm sorry to announce that our sup-ply of wedding wine has been depleted. But never fear, there is plenty of tea and ice water."

"Isn't that a shame, Son. I know Salema and her family are embarrassed . . ."

"Yes, Mother."

"Isn't there something you can do?"

"What are you getting at, Mother?"

"Oh, I don't know, Son, it just seems like you could help them out of this predicament."

"But Mother . . ."

"Please, Jesus. I'll look for the wine stewards."

"May we help you, ma'am?"

"I believe my son can remedy your problem with the marriage wine."

Father, what shall I do now? Is this the time for everybody at this wedding to discover my mission? That I have come that they might have life—abundant life?

"Now, boys, whatever my son tells you to do—do it!"

"Sir, your mother tells us that if we are to have more wedding wine, you'll tell us what to do."

"Yes, of course. Are there water jars handy?"

"Sure, there are six of them right there."

"Yeah, each one holds from twenty to thirty gallons."

"So, what do you want us to do?"

"Fill each of the jars to the very brim with water."

"Sure, it'll take us a while to do it."

"But we'll get it done. Come on, boys."

"Son?"

"Yes, Mother."

"Son, how do you plan to supply more wedding wine with those six jugs?"

"My Father will do it, Mother."

"Son, I'm thinking about when you were a little boy, when

Joseph took us up to the temple. Do you remember what you said when we found you with the temple elders?"

"I remember very well, Mother. That's why I'm here at this wedding—to do my Father's business."

"There, the six water jars are filled."

"Fine. Now dip some of the water out, and take it to your master."

"Son, what have you done?"

"Listen, Mother . . ."

"Ladies and gentlemen, your attention, please. This wedding reception has surprised us all. We will now toast our happy couple, Joel and Salema, with the finest wine I have ever tasted, thanks to Mary's Son, Jesus."

"Andrew, Peter, Nathaniel, did you see that? Jesus turned six jars of water into six jars of wine."

"Simon, I think we have put our trust in the right person, Jesus of Nazareth."

"To our bride and groom, Salema and Joel, may this miracle of turning water into wine, remain in your mind and heart and be a reminder of God's glory in your individual lives, and in your life as husband and wife."

THE CREATION

Then God sat down—on the side of a hill where He could think;
by a deep, wide river He sat down; with His head on His hands,
God thought and thought, till He thought: I'll make me a man!

Up from the bed of the river God scooped the clay; and by the bank of
the river He kneeled Him down; and there the great God Almighty
Who lit the sun and fixed it in the sky, Who flung the stars to the
most far corner of the night, Who rounded the earth in the middle of
His hand; this Great God, like a mammy bending over her baby,
kneeled down in the dust toiling over a lump of clay till He shaped it
in His own image; Then into it He blew the breath of life, and man
became a living soul.

Amen. Amen.[76]

JAMES WELDON JOHNSON

Adam and Eve

In the day that the Lord God made the earth and the heavens, when no plant of the field was yet in the earth and no herb of the field had yet sprung up . . . the Lord God formed man from the dust of the ground, and breathed into his nostrils the breath of life; and the man became a living being. . . . Then the Lord God said, "It is not good that the man should be alone; I will make him a helper as his partner. . . . So the Lord God caused a deep sleep to fall upon the man, and he slept; then he took one of his ribs and closed up its place with flesh. And the rib that the Lord God had taken from the man he made into a woman and brought her to the man. Then the man said, "This at last is bone of my bones and flesh of my flesh; this one shall be called Woman, for out of Man this one was taken." Therefore a man leaves his father and his mother and clings to his wife, and they become one flesh.

GENESIS 2:4-5.7.18.21-24 NRSV

CREATED IN THE IMAGE OF GOD

MARK TWAIN

From *The Diary of Adam and Eve*

From Adam's Diary

Monday. This new creature with the long hair is a good deal in the way. It is always hanging around and following me about, I don't like this; I am not used to company. I wish it would stay with the other animals. . . . Cloudy today, wind in the east; think we shall have rain. . . . *We?* Where did I get that word?—I remember now—the new creature uses it.

Wednesday. Built me a shelter against the rain, but could not have it to myself in peace. The new creature intruded. When I tried to put it out it shed water out of the holes it looks with, and wiped it away with the back of its paws, and made a noise such as some of the other animals make when they are in distress. I wish it would not talk; it is always talking. . . . This new sound is so close to me; it is right at my shoulder, right at my ear, first on one side and then on the other, and I am used only to sounds that are more or less distant from me.

From Eve's Diary

Thursday. My first sorrow. Yesterday he avoided me and seemed to wish I would not talk to him. I could not believe it, and thought there was some mistake, for I loved to be with him, and loved to hear him talk, and so how could it be that he could feel unkind toward me when I had not done anything? But at least it seemed true, so I went away and sat lonely in the place where I first saw him the morning that we were made and I did not know what he was and was indifferent about him; but now it was a mournful place, and every little thing spoke of him, and my heart was very sore. I did not know why very clearly, for it was a new feeling; I had not experienced it before, and it was all a mystery, and I could not make it out.

After the Fall

The Garden is lost, but I have found *him*, and am content. He loves me as well as he can; I love him with all the strength of my passionate nature, and this, I think, is proper to my youth and sex. If I ask myself why I love him, I find I do not know, and do not really much care to know; so I suppose that this kind of love is not the product of reasoning and statistics, like one's love for other reptiles and animals. I think that this must be so. I love certain birds because of their song; but I do not love Adam on account of his singing—no, it is not that; the more he sings the more I do not get reconciled to it. Yet I ask him to sing, because I wish to learn to like everything he is interested in. I am sure I can learn, because at first I could not stand it, but now I can. It sours the milk, but it doesn't matter; I can get used to that kind of milk.

At Eve's Grave

Adam: Wheresoever she was, *there* was Eden.[77]

HOSEA AND GOMER: A LOVE THAT WILL NOT LET GO

PAUL MEDFORD

Oh sure, I've been a preacher for most of my life. I can hardly remember when I wasn't. Successful? What do you mean by "successful"? I never made much money. And, frankly, the crowds never stopped to listen—that is until *she* came into my life. That's when everything changed.

She? Oh, I think that's a story your readers would find interesting. Like I said, I wasn't a major league preacher, you know, like the men you see on television. I never went to college, much less seminary. No one ever heard of me, not at first anyway. I wasn't very happy, not by any stretch of the imagination. Of course being a bachelor didn't help much. I always felt kinda out of step with most of the folks in town.

I remember so well what it was like going home at night after a day of street preaching; getting off the bus at the corner of my street and walking the half block to my house. I was tired and discouraged. There really wasn't much incentive to go home, but I couldn't afford to eat out. So, I'd go home after a day of exhorting and warm up a can of something in a saucepan.

Like I said, I wasn't very successful.

I used to stand on the corner across from the public library, where the taxi stand is, and warn passersby about God's wrath—about how He was going to smite those hardened hearts and condemn them to eternal punishment. I really worked over those folks who waited for the bus at Main and Third Avenue—from old man Gilbertson, the bank manager, to that red-headed paper boy who later got killed in Southeast Asia. Everyone was fair game for the fires of hell.

The discouraging thing was that nobody listened to me. The tracts I pushed into the reluctant hands ended up on the sidewalk. I suspect the Almighty Himself would have been rejected if He had preached on that corner. I know what I preached was true—I believed it with all my heart. But people were not interested in hearing about the wrath to come. Frankly, as I look back on those days, I'm afraid my view of Father God was pretty much limited to the dark-side of His nature. I just couldn't get excited about a loving God—that is until Gomer entered my life.

Yeah, I know, I'm getting ahead of my story, but it's true. She made all the difference in the world. You just have to understand how unhappy and unsuccessful I was.

Well, on a particular warm Sunday evening, when I walked the half block to my house, I began to get an overpowering feeling that my luck was going to change. Yes, sir, when I scooped up the Times from the front yard, I distinctly heard a voice from somewhere say, "Happy days are almost here again!"

The house was stifling, so I left the front door open and pushed up a couple of windows. As I always did, I tossed my tract case onto a dining room chair and went out to the kitchen for a cold drink. The cold air from the fridge felt good on my face, but electric bills being what they are, I closed the door quickly and poured a glass of tea.

Sitting down at the table I glanced over the front page— that's when I noticed a small story about a call girl operation that had been raided. Accompanying the article was a photo of a vice squad officer leading a girl to the paddy wagon. The girl looked so forlorn that my heart went out to her. In the caption, she was quoted as saying, "I don't have the money to post bail, so I guess I'll have to spend the rest of my life in jail."

Like I said, I was smitten by the girl's picture and her words. Her face burned in my mind while my dinner boiled over on the stove. I studied the young woman's features and reread her admission, "I don't have the money." I can't say she was particularly beautiful, but there was something about her face that spoke to my heart.

Then it was as if God in heaven spoke to me right there at my kitchen table. I swear, I heard Him say, "I want you to go down to the Municipal Court Building and find this girl. She is part of My design for your life."

"A prostitute?" I asked aloud to no one in particular. "What about my ministry? What about the neighbors?"

All that night I sat up at my table. I was unable to shake the feeling that my life was in for a big change.

By morning I was reconciled to the idea of going down to the court building and finding her. I skipped my usual cereal for a cup of black coffee and reached for my briefcase, then decided to leave it; to forget God's wrath for a few hours.

I'd never been inside the county building before, much less visited the lock-up area on the third floor.

Did I know why I was doing what I was doing? I don't think so. I have to admit I had a romantic notion about the woman in that newspaper photo, but I think there was more to it than that; I had a distinct sense of oughtness. I knew that providence had something to do with my being there.

You better believe how nervous I was sitting there in the visitors' room waiting to meet her. When the door opened a guard stuck his head in and asked, "Are you here to see Gomer?" I remember jumping to my feet and feeling my legs go to jelly, so I sat down. Then into the room moved a frightened young woman dressed in a shapeless gray dress.

It's funny, to this day I am unable to remember what we talked about in the forlorn room on that momentous morning. Also, I am unable to tell you when I first decided to take Gomer as my wife.

But I did, and in time God gave us a daughter and two sons. Many a time on a warm summer evening when the kids played at the corner under the streetlight, and we sat on the front steps, I'd recall the face of that frightened woman who felt the wrath of society. Many times when I'd reach over and take her hand, she'd ask me to tell her one more time why I "redeemed" her. My answer was always the same, "Because I love you."[78]

O love that will not let me go,
I rest my weary soul in Thee.
I give Thee back the life I owe,
That in Thine ocean depths it flow
May richer fuller be.

GEORGE MATHESON

Chapter 10
SEEING LOVE FACE TO FACE

The beautiful face of a woman has long been

known to spark undying devotion in a man's

heart. It was in praise of Helen of Troy's fabled

beauty that Christopher Marlow wrote:

Was this the face that launch'd a thousand ships,

And burnt the topless towers of Ilium?

Sweet Helen, make me immortal

with a kiss. . . .

Lovely sentiment, classic poetry, but that is not the focus of 1 Corinthians 13:

"Now we see in a mirror dimly,

but then we shall see face to face.

Now I know only in part;

then I will know fully,

even as I have been fully known."

The gift of self-giving love demands an acceptance of patience, growth, understanding, and knowledge. Until then, we see God dimly. Is it any different with human love? All of the selections in this chapter remind us that maturing love is a process, albeit, a lovely process.

SEVEN DAFFODILS

Haven't got a mansion, haven't any land

Not one paper dollar to crumple in my hand

But I can show you morning on a thousand hills

And kiss you and give you seven daffodils

Haven't got a fortune to buy you pretty things

But I can give you moonbeams for necklaces and rings

But I can show you morning on a thousand hills

And kiss you and give you seven daffodils

Seven golden daffodils shining in the sun

Light our way to evening when the day is done

And I can give you music and a crust of bread

A pillow of piney bows to rest your head.

TRADITIONAL, AMERICAN

WAS THIS THE FACE?

Was this the face that launched a thousand ships

And burned the topless towers of Ilium?

Sweet Helen, make me immortal with a kiss!

Her lips suck forth my soul—see where it flies.

Come, Helen, come give me my soul again;

Here will I dwell, for heaven is in these lips,

And all is dross that is not Helena. . . .

O thou art fairer than the evening air,

Clad in the beauty of a thousand stars![79]

CHRISTOPHER MARLOWE

LOVE QUOTES

Love, like a bird, hath perch'd upon a spray
For thee and me to hearken what he sings.
Contented, he forgets to fly away;
But hush! . . . remind not Eros of his wings.

SIR WILLIAM WATSON

I would that the loving were loved, and
I would that the weary should sleep,
And that man should hearken to man,
And that he that soweth should reap.

WILLIAM MORRIS

Love does not consist
In gazing at each other
But in looking outward together
In the same direction.

ANTOINE DE SAINT-EXUPERY

To love is to find pleasure
In the happiness of the person loved.

LEIBNITZ

The sea has its pearls,
The heaven its stars—
But my heart, my heart,
My heart has its love.

HEINRICH HEINE

Compose a tender symphony;
gather robins, whippoorwills,
and larks;
but still the music
could not express
the love for you
within my heart.

ELIZABETH ST. JACQUES

Love cannot be forced;
Love cannot be coaxed and teased.
It comes out of Heaven,
Unasked and unsought.

PEARL S. BUCK

O Fair! O Sweet!

O fair! O sweet! when I do look on thee.

In whom all joys so well agree,

Heart and soul do sing in me,

Just accord all music makes;

In thee just accord excelleth,

Where each part in such peace excelleth,

One of other beauty takes,

Since, then, truth to all minds telleth

That in thee lives harmony,

Heart and soul do sing in me.

Sir Phillip Sidney

Johnny: Oh, Mollie, Oh Mollie, would you take it unkind
For me to sit by you and tell you my mind?
For my mind is to marry and never to part
For the first time I saw you, you wounded my heart.

Mollie: Yes, you may be seated and say what you will
For I've time a-plenty, will listen, be still;
The subject of marriage means much in my life
Should I need a husband and you want a wife.

Johnny: Oh Mollie, consider for you sure understand
That love now is speaking, Oh heed her command;
We will ramble together in ways of true love
Until life is passed, then renew it above.

Mollie: Put your horse in the stable and feed him some hay,
Come and seat yourself by me so long as you may,
For who would be hasty in matters like this,
Repent at our leisure, the true object miss?

Johnny: My horse is not hungry and won't eat your hay,
So fare you well, Mollie, I'll be on my way.
You take all things lightly, my heart is like a toy
Toss about like a plaything and count it a joy.

Mollie: You really surprise me, for all this is new,
I need time for thought and consider your view.
I will marry for love or not wed at all,

My mate will be waiting and answer my call.
Johnny: A meeting is a pleasure but parting is grief,
An inconsistent lover is worse than a thief,
For a thief can but rob you and take all you have
But an inconsistent lover can lead you to the grave.

Mollie: My heart you have wounded,
but wounds they will heal,
And this changes all things, you know how I feel,
When you fall from your high horse and could happy be,
So whatever happens, just remember me.

Johnny: The grave it will rob you and turn you to dust,
So where's a fair lady, a young man to trust?
A cuckoo's a pretty bird and sings as she flies,
Yes, she brings us glad tidings and tells us no lies.

Mollie: Now don't be presumptuous, all things have two sides,
There's nothing worthwhile if it's never been tried.
I know what you have said in some cases is true
But my love for you, Johnny, will sure change your view!

ANONYMOUS, AMERICAN

A FABLE

ROBERT FOX

The young man was clean and neatly dressed. It was early Monday morning and he got on the subway. It was the first day of his first job and he was slightly nervous; he didn't know exactly what his job would be. Otherwise he felt fine. He loved everybody he saw. He loved everybody on the street and everybody disappearing into the subway, and he loved the world because it was a fine clear day and he was starting his first job.

Without kicking anybody, the young man was able to find a seat on the Manhattan-bound train. The car filled quickly and he looked up at the people standing over him envying his seat. Among them were a mother and daughter who were going shopping. The daughter was a beautiful girl with blond hair and soft-looking skin, and he was immediately attracted to her.

"He's staring at you," the mother whispered to the daughter.

"Yes, Mother, I feel so uncomfortable. What shall I *do*?"

"He's in love with you."

"In love with me? How can you tell?"

"Because I'm your mother."

"But what shall I do?"

"Nothing. He'll try to talk to you. If he does, answer him. Be nice to him. He's only a boy."

The train reached the business district and many people got off. The girl and her mother found seats opposite the young man. He continued to look at the girl who occasionally looked to see if he was looking at her.

The young man found a good pretext for standing by giving his seat to an elderly man. He stood over the girl and her mother. They whispered back and forth and looked up at him. At another stop the seat next to the girl was vacated, and the young man blushed but quickly took it.

"I knew it," the mother said between her teeth. "I knew it, I *knew* it."

The young man cleared his throat and tapped the girl. She jumped.

"Pardon me," he said. "You're a very pretty girl."

"Thank you," she said.

"Don't talk to him," her mother said. "Don't answer him. I'm warning you. Believe me."

"I'm in love with you," he said to the girl.

"I don't believe you," the girl said.

"Don't answer him," the mother said.

"I really do," he said. "In fact, I'm so much in love with you that I want to marry you."

"Do you have a job?" she said.

"Yes, today is my first day. I'm going to Manhattan to start my first day of work."

"What kind of work will you do?" she asked.

"I don't know exactly," he said. "You see, I didn't start yet."

"It sounds exciting," she said.

"It's my first job, but I'll have my own desk and handle a lot of papers and carry them around in a briefcase, and it will pay well, and I'll work my way up."

"I love you," she said.

"Will you marry me?"

"I don't know. You'll have to ask my mother."

The young man rose from his seat and stood before the girl's mother. He cleared his throat very carefully for a long time. "May I have the honor of having your daughter's hand in marriage?" he said, but he was drowned out by the subway noise.

The mother looked up at him and said, "What?" He couldn't hear either, but he could tell by the movement of her lips and by the way her face wrinkled up that she said, "What."

The train pulled to a stop.

"May I have the honor of having your daughter's hand in marriage!" he shouted, not realizing there was no subway noise. Everybody on the train looked at him, smiled, and then they all applauded.

"Are you crazy?" the mother asked.

The train started again.

"What?" he said.

"Why do you want to marry her?" she asked.

"Well, she's pretty—I mean, I'm in love with her."

"Is that all?"

"I guess so," he said. "Is there supposed to be more?"

"No, not usually," the mother said. "Are you working?"

"Yes. As a matter of fact, that's why I'm going to Manhattan so early. Today is the first day of my first job."

"Congratulations," the mother said.

"Thanks," he said. "Can I marry your daughter?"

"Do you have a car?" she asked.

"Not yet," he said. "But I should be able to get one pretty soon. And a house, too."

"A house?"

"With lots of rooms."

"Yes, that's what I expected you to say," she said. She turned to her daughter. "Do you love him?"

"Yes, Mother, I do."

"Why?"

"Because he's good, and gentle, and kind."

"Are you sure?"

"Yes."

"Then you really love him?"

"Yes."

"Are you sure there isn't anyone else that you might love and might want to marry?"

"No, mother," the girl said.

"Well, then," the mother said to the young man. "Looks like there's nothing I can do about it. Ask her again."

The train stopped.

"My dearest one," he said, "will you marry me?"

"Yes," she said.

Everybody in the car smiled and applauded.

"Isn't life wonderful?" the boy asked the mother.

"Beautiful," the mother said.

The conductor climbed down from between the cars as the train started up and straightening his dark tie, approached them with a solemn black book in his hand.

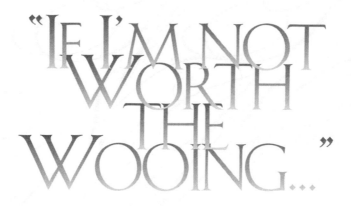

"IF I'M NOT WORTH THE WOOING..."

HENRY WADSWORTH LONGFELLOW
From *"The Courtship of Miles Standish"*

Military Captain of great repute, and now Captain of the Plymouth colony, Miles Standish was a no-nonsense man's man who knew more about armaments and warfare than about courting his beloved Priscilla. So, as the legend and Mr. Longfellow tell, the Captain turns to his trusted John Alden to court the beautiful Priscilla for him. The painful point of this epic poem is that John Alden loved Priscilla himself. On an eventful Spring morning Miles Standish called for his friend and military cohort and began phrasing a request that has become a classic model for bashful suitors the world around. The Captain speaks:

Love and Friendship

"'Tis not good for a man to be alone,
say the Scriptures.
This I have said before,
and again and again I repeat it;
Every hour in the day,
I think it, and feel it, and say it.
Since Rose Standish died,
my life has been weary
And dreary;
Sick at heart I have been,

beyond the healing
of friendship;
Oft in my lonely hours,
I have thought of the maiden
Priscilla.
She is alone in the world;
her father and mother and brother
Died in the winter together;
I saw her going and coming,
Now to the grave of the dead,
and now to the bed of the dying,
Patient, courageous, and strong,
and said to myself, that if ever
There were angels on earth,
as there are angels in heaven,
Two have I seen and known;
and the angel whose name is Priscilla
Holds in my desolate life,
the place which the other abandoned.
Long have I cherished the thought,
but never have dared to reveal it,
Being a coward in this,
though valiant enough for the most part.
Go to the damsel Priscilla,
the loveliest maiden of Plymouth,
Say that the blunt old Captain,
a man not of words but of actions,
Offers his hand and his heart,
the hand and heart of a soldier.
Not in these words, you know,
but this in short is my meaning;
I am a maker of war,
and not a maker of phrases.

You, who are bred as a scholar,
can say it in elegant language,
Such as you read,
in your books of the pleadings and wooings of lovers,
Such as you think best adapted,
to win the heart of a maiden."
When he had spoken, John Alden,
the fair-haired, taciturn stripling,
All aghast at his words,
surprised, embarrassed, bewildered,
Trying to mask his dismay,
by treating the subject with Lightness,
Trying to smile,
and yet feeling his heart stand still in His bosom,
Just as a timepiece stops,
in a house that is stricken by lightning,
Thus made answer and spake,
or rather stammered than answered:
"Such a message as that,
I am sure I would mangle and mar it;
If you would have it well done
—I am only repeating your maxim,—
You must do it yourself,
you must not leave it to others!"
But with the air of a man,
whom nothing can turn from his purpose,
Gravely shaking his head,
made answer the Captain of Plymouth:
"Truly the maxim is good,
and I do not mean to gainsay it;
But we must use it discreetly,
and not waste powder for nothing.
Now, as I said before,

I was never a maker of phrases.
I can match up to a fortress,
and summon the place to surrender,
But march up to a woman with such a proposal,
I dare not.
I'm not afraid of bullets,
nor shots from the mouth of a cannon,
But of a thundering 'No!'
point blank from the mouth of a woman,
That I confess I'm afraid of,
nor am I ashamed to confess it!
So you must grant my request,
for you are an elegant scholar,
Having the graces of speech,
and skill in the turning of phrases."
Taking the hand of his friend,
who still was reluctant and doubtful,
Holding it long in his own,
and pressing it kindly, he added:
"Though I have spoken thus lightly,
yet deep is the feeling that prompts me;
Surely you cannot refuse what I ask,
in the name of our friendship!"
Then made answer John Alden:
  "The name of friendship is sacred;
What you demand in that name,
I have not the power to deny you!"
So the strong will prevailed,
subdoing and moulding the gentler,
Friendship prevailed over love,
and Alden went on his errand.

So the strong will prevailed,
and Alden went on his errand,
Out of the street of the village,
and into the paths of the forest,
Into the tranquil woods,
where bluebirds and robins were building.
Towns in the populous trees,
with hanging gardens of verdure,
Peaceful,
aerial cities and affection and freedom.
All around him was calm,
but within him commotion and conflict,
Love contending with friendship,
and self with each generous impulse.

So through the Plymouth woods,
John Alden went on his errand;
Crossing the brook at the ford,
where it brawled over
pebble and shallow,
Gathering still, as he went,
the May flowers blooming around him,
Fragrant,
filling the air with a strange and wonderful
sweetness.
Children lost in the woods,
and covered with leaves in their slumber.
"Puritan flowers," he said,
"and the type of Puritan maidens,
Modest and simple and sweet,

the very type of Priscilla!
So I will take them to her,
to Priscilla the Mayflower of Plymouth,
Modest and simple and sweet,
as a parting gift will I take them;
Breathing their silent farewells,
as they fade and wither and perish,
Soon to be thrown away,
as is the heart of the giver."
So through the Plymouth woods,
John Alden went on his errand;
Came to an open space,
and saw the disk of the ocean,
Sailess,
sombre and cold with the comfortless breath
of the east wind;
Saw the new built house,
and people at work in the meadow;
Heard, as he drew near the door,
the musical voice of Priscilla
Singing the hundredth Psalm,
the grand old Puritan anthem,
Music that Luther sang,
to the sacred words of the Psalmist,
Full of the breath of the Lord,
consoling and comforting many.
Then as he opened the door,
he beheld the form of the maiden
Seated beside her wheel,
and the carded wool like a snowdrift
Piled at her knee,
her white hands feeding the ravenous spindle,
While with her foot on the treadle,

she guided the wheel in its motion.

So he entered the house:
and the hum of the wheel and the singing
Suddenly ceased;
for Priscilla, aroused by his step on the threshold,
Rose as he entered,
and gave him her hand, in signal of welcome,
Saying, "I knew it was you,
when I heard your step in the passage;
For I was thinking of you,
as I sat there singing and spinning."
Awkward and dumb with delight,
that a thought had been mingled
Thus in the sacred psalm,
that came from the heart of the maiden,
Silent before her he stood,
and gave her the flowers for an answer.

"So I have come to you now,
with an offer and proffer of marriage
Made by a good man and true,
Miles Standish, the Captain of Plymouth!"
Thus he delivered his message,
the dexterous writer of letters—
Did not embellish the theme,
nor array it in beautiful phrases,
But came straight to the point,
and blurted it out like a school boy;
Even the Captain himself
could hardly have said it more bluntly.

Mute with amazement and sorrow,
Priscilla the Puritan maiden
Looked into Alden's face,
her eyes dilated with wonder,
Feeling his words like a blow,
that stunned her and rendered her speechless;
Till at length she exclaimed,
interrupting the ominous silence:
"If the Captain of Plymouth
is so very eager to wed me,
Why does he not come himself,
and take the trouble to woo me?
If I am not worth the wooing,
I surely am not worth the the winning!"
Then John Alden began
explaining and smoothing the matter,
Making it worse as he went,
by saying the Captain was busy—
Had no time for such things
—such things! The words grating harshly
Fell on the ear of Priscilla;
and swift as a flash she made an answer:
"Has he no time for such things,
as you call it, before he is married,
Would he be likely to find it,
or make it, after the wedding?
That is the way with you men;
you don't understand us, you cannot.
When you have made up your minds,
after thinking of this one and that one,
Choosing, selecting, rejecting,
comparing one with another,
Then you make known your desire,

with abrupt and sudden avowal,
And are offended and hurt,
and indignant perhaps, that a woman
Does not respond at once
to a love that she never suspected,
Does not attain at a bound
the height to which you have been climbing.
This is not right nor just:
for surely a woman's affection
Is not a thing to be asked for,
and had only for the asking.
When one is truly in love,
one not only says it, but shows it.
Had he but waited awhile,
had he only showed that he loved me,
Even this Captain of yours—who knows?
—at last might have won me,
Old and rough as he is;
but now it can never happen."
Still John Alden went on,
unheeding the words of Priscilla,
Urging the suit of his friend,
explaining, persuading, expanding;
Spoke of his courage and skill,
and of all his battles in Flanders,
How with the people of God
he had chosen to suffer affliction;
How, in return for his zeal,
they had made him Captain of Plymouth;
He was a gentleman born,
could trace his pedigree plainly.

Any woman in Plymouth,
nay, any woman in England,
Might be happy and proud
to be called the wife of Miles Standish!
But as he warmed and glowed,
in his simple and eloquent language,
Quite forgetful of self,
and full of the praise of his rival,
Archly the maiden smiled,
and with eyes overrunning
with laughter, Said in a tremulous voice,
"Why don't you speak for yourself, John?"[80]

You will want to read the rest of the story.

THE LIFE OF LOVE

KAHLIL GIBRAN
From *The Beloved*

Spring

Come, my beloved, let us walk among the ruins, for the snows have melted. Life stirs from its couch and swirls among the valleys and hills. Go with me and we will trace the footsteps of spring in the distant field. Come, let us go up to the hilltops and see the plains in waves of green around us.

For spring has unfolded the garment that the winter night had rolled up. The plum tree and the apple wear it, arrayed like brides on the Holy Night. The orchards have shaken off their slumber. Their branches embrace like crowds of lovers. The streams flow, dancing among the stones, echoing songs of joy. Flowers burst from the heart of nature like froth on the sea.

Come, let us drink the last raindrop tears from a narcissus cup and fill our souls with the songs of larks.

Now is our time to breath deeply of the scent of spring breezes.

Let us sit by the stone where the violet is hidden, exchanging kisses of love.

Summer

Come, let us go to the field, for the days of the harvest have come. The crop is now grown, and the heat of the sun's love for nature has ripened it. Come, before the birds forestall us and reap the fruits of our toil, or before a colony of ants takes our land. Come, let us reap the fruits of the soil, as the soul reaps the fruits of happiness grown from the seeds of fidelity—seeds planted by love in the depths of our two hearts. Let us fill storehouses with the products of the elements, even as life fills up the granaries of our emotions.

Come, my companion, let us lie upon the grass with heaven as our blanket. Let us lay our heads upon fresh hay and rest from the labor of the day, listening to the night whispers of the brook in the valley below.

Autumn

Let us go to the vineyard, my beloved, and press the grapes, filling the vats with juice as the soul is filled with the wisdom of generations. Let us gather the dried fruits and distill the blossoms, sacrificing the flower itself to preserve its lingering scent.

Let us return to the dwellings, for the leaves of the trees are now brown and scatter before the wind. The wind will make them a shroud for flowers dead in their longing for the summer that has forsaken them. Let us go, for the birds have journeyed toward the shore, carrying with them the friendliness of the meadows and leaving behind in desolation the jasmine and the myrtle to weep their last tears onto the ground.

Let us go back, for the brooks have ceased to flow. The springs have dried their tears of joy. The hills are stripped of their splendid robes. Come, my beloved, for nature is seduced by lethargy and says its evening farewells to wakefulness in the plaintive strains of Nihavand.

Winter

Come near, my life's companion. Come near to me, and do not let the icy breaths separate our two bodies. Sit beside me before the hearth, for fire is the sweetest fruit of winter.

Tell me stories of bygone times, for my ears weary of the wind's sighs and the keening of the elements. Bolt the doors and windows, for the sight of angry weather saddens my soul and the sight of the town, sitting like a bereaved mother beneath layers of ice, oppresses my heart. . . . Fill the lamp with oil, O my life's companion, for it burns low. Place it near me so I can see what the nights have written on your face.

Bring a jug of wine for us to drink, and we will remember the days when it was pressed.

Come, come near to me, beloved of my soul, for the fire has burned down and the ashes cover it. Embrace me, for the lamp has gone out and darkness presses in. Our eyes have grown heavy with the wine of years. Look on me with eyes shadowed with sleep.

Embrace me before slumber embraces me. Kiss me, for the ice has conquered all but your kiss. And oh, my beloved, how deep is the sea of sleep, how far distant is the morning . . . in this world![81]

ABSENCE AND
THE HEART

*Clementine Churchill, the wife of England's prime minister Winston
Churchill, was acutely aware of having to say Godspeed and
good-bye to the one she loved above all others. Those frequent and
long absences were filled with loving letters that sprang from deep
trust and affection. In January of 1935 the tables were turned, and
Clementine was on the high seas on her way to India.
Upon arrival she wrote to Winston,*

"Oh my Darling, I am thinking so much of you and how you
have enriched my life. I have loved you very much but wish I
had been a more amusing wife to you. How nice it would be if
we were both young again."

Winston Churchill's answer . . .

January 23, 1935

My darling Clemmie,

"In your letter from Madras you wrote some words very dear to
me, about my having enriched your life. I cannot tell you what
pleasure this gave me, because I always feel so overwhelmingly
in your debt, if there can be accounts in love. It was sweet of
you to write this to me, and I hope and pray I shall be able to
make you happy and secure during my remaining years, and
cherish you, my darling one, as you deserve, and leave you in
comfort when my race is run. What it has been to me to live all
these years in your heart and companionship no phrases can
convey. Time passes swiftly, but is it not joyous to see how

great and growing is the treasure we have gathered together, amid the storms and stresses of so many eventful, and to millions, tragic and terrible years? . . ."

Your loving husband,
W.

Winston and Clementine Churchill were married fifty-seven years.
They met at a ball in London in 1904.
Four years later they met again, and were engaged in five months.
After their second meeting Winston wrote,

"What a comfort and pleasure it was to meet a girl with so much intellectual quality and such strong reserves of noble sentiment."

And after four years of marriage
and the birth of their second child, she wrote,

"My sweet beloved Winston, I am so happy with you my Dear. You have so transformed my life that I can hardly remember what it felt like . . . before I knew you."

P.S. "Please be a good Pug [her nickname for him] and not destroy the good of your little open air holiday by smoking too many fat cigars."

On their 11th wedding anniversary Winston wrote,

"It is a rock of comfort to have your love and companionship at my side."[82]

GOD KEEP YOU

God keep you, dearest, all this lonely night:

The winds are still,

The moon drops down behind the western hill;

God keep you safely, dearest, till the light.

God keep you then when slumber melts away,

And care and strife

Take up new arms to fret out waking life,

God keep you through the battle of the day.

God keep you. Nay, beloved soul, how vain,

How poor is prayer!

But I can but say again, and yet again,

God keep you every time and everywhere.

MADELINE BRIDGES

CROSSING OVER
WILLIAM MEREDITH

It was now early spring, and the river was swollen and turbulent; great cakes of floating ice were swinging heavily to and fro
in the turbid waters. Owing to a peculiar form of the shore, on
the Kentucky side, the land bending far out into the water, the
ice had been lodged and detained in great quantities, and the
narrow channel which swept round the bend was full of ice,
piled one cake over another, thus forming a temporary barrier to
the descending ice, which lodged, and formed a great undulating raft. . . . Eliza stood, for a moment, contemplating this
unfavorable aspect of things.

Uncle Tom's Cabin
(Chapter VII, "The Mother's Struggle")
Harriet Beecher Stowe

That's what love is like. The whole river
is melting. We skim along in great peril,

having to move faster than ice goes under
and still find foothold in the soft floe.

We are one another's floe. Each displaces the weight
of his own need. I am fat as a bloodhound,

hold me up. I won't hurt you. Though I bay,
I could swim with you on my back until the cold

seeped into my heart. We are committed, we
are going across this river willy-nilly.

No one, black or white, is free in Kentucky,
old gravity owns everyone. We're weighty.

I contemplate this unfavorable aspect of things.
Where is something solid? Only you and me.

Has anyone ever been to Ohio?
Do the people there stand firmly on icebergs?

Here all we have is love, a great undulating
raft, melting steadily. We go out on it

anyhow. I love you, I love this fool's walk.
The thing we have to learn is how to walk light.

SWEETHEARTS ALWAYS

From *More Heart Throbs*

If sweethearts were sweethearts always,
Whether as maid or wife,
No drop would be half as pleasant
In the mingled draught of life.

But the sweetheart has smiles and blushes
When the wife has frowns and sighs,
And the wife's have a wrathful glitter
For the glow of the sweetheart's eyes.

If lovers were lovers always—
The same to sweetheart and wife,
Who would change for a future of Eden
The joys of this checkered life?

But husbands grow grave and silent,
And care on the anxious brow
Oft replaces the sunshine that perished
With the words of the marriage vow.

Happy is he whose sweetheart
Is wife and sweetheart still—
Whose voice, as of old, can charm;
Whose kiss, as old, can thrill;

Who has plucked the rose to find ever
Its beauty and fragrance increase,
As the flush of passion is mellowed
In love's unmeasured peace.

DANIEL O'CONNELL

BE MY MISTRESS
SHORT OR TALL

Be my mistress short or tall

And distorted therewithal

Be she likewise one of those

That an acre hath of nose

Be her teeth ill hung or set

And her grinders black as jet

Be her cheeks so shallow too

As to show her tongue wag through

Hath she thin hair, hath she none

She's to me a paragon.

ROBERT HERRICK

Chapter 11

ABIDE WITH ME

*Abide \ abode \ abided \ abiding: 1: to wait
for; 2: to endure without yielding;
3: to bear patiently; 4: to accept without
objection; 5: to remain stable or fixed;
6: to continue in a place. (Webster)*

*"And now faith, hope, and love abide, these
three; and the greatest of these is love."
(The Apostle Paul)*

*In the literature of the heart, love's abiding
assumes a myriad of roles.*

Perhaps the favorite literary call to abiding
is found in Robert Browning's
"Rabbi Ben Ezra":

Grow old along with me!
The best is yet to be,
The last of life, for which the first was made:
Our times are in His hand
Who saith, "A whole I planned,
Youth shows but half; trust God: see all,
nor be afraid!"

And now, come, let us abide with these
love treasures . . .

MUSIC I HEARD

Music I heard with you was more than music,

And bread I broke with you was more than bread,

Now that I am without you, all is desolate;

All that was once beautiful is dead.

Your hands once touched this table and this silver,

And I have seen your fingers hold this glass.

These things do not remember you, beloved—

And yet your touch upon them will not pass.

For it was in my heart you moved among them.

And blessed them with your hands and with your eyes;

And in my heart they will remember always—

They knew you once, O beautiful and wise.[83]

CONRAD AIKEN

HER BRIGHT SMILE
HAUNTS ME STILL

It's been a year since last we met
We may never meet again
I have struggled to forget,
But the struggle was in vain.
For her voice lives in the breeze,
Her spirit comes at will.
In the midnight on the seas
Her bright smile haunts me still.

In the midnight on the seas
Her bright smile haunts me still.

I have sailed a falling sky
And I have charted hazard's paths
I have seen the storm arise
Like a giant in his wrath.
Every danger I have known
That a reckless life can fill,
Though her presence is now flown
Her bright smile haunts me still.

Though her presence is now flown
Her bright smile haunts me still.

At the first sweet dawn of light
When I gaze upon the deep,
Her form still greets my sight
While the stars their vigil keep.
When I close my aching eyes
Sweet dreams my memory fill.
And from sleep when I arise
Her bright smile haunts me still.

And from sleep when I arise
Her bright smile haunts me still.

TRADITIONAL, AMERICAN

RABBI BEN EZRA

"GROW OLD WITH ME"
ROBERT BROWNING

Grow old along with me!
The best is yet to be,
The last of life, for which the first was made:
Our times are in His hand
Who saith "A whole I planned,
Youth shows but half; trust God: see all, nor be afraid!"

Not that, amassing flowers,
Youth sighed "Which rose make ours,
Which lily leave and then as best recall?"
Not that, admiring stars,
It yearned "Nor Jove, nor Mars;
Mine be some figured flame which blends,
transcends them all!"

Not for such hopes and fears
Annulling youth's brief years,
Do I remonstrate: folly wide the mark!
Rather I prize the doubt
Low kinds exist without,
Finished and finite clods, untroubled by a spark.

Poor vaunt of life indeed,
Were man but formed to feed

On joy, to solely seek and find and feast:
Such feasting ended, then
As sure an end to men;
Irks care the crop-full bird?
Frets doubt the maw-crammed beast?

Rejoice we are allied
To that which dash provide
And not partake, effect and not receive!
A spark disturbs our clod;
Nearer we hold of God
Who gives, than of His tribes that take, I must believe.

Then, welcome each rebuff
That turns earth's smoothness rough,
Each sting that bids nor sit nor stand but go!
Be our joys three-parts pain!
Strive, and hold cheap the strain;
Learn, nor account the pang;
dare, never grudge the three!

For thence—a paradox
Which comforts while it mocks—
Shall life succeed in that it seems to fail:
What I aspired to be,
And was not, comforts me:
A brute I might have been, but would not sink i' the scale.

What is he but a brute
Whose flesh has soul to suit,
Whose spirit works lest arms and legs want play?
To man, propose this test—
Thy body at its best,
How far can that project thy soul on its lone way?

Yet gifts should prove their use:
I own the Past profuse
Of power each side, perfection every turn:
Eyes, ears took in their dole,
Brain treasured up the whole;
Should not the heart beat once
"How good to live and learn?"

Not once beat "Praise be Thine!
I see the whole design,
I, who saw power, see now love perfect too:
Perfect I call Thy plan:
Thanks that I was a man!
Maker, remake, complete—I trust what Thou shalt do!"

For pleasant is this flesh;
Our soul, in its rose-mesh
Pulled ever to the earth, still yearns for rest;
Would we some prize might hold
To match those manifold
Possessions of the brute—gain most, as we did best!

Let us not always say,
"Spite of this flesh to-day
I strove, made head, gained ground upon the whole!"
As the bird wings and sings,
Let us cry "All good things
Are ours, nor soul helps flesh more,
now, than flesh helps soul!"

Therefore I summon age
To grant youth's heritage,
Life's struggle having so far reached its term:
Thence shall I pass, approved
A man, for aye removed

From the developed brute;
a god though in the germ.

And I shall thereupon
Take rest, ere I be gone
Once more on my adventure brave and new:
Fearless and unperplexed,
When I wage battle next,
What weapons to select, what armour to indue.

Youth ended, I shall try
My gain or loss thereby;
Leave the fire ashes, what survives is gold:
And I shall weigh the same,
Give life its praise or blame:
Young, all lay in dispute; I shall know, being old.

For note, when evening shuts,
A certain moment cuts
The deed off, calls the glory from the grey:
A whisper from the west
Shoots—"Add this to the rest,
"Take it and try its worth: here dies another day."

So, still within this life,
Though lifted o'er its strife,
Let me discern, compare, pronounce at last,
This rage was right i' the main,
That acquiescence vain:
"The Future I may face now I have proved the Past."

For more is not reserved
To man, with soul just nerved
To act to-morrow what he learns to-day:
Here, work enough to watch

The Master work, and catch
Hints of the proper craft, tricks of the tool's true play.

As it was better, youth
Should strive, through acts uncouth,
Toward making, than repose on aught found made:
So, better, age, exempt
From strife, should know, than tempt
Further. Thou waitedst age: wait death nor be afraid!

Enough now, if the Right
And Good and Infinite
Be named here, as thou callest thy hand thine own
With knowledge absolute,
Subject to no dispute
From fools that crowded youth,
nor let thee feel alone.

Be there, for once and all,
Severed great minds from small,
Announced to each his station in the Past!
Was I, the world arraigned,
Were they, my soul disdained,
Right? Let age speak the truth and give us peace at last!

Now, who shall arbitrate?
Ten men love what I hate,
Shun what I follow, slight what I receive;
Ten, who in ears and eyes
Match me: we all surmise,
They this thing, and I that: whom shall my soul believe?

Not on the vulgar mass
Called "work," must sentence pass,
Things done, that took the eye and had the price;
O'er which, from level stand,

The low world laid its hand,
Found straightway to its mind, could value in a trice:

But all, the world's coarse thumb
And finger failed to plumb,
So passed in making up the main account;
All instincts immature,
All purposes unsure,
That weighed not as his work, yet swelled the man's amount:

Thoughts hardly to be packed
Into a narrow act,
Fancies that broke through language and escaped;
All I could never be,
All, men ignored in me,
This, I was worth to God, whose wheel the pitcher shaped.

Ay, note that Potter's wheel,
That metaphor! and feel
Why time spins fast, why passive lies our clay,—
Thou, to whom fools propound,
When the wine makes its round,
"Since life fleets, all is change; the Past gone, seize to-day!"

Fool! All that is, at all,
Lasts ever, past recall;
Earth changes, but thy soul and God stand sure:
What entered into thee,
That was, is, and shall be:
Time's wheel runs back or stops: Potter and clay endure.

He fixed thee mid this dance
Of plastic circumstance,
This Present, thou, forsooth, wouldst fain arrest:
Machinery just meant

To give thy soul its bent,
Try thee and turn thee forth, sufficiently impressed.

What though the earlier grooves,
Which ran the laughing loves
Around thy base, no longer pause and press?
What though, about thy rim,
Skull-things in order grim
Grow out, in graver mood,
obey the sterner stress?

Look not thou down but up!
To uses of a cup,
The festal board, lamp's flash and trumpet's peal,
The new wine's foaming flow,
The Master's lips a-glow!
Thou, heaven's consummate cup,
what need'st thou with earth's wheel?

But I need, now as then,
Thee, God, who mouldest men;
And since, not even while the whirl was worst,
Did I—to the wheel of life
With shapes and colours rife,
Bound dizzily—mistake my end, to slake Thy thirst:

So, take and use Thy work:
Amend what flaws may lurk,
What strain o' the stuff, what warpings past the aim!
My times be in Thy hand!
Perfect the cup as planned!
Let age approve of youth, and death complete the same!

BARTER

Life has loveliness to sell
All beautiful and splendid things,
Blue waves whitened on a cliff,
Soaring fire that sways and sings,
And children's faces looking up
Holding wonder like a cup.
Life has loveliness to sell,
Music like a curve of gold,
Scent of pine trees in the rain,
Eyes that love you, arms that hold,
And for your spirit's still delight,
Holy thoughts that star the night.
Spend all you have for loveliness,
Buy it and never count the cost;
For one white singing hour of peace
Count many a year of strife well lost,
And for a breath of ecstasy
Give all you have been, or could be.[84]

SARA TEASDALE

LONDONDERRY AIR

Would God I were the tender apple blossom
That floats and falls from off the twisted bough,
To lie and faint within your silken bosom
Within your silken bosom as that does now!
Or would I were a little burnish'd apple
For you to pluck me, gliding by so cold,
While sun and shade your robe of lawn with dapple,
Your robe of lawn, and your hair's spun gold.
Yea, would to God I were among the roses
That lean to kiss you as you float between,
While on the lowest branch a bud uncloses,
A bud uncloses, to touch you, queen.
Nay, since you will not love, would I were growing,
A happy daisy, in the garden path;
That so your silver foot might press me going,
Might press me going even unto death.

TRADITIONAL, IRISH

YOUR FRIEND, BILLY: A LOVE STORY

P. MOLINERO

Franklin, Missouri
June 30, 1973

Dear Nancy,

Mom says I need to thank you for the birthday present you gave me. Thank you. I like it very much.

Your friend,
Billy

> *Licking the envelope, Billy Pierce folded down the flap and rubbed a grimey seven-year-old hand over it. "That's that," he said to himself. "Mom, will you mail my letter for me? I'm going over to Eddie's."*

June 29, 1976
Dear Billy:

I really had a good time at your twelfth birthday party. It doesn't seem possible that we're going to be in junior high school, does it? The punch came out of my skirt okay. Angie says that she's going to give me a great party in August for my twelfth. I'll make sure she invites you.

Your friend,
Nancy

"Mom, do we have any stamps?"

"Look in the top drawer of the desk, honey. Who'd you write to?"

"Oh, just that pest Billy Pierce."

October 28, 1977

Billy:
I've called you up a couple of times, but no one was home. Before I leave town, I want you to know that I won't be going to the church Pumpkin Patch Party. My grandma died this morning, and we are going to Detroit this afternoon to take care of things and for her funeral, I guess. No one in our family has ever died before—at least as long as I can remember. I'm sort of scared.

Your friend,
Nancy

October 31, 1977

Dear Nancy:

I really don't know what to say. My grandfather died two years ago. It was just terrible. Everybody was crying about it. I felt pretty sad, too. The Pumpkin party was fun. Everyone said they missed you. Eddie Nelson broke his arm playing some stupid game.

Mr. Cheever says he'll let you take a makeup on the math test. Well, I gotta go.

Your friend,
Billy

> *"Mom, was it two years ago that grandpa died?"*

> *"No Billy, not quite. It was just after you began junior high. Remember?"*

> *"Oh, yeah. . . ."*

P.S. My mom says it hasn't been two years since grandpa died. You should have seen Angie try to give Eddie Nelson first aid.

July 3, 1979
Orlando, Florida

Dear Billy:

Walt Disney World is sure fun. I put an "X" on the car we rode in on Magic Mountain. Scary!!! My brother Tony threw up. Gross!!!!

Nancy

"Dad, when are we leaving in the morning?"

"Well, honey, because of 4th of July traffic, we ought to get an early start for home."

"Good!"

Nancy, I found your note stuck in my locker. What do you mean I've been paying more attention to Lisa Marie than to you? That's really stupid. Bill

Nancy, No, I wasn't calling you stupid. But you shouldn't believe everything Angie tells you. I've got soccer practice tonight. Won't be at youth group. Bill

Nancy, if you want to be that way just go ahead. I thought when we left junior high you'd be a lot more mature. Maybe Lisa Marie is more ready for high school. Let me know when you're ready to be a freshman. Bill

December 15, 1979

Dear Bill:

For one of my Christmas gifts, my folks are taking me to see *The Nutcracker.* They said I could invite a friend to go with us. I'd like you to be that friend. We'll see if you're "mature" enough to handle a ballet. If you can make it, I'll get the details to you.

Your freshman friend,
Nancy

P.S. I'm putting this in a letter because it's the proper way of doing it.

December 18, 1979

Dear Nancy,

If a letter is the proper way, then I'll answer you with one. (Seems to me that the phone or on the school bus would be just as good.) If going to see *The Nutcracker* with you and your family will convince you of my maturity, I accept.

My mother says ballet is beautiful. Dad just kept reading the paper when she tried to get him to agree. It should be an experience. Thanks for inviting me.

Your friend,
Bill

> *"Can I speak to Eddie, please? . . . 'May I'—sorry, Mrs. Nelson. . . . Hey, Eddie, guess where I'm goin'? (Pause.) "No, I didn't get accepted for baseball camp yet. (Pause.) No, not that either. I'm goin' to the ballet! (Pause) . . . Eddie? Eddie, are you there?"*

December 23, 1979

Dear Mr. and Mrs. Wyatt,

Thank you very much for the invitation to go to see *The*

Nutcracker with you folks and Nancy. I enjoyed it very much. I had never seen a ballet before. It was really better than I thought it would be.

Merry Christmas,
Bill Pierce

> *"Billy, are you going caroling with the youth group tonight?"*
> *"Yeah, Mom, can . . .ah . . .may I borrow the car to go to the church? Eddie can't get his started."*

January 2, 1980

Dear Grandma Pierce,

Happy 1980! Thank you for the Christmas gifts. I really like the wallet, and the $5.00 bill you put in it. I'm saving for a car, so the money will come in handy. We missed having you here for Christmas. I hope you had a good time with Uncle Charles and Aunt Vivian. Dad says to tell you to help me pray about what college I ought to go to. I graduate from high school next year. No, I really don't have a real steady girlfriend. I guess Nancy is about as close to a girlfriend as I have. Hurry up and visit us. Excuse the mistakes. I'm writing this and watching the Rose Bowl game at the same time.

Love,
Bill

Bill: I hope you come by your locker before second hour. I have something really important to tell you. Nancy

Nancy: Sorry I missed you. I had an emergency student council meeting to go to. What'cha got to tell me? You know I can't buy anymore band candy. Bill

April 14, 1980

Dear Nancy:

I can't bring myself to tell you this in person. I'm still shocked by your news. Why can't your dad turn down a job transfer? My dad did that once when his dad—my grandfather—died. He had to stay in this part of the country.

Nancy, you have to stay here, too—because I'm here. Don't we have to have our senior year together? I can't imagine what it would be like to march in the graduation line—and you're not there. I'm really praying about this. You pray, too. I'm going to get my nerve up and sign this. . . .

Love,
Bill

June 24, 1981

Dear Grandma:

I hope you're feeling better. I'm sorry you couldn't be at my graduation. We all missed you. Thank you for the check. I'll add it to my first-year college fund. I'm going to need every dime I can scrape together. Since I decided not to go to State, but to go to a Christian college, scholarship money is harder to come by. But I know I made the right decision.

Thank you for sending Nancy a card. She really appreciated it. Her graduation was very nice—but it would have been nicer if we'd been together. But of course, the good news is we'll both be at Covenant College in September.

One time you asked me if I had a steady girlfriend. I think I said that Nancy came the closest. Well, today I can honestly say she *is* the closest.

Please get well, Grandma.

Your loving grandson,
Bill

Columbus, Ohio
August 3, 1981

Dear Bill:

Does it seem possible we are going to be living on the same campus in just a little over three weeks? Have you figured out that if you're in Mayfield Hall and I'm in Goodwin House, we'll be right across the quad from each other? Maybe we can work out a signal system with our Venetian blinds? . . .

Love,
Nance

Franklin, Missouri
August 6, 1981

Nance:

Thanks for writing me so faithfully. I'm afraid I haven't held up
my end of our letter writing. Usually by the time I get home
from Acme, take a shower and eat I'm about ready to go to bed.
Five o'clock comes pretty early. Sorry to be moaning, I know
you're working lousy hours, too. Are you getting along better
with your boss?

Yeah, I'm unhappy that I can't pick you up and move you to college with me. It wouldn't be that far out of my way. But obviously, your parents want to take their "little girl" themselves. . . .

August 9, 1981

Bill:

That was a cheap shot on my parents. I don't think you're being
very fair to them.

Nance

August 13, 1981

Honest, Nancy, I'm not unhappy. Sorry. I'll make it up to you
our first day on campus.

Love,
Bill

Beep. "Hello, Nancy?" Sorry you're not there. I just wrote a note, but I want you to know how bad I feel about the letter. If your folks hear this message you can explain what happened. I love you, Nancy."

Covenant College / St. Louis, Missouri
Mayfield Hall

October 15, 1981

Nance:
It's with pleasure that I accept your invitation to be your twerp date for the Sadie Hawkins party. Remember, I don't kiss on the first date!

Bill

Covenant College / St. Louis, Missouri
Mayfield Hall

October 29, 1983

Dear Nancy:

I guess our Sadie Hawkins twerp date has been a tradition, but Pam thinks I need to go home with her to Columbia for that weekend. I've never met her folks.

Hope you understand. I imagine you can tell that Pam and I are getting pretty serious. Since she graduates this spring we need to think seriously about where our relationship is heading. I don't have to tell you, Nance, you already know that next to Pam, you're the best friend I have. We've both been praying about the future. Right now, all we know is that she's going to start grad school and I have to get through my senior year.

Nance, I'm sure we can all be friends. I know Pam really likes you. It's just that sometimes she feels left out because you and I have known each other for so long.

Well, gotta study. Please call or leave a note in my mailbox. (I decided that what I had to say here worked better in a letter.) Pam says hello.

Your friend,
Bill

The Covenant Clarion

> *Dateline: December 10, 1983. Dr. and Mrs. Frederick Medford of Columbia, Missouri, announce the engagement of their daughter Pamela Lea Medford to William Pierce, son of Flora and Max Pierce of Franklin, Missouri. A Christmas 1984 wedding is planned.*

Franklin, Missouri
December 15, 1983

Honey,

Thanks for sending the clipping about Billy's engagement. Your father and I understand you're hurt. If Billy and his young lady prayed about their decision, then you shouldn't question God. But that doesn't keep it from hurting, I know. We'll talk about it next week when you get here for Christmas. Guess what, Tony is going to have a girlfriend here Christmas Eve. He's really anxious for you to meet her.

All our love,
Mother and Daddy

Covenant College / St. Louis, Missouri
December 18, 1983

Dear Mom:

Thank you for the letter. I have so much to tell you when I get
home this weekend. My roommates are treating me like Bill is
dead or something! Actually, I do sort of feel that way.

Tony's girlfriend! That's all I need, my little brother getting
married before I do!

x x x
N.

> *Beep. "Sorry you're not there, Nance. Pam and I have
> gotten in from Columbia. I just dropped her off at her
> apartment. I had no idea wedding plans can be such a
> big deal. Just a tip: expect a call from Pam, she wants
> you to do something at the reception. It's up to you, I
> know. But I'd sure like to have you there. I'll get back
> in touch. Have an economics exam tomorrow. How'd
> you make out with Shakespeare?*

The Parents of Pamela Lea Medford
and William Jerome Pierce
invite you to a rite of celebration,
as they pledge their vows of
Christian Marriage to one another
December 24, 1984, in Covenant College Chapel
St. Louis, Missouri
at two o'clock in the afternoon.
RSVP

Franklin, Missouri
December 5, 1984

Dear Pam:

Thank you for the wedding invitation and the request that I
help serve at your reception table. I'm sorry I have been so slow
in responding. I am afraid that my family and I are not going
to be able to attend. My brother Tony is entering the hospital
earlier that week for a second opinion on what may or may not
be lymphoma. Our doctor detected an abnormality in his
lymph glands when he was getting a football physical. You can
imagine how we really need to stick together for Christmas.

Please give my regrets to Bill.

Sincerely,
Nancy

Columbia, Missouri
December 10, 1984

Dear Nancy:

I had no idea about Tony. That's a real shock. What can I do?
If he needs blood or something, please remember that we have
the same type. I'll be praying for you and your family.

Who would have thought in a million years that I'd ever get
married without you there? When we were growing up I think
I depended upon your approval more than I did Eddie Nelson's.
Remember the first time I tried to wear a bow tie—the night
we went to see *The Nutcracker?* You said it made me look like a
Halloween jack-o-lantern. Well, I'm putting one on for my

wedding—and you won't be there.

Please know, Nance, you will always be a very special person to me. Pam is aware of how I feel. In fact she says she wants you to feel comfortable around her and in our home. I hope you will. I need you as my friend.

Even though you won't be there, when Eddie toasts Pam and me at the reception, he'll be toasting all the things that make me, me—and that includes our memories and your family.

Lovingly,
Bill

"Miss Wyatt, the mail has come."

"Just put it down on the table, please."

"The Franklin Times is there. . . ."

The Franklin Times
Franklin, Missouri

Dateline: June 12, 1998. Sources report that Dr. William J. Pierce is returning to Franklin on a fact-finding mission to establish a national cancer clinic specializing in the treatment of the young. Pierce is the son of the late Maxwell and Flora Pierce of the city. He has been involved with a highly touted oncology practice in Chicago. The doctor is quoted as saying, "I want to return to my roots. There's a very dear friend here whose young brother died of this cursed blight. It's time for someone to give the Tony's of this world a chance. I want to see what I can do."

Chicago, Illinois
July 3, 1998

Dear Nancy:

Recognize the handwriting? You've seen an awful lot of it through the years, though none for the past several. I'm coming out of hibernation. It's time to get back to Franklin. I want to investigate the possibilities of establishing a cancer clinic. I can still see that hillside meadow outside of town, where you and Angie used to go to pick flowers. I have always imagined a medical research facility sitting there.

I'd like to tell you more about it, Nancy. May I visit you when I am in town in a month or so? There's a lot I need to bring you up to speed about. I'll call when I get there. Ed Nelson gave me your phone number when he was in Chicago recently. I hear you have become a successful writer. I don't read much fiction, so I have never seen any of your books. You can tell me all about them when we're together.

Your friend,
Billy

July 15, 1998

> To: The Research Librarian of the Chicago Tribune
> Fr: Nancy Wyatt
> Re: Background information about a certain William
>   Jerome Pierce, M.D.

August 1, 1998

Dear Miss Wyatt:

First of all, let me say how honored I was to receive your letter.
I believe I have devoured every book you have written. As an
amateur writer, I can appreciate the depth of emotion you are
able to conjure up with words. I am particularly intrigued by
your understanding of the single life.

Now, to the real point of this letter; Dr. William J. Pierce has
practiced here in Chicago for the past eight years. He has had a
profitable practice, in that his clientele has represented the city's
more influential. His wife, Pamela Pierce, was a Medford from
Columbia, Missouri, where her father, Frederick Medford, was
head of Missouri University Medical School. Pamela Pierce
died in childbirth in 1996. . . .

"Miss Wyatt, there is a Dr. Pierce here to see you."

"Show him in, please. . . ."

BEAUTIFUL DREAMER

Beautiful dreamer, awake unto me
Starlight and dewdrops are waiting for thee
Sounds of the rude world heard in the day
Lulled by the moonlight are all passed away.

Beautiful dreamer, queen of my song,
Gone are the cares of life's busy throng
List while I woo thee with soft melody
Beautiful dreamer, awake unto me!
Beautiful dreamer, awake unto me.

STEPHEN FOSTER

TO CELIA

Drink to me only with thine eyes,
And I will pledge with mine;
Or leave a kiss but in the cup,
And I'll not look for wine.
The thirst that from the soul doth rise,
Doth ask a drink divine:
But might I of Jove's nectar sup,
I would not change for thine.

I sent thee late a rosy wreath,
Not so much honoring thee,
As giving it a hope, that there
It could not withered be.
But thou thereon did'st only breathe,
And sent'st it back to me;
Since when it grows and smells, I swear,
Not of itself, but thee.

BEN JOHNSON

LOVE

Come, let us make love deathless, thou and I,
Seeing that our footing on earth is brief. . . .

HERBERT TRENCH

THE REAL PRINCESS

HANS CHRISTIAN ANDERSON

Sometimes called "The Princess and the Pea," this 19th century fairy tale may not be as romantic as some of the other Anderson stories, but it might prove to be quite beneficial to males today.

There once was a prince, and he wanted a princess, but then she must be a real princess. He traveled right around the world to find one but there was always something wrong. There were plenty of princesses, but whether they were real princesses he had great difficulty in discovering; there was always something which was not quite right about them. So at last he had to come home again and he was very sad because he wanted a real princess so badly.

One evening there was a terrible storm; it thundered and lightninged and rain poured down in torrents. Indeed it was a fearful night.

In the middle of the storm somebody knocked at the town gate, and the old King himself went to open it.

It was a princess who stood outside but she was in a terrible state from the rain and the storm. The water streamed out of her hair and her clothes; it ran in at the top of her shoes and out at the heel, but she said that she was a real princess. "Well, we shall soon see if that is true," thought the old Queen, but she said nothing. She went into the bedroom, took all the bed clothes off and laid a pea on the bedstead. Then she took twenty mattresses and piled them on the top of the pea, and then twenty feather beds on the top of the mattresses. This was where the princess was to sleep that night.

In the morning they asked her how she had slept.

"Oh, terribly badly!" said the Princess. "I have hardly closed my eyes the whole night! Heaven knows what was in the bed! I seemed to be lying upon some hard thing, and my whole body is black and blue this morning. It is terrible!"

They saw at once she must have been a real princess when she had felt the pea through twenty mattresses and twenty feather-beds. Nobody but a real princess could have such a delicate skin.

So the prince took her to be his wife, for now he was sure that he had found a real princess, and the pea was put into a Museum where it may still be seen if no one has stolen it.

Now this is a true story.[85]

Chapter 12
LOVE IS ETERNAL

O God, the protector of all who trust in thee,

without whom nothing is strong, nothing is

holy . . . may we so pass through things

temporal, that we lose not the things eternal.

—Book of Common Prayer

Inside the wedding band that Abraham Lincoln

gave Mary Todd was engraved

the words, "Love is eternal." As Lincoln lay

dying in a rooming house across the

street from Ford's Theatre, where he had been

the victim of an assassin's bullet,

Mary Todd Lincoln twisted the gold band on
her left hand. Had any other marriage ever
undergone the strain of theirs? The war . . . the
loss of a son . . . Mary's irrational
behavior . . . and now this.

When the President breathed his last,
someone in the room declared, "He belongs to the
ages." Mary's response was, "He belongs to me.
Our love is eternal."

Like the proverbial a gift that keeps
on giving;
"Love never ends."

THE FINAL TOLL

CHARLES R. SWINDOLL

Sleep came hard for me last night, which for me is a rarity. I'm usually out in less than ten seconds. Last night I must have been awake for an hour and a half . . . thinking, musing, and praying.

Earlier that evening, [my wife] Cynthia and I had read together a letter from our longtime friend Wally Norling, who had just returned from the bedside of Betty, his "loving partner in life for forty-two years." Betty is dying of cancer of the liver, and Wally's letter, written in the midst of that, was a gracious, understated masterpiece of faith.

His words left us both pensive. In silence, we dressed for bed, and I'm sure we were thinking the same thing: it could happen to us. If it does, I know this . . . I would not be nearly so brave as my friend, certainly not as eloquent in expressing such feelings.

And so I lay there wide awake, reviewing our almost forty years together. I thought about those innocent early years, which seemed so tough back there. Years of enforced separation (thanks to the military), of a career change, of the first years in graduate school, of financially lean times, of learning and grow- ing closer together.

Then came our child bearing years—wonderful years, so incredibly surprising to both of us. The loss of two precious children by miscarriage, the healthy births of four. Yes, four! (And to think I felt one was enough, certainly not more than two.) The simple joys of tent camping, of early schooling, of struggling with "finding myself," in pulpit style, philosophy of ministry, confronting criticism for the first time, and discovering much of what "being a pastor" meant. And all the while,

Cynthia was right there . . . understanding, affirming, being mother to our four children and partner with me, assuring me that it was worth all the effort. Though she never bragged about it, I know she prayed me through many a sermon. As I improved, I got the credit, but she deserved the applause. As the song goes, she was the wind beneath my wings . . . and boy, did I need healthy gusts at times! Still do.

Before dropping off to sleep, I did a quick recap of the balance of our years together. Wow! Giant steps through big-time changes. A surprising move to California . . . the teenaged years (among our favorite!), an endless number of high school football games . . . dating, four unforgettable weddings, the birth of new dimensions of ministry, wild 'n' crazy family times, eight grandchildren, summer vacations, backyard barbecues, gaining weight and dieting together, jogging and laughing together, feeling loved, blending strengths with weaknesses, refusing to quit no matter what. Two people so different, yet so close. And now, a whole new direction in training men and women for ministry.

As I remembered all this, I realized anew the enormity of Wally's loss, and that reminds me of what John Donne wrote in 1624:

No man is an island, entire of itself; every man [or woman] is a piece of the continent, a part of the main . . . any man's [or woman's] death diminishes me, because I am involved in mankind; and therefore never send to know for whom the bell tolls; it tolls for thee.

Last night, in the arms of my wife, I couldn't help but imagine the night that ominous final bell might toll on our marriage. I tried to picture life without my loving partner . . . that dark era when the other side of my bed will be empty and lonely memories will replace the warmth of reality. And, sadly, I fell asleep.[86]

DANNY BOY

Oh Danny boy, the pipes, the pipes are calling
From glen to glen, and down the mountainside
The summer's gone, and all the flowers are dying
'Tis you, 'tis you must go and I must bide.
But come you back when summer's in the meadow
Or when the valley's hushed and white with snow
'Tis I'll be there in sunshine or in shadow
Oh Danny boy, oh Danny boy, I love you so.
And if you come, when all the flowers are dying
And I am dead, as dead I well may be
You'll come and find the place where I am lying
And kneel and say an "Ave" there for me.
And I shall hear, tho' soft you tread above me
And all my dreams will warm and sweeter be
If you'll not fail to tell me that you love me
I simply sleep in peace until you come to me.

TRADITIONAL, IRISH

TO MY DEAR
LOVING HUSBAND

If ever two were one then surely we.
If ever man were loved by wife, then thee;
If ever wife were happy in a man,
Compare with me, ye women, if you can.
I prize thy love more than whole minds of gold
Or all the riches that the East cloth hold.
My love is such that rivers cannot quench,
Nor aught but love from thee give recompense.
Thy love is such I can no way repay,
The heavens reward thee manifold, I pray.
Then while we live, in love let's so persevere
That when we live no more, we may live ever.

ANNE BRADSTREET

LOVE POEM

Because I love

There is an invisible way across the sky,

Birds travel by that way, the sun and moon

And all the stars travel that path by night.

Because I love

There is a river flowing all night long.

Because I love

All night the river flows into my sleep,

Ten thousand living things are sleeping in my arms,

And sleeping wake, and flowing are at rest.

KATHLEEN RAINE

An Epitaph Upon Husband and Wife Who Died and Were Buried Together

To these, whom death again did wed,
This grave's the second marriage bed,
For though the hand of fate could force
'Twixt soul and body a divorce,
It could not sunder man and wife,
Because they both lived but one life.
Peace, good reader. Do not weep.
Peace, the lovers are asleep.
They, sweet turtles, folded lie
In the last knot love could tie.
And though they lie as they were dead,
Their pillow stone, their sheets of lead
(Pillow hard, and sheets not warm),
Love made the bed; they'll take no harm.
Let them sleep: let them sleep, on,
Till this stormy night be gone,
Till the eternal morrow dawn.
Then the curtains will be drawn
And they wake into a light
Whose day shall never die in night.

RICHARD CRASHAW

LOVE, FAITH AND ETERNAL LIFE

From *The Greatest Thing in the World*

Did you ever notice how continually John associates love and faith with eternal life? I was not told when I was a boy that "God so loved the world that He gave His only begotten Son, that whosoever believeth in Him should have everlasting life." What I was told, I remember, was that God so loved the world that, if I trusted in Him, I was to have a thing called peace, or I was to have rest, or I was to have joy, or I was to have safety. But I had to find out for myself that whosoever trusteth in Him—that is, whosoever loveth Him, for trust is only the avenue to love—hath everlasting life. The Gospel offers life.

To love abundantly is to live abundantly, and to love forever is to live forever. Hence, eternal life is inextricably bound with love.[87]

HENRY DRUMMOND

A Deathbed Letter from Catherine of Aragon to Henry VIII

Henry VIII had six wives. The first, when he was seventeen, was Catherine of Aragon, the youngest daughter of Spain's royal couple Ferdinand and Isabella of Columbus fame. After a marriage that produced no male heir to the throne (all male babies died in infancy), Henry requested an annulment from the Pope in Rome, which was denied. As a renouncement against the Catholic church, though never recognized by the church, Henry arranged a divorce from Catherine after twenty-two years of marriage. During this time he illegally married and had beheaded, Anne Boleyn. Dying of natural causes, one of only two of Henry's wives to do so, Catherine wrote this letter to her King two days before her death, certainly a love letter from one who was so wronged.

January, 1536

My most dear, king and husband,

The hour of my death now approaching, I cannot choose but out of the love I bear you, advise you of your soul's health, which you ought to prefer before all considerations of the world or flesh whatsoever. For which yet you have cast me into many calamities, and yourself into many troubles.

But I forgive you all; and pray to God to do likewise. For the rest, I commend unto you Mary, our daughter, beseeching you to be a good father to her, as I have heretofore desired. I must entreat you also, to respect my maids, and give them in marriage, which is not much, they being but three; and to all my other servants a year's pay, besides their due, lest otherwise they should be unprovided for; lastly, I make this vow, that mine eyes desire you above all things. Farewell.

THE TWO LEAVES

From *Bambi*

FELIX SALTEN

One of this compiler's favorite love pieces takes place deep in a forest where the sounds of passionate breathing and the whispers of lovers are but the west wind stirring in the treetops. Only a writer with deep appreciation for the natural world, who gave us the original "Bambi," from which Disney took his story, could personify nature with such feeling and romance.

The leaves were falling from the great oak at the meadow's edge. They were falling from all the trees.

One branch of the oak reached high above the others and stretched far out over the meadow. Two leaves clung to the very tip.

"It isn't the way it used to be," said one leaf to the other.

"No," the other leaf answered. "So many of us have fallen off tonight, we're almost the only ones left on our branch."

"You never know who's going to go next," said the first leaf.

"Even when it was warm and the sun shone, a storm or a cloudburst would come sometimes and many leaves were torn off, though they were still young. You never know who's going to go next."

"The sun seldom shines now," sighed the second leaf, "and when it does it gives no warmth. We must have warmth again."

"Can it be true," said the first leaf, "can it really be true, that others come to take our places when we're gone and after them still others, and more and more?"

"It is really true," whispered the second leaf. "We can't even begin to imagine it, it's beyond our powers."

"It makes me very sad," added the first leaf.

They were silent for a while. Then the first leaf said quietly to herself, "Why must we fall . . .?"

The second leaf asked, "What happens to us when we have fallen?"

"We sink down. . . ."

"What is under us?"

The first leaf answered, "I don't know, some say one thing, some another, but nobody knows."

The second leaf asked, "Do we feel anything, do we know anything about ourselves when we're down there?"

The first leaf answered, "Who knows? Not one of all those down there has ever come back to tell us about it."

They were silent again. Then the first leaf said tenderly to the other, "Don't worry so much about it, you're trembling."

"That's nothing," the second leaf answered, "I tremble at the least thing now. I don't feel so sure of my hold as I used to."

"Let's not talk anymore about such things," said the first leaf.

The other replied, "No, we'll let be. But—what else shall we talk about?" She was silent and went on after a little while, "Which of us will go first?"

"There's still plenty of time to worry about that," the other leaf assured her. "Let's remember how beautiful it was, how wonderful. When the sun came out and shone so warmly that we thought we'd burst with life. Do you remember? And the morning dew, and the mild and splendid nights."

"Now the nights are dreadful," the second leaf complained, "and there is no end to them."

"We shouldn't complain," said the first leaf gently. "We've outlived many, many others."

"Have I changed much?" asked the second leaf shyly but determinedly.

"Not in the least," the first leaf assured her. "You only think so because I've gotten to be so yellow and ugly. But it's different in your case."

"You're fooling me," the second leaf said.

"No, really," the first leaf exclaimed eagerly, "believe me, you're as lovely as the day you were born. Here and there may be a little yellow spot but it's hardly noticeable and only makes you handsomer, believe me."

"Thanks," whispered the second leaf, quite touched. "I don't believe you, not altogether, but I thank you because you are so kind, you've always been so kind to me. I'm just beginning to understand how kind you are."

"Hush," said the other leaf, and kept silent herself for she was too troubled to talk anymore.

Then they were both silent. Hours passed.

A moist wind blew cold and hostile, through the treetops.

"Ah, now," said the second leaf, "I. . . ." Then her voice broke off. She was torn from her place and spun down.

Winter had come.[88]

ON LOVE

From *The Prophet*

Love has no other desire but to
fulfill itself.
But if you love and must needs have
desires, let these be your desires:
To melt and be like a running brook
that sings its melody to the night.
To know the pain of too much
tenderness.
To be wounded by your own
understanding of love;
And to bleed willingly and joyfully.
To wake at dawn with a winged
heart and give thanks for another day
of loving.
To rest at the noon hour and
meditate love's ecstasy;
To return home at eventide with
gratitude;
And then to sleep with a prayer for
the beloved in your heart and a song
of praise upon your lips.[89]

KAHLIL GIBRAN

EPITAPH

This epitaph was placed on the
tomb of his wife by Mark Twain.

Warm summer sun,
Shine kindly here.
Warm southern wind
Blow softly here.
Green sod above
Lie light, lie light.
Good-night, dear heart,
Good-night, good-night.

The Angelus

Paul M. Miller

Every evening after sunset, when the most wonderful soft light is in the sky and it is very still everywhere, the old bell in the steeple chimes out over the village and the fields around. No one quite knows what the evening bell sings, but the tone is so beautiful that everyone stands still and listens.

Ever since the oldest grandfather can remember, the dear old bell has sung at evening and everyone has listened, for the message.

A great many people said there was really no message at all, and one very learned man wrote a whole book to show the song of the evening bell was nothing but the clanging of brass and iron; and almost everyone who read it believed it.

But Franz and Anna knew that the bell's ring had a message. Every evening before they returned to their cottage from the field, they'd anticipate the steeple song. When it began, Franz removed his work cap, and Anna folded her hands and bowed her head.

When Franz would look at her standing there against the setting sun with bowed head, his heart whelmed up within him. To Franz, the bell's song expressed all the feeling he had for Anna. As children they had played in those very fields. Even then, when they heard the Angelus, they knew there was something special about the bell. Even then, Franz knew that someday he and Anna would be married and would work this field as their own. The bell, the church steeple, and the closing sun combined to make him think of his Father who was in heaven, and his love who stood next to him.

Sometimes when the sweet music pealed out, Anna would glance up at Franz, before she bowed her head. In that moment, she felt such love in her heart for Franz. She could see his gray hair and rough worker's hands. She knew that her beloved husband had toiled all these years for her, and to be able to give to God's work at the church where the angelus music came from each evening. Her love for Franz was somehow all mixed up with her love for God, and her dependence upon Him.

One evening the great painter Jean Francois Millet strolled through the village and out into the countryside looking for a scene of true love. At the ringing of the Angelus, Millet discovered Anna and Hans standing together in their field. In the soft light he could sense their love for each other. There was something about the way the light fell upon their faces, and the way Franz stole glances of his dear one, that inspired Millet to paint what became his most popular work, "The Angelus."

"Why didn't you title it after the elderly couple who are the center of interest in this work?" inquired a gallery owner.

"I wanted this painting to reflect what put the love in their hearts; the Angelus bell at the old church was a voice that spoke to their hearts; the voice of God's love, and their love for one another."

REFERENCES

1. From *Love's Witness*, Sonnets from Portuguese, Sonnet 38, 'If Thou Must Love Me, Let It Be for Naught,' by Elizabeth Barrett Browning (New York, NY: Carroll & Graf, Inc., 1993), 11.

2. From *The Book of Love* (Diane Ackerman & Jeanne Mackin, Eds.), 'Letters of Love' (New York, NY: W. W. Norton & Co., Inc., 1998).

   Mary Wordsworth Letter to Her Husband William Wordsworth.

   Jack London Letter to His Wife, 750.

   Britain's Queen Victoria About Albert, 716,717.

   Russian Playwright Anton Chekhov to His Wife.

   Mark Twain to His Future Wife.

   John Steinbeck to His Wife.

   Robert Schumann to Clara Wiech.

   Elizabeth Barrett to Robert Browning, 720,721.

3. From *Sonnets from the Portuguese*, 'How Do I Love Thee,' by Elizabeth Barrett Browning (New York, NY: Carroll & Graf, Inc., 1993).

4. From *The White Cliffs*, 'Young and in Love,' by Alice Duer Miller (New York, NY: Coward-McCann, Inc., 1940), 8.

5. From Act Three, *'Cyrano de Bergerac,'* by Edmond Rostand (Houghton Mifflin Co./The Riverside Press Cambridge, 1931), 299 ff.

6. From *The Greatest Thing in the World*, 'Though I Give My Body To Be Burned,' by Henry Drummond (Uhrichsville, OH: Barbour & Co., Inc., 1994), 55.

7. From *True Stories*, 'Variations on the Word Love,' by Margaret Atwood (New York, NY: Carroll & Graf, Inc., 1993), 20.

8. From *The Book of Love* (Diane Ackerman & Jeanne Mackin, Eds.), 'She Walks in Beauty,' by Lord Byron (New York, NY: W. W. Norton & Co., Inc., 1998), 331.

9. From *The Book of Love* (Diane Ackerman & Jeanne Mackin, Eds.), 'A Midsummer Night's Dream (On Falling in Love)' by Robert Louis Stevenson (New York, NY: W. W. Norton & Co.), 573.

10. From *Sonnet 38: Sonnets from the Portuguese*, 'First Time He Kissed Me,' by Elizabeth Barrett Browning (New York, NY: Carroll & Graf, Inc., 1993), 11.

11.	From *The Love Book,* 'Jenny Kissed Me,' by Leigh Hunt. (New York, NY: W. W. Norton & Co., Inc., 1998), 357.

12.	From *The Book of Love* (Diane Ackerman & Jeanne Mackin, Eds.), 'First Love,' by John Clare. (New York, NY: W. W. Norton & Co., Inc. 1998), 320.

13.	From *William Blake,* 'The Lamb,' by William Blake. (Alfred A. Knopf, Inc., 1994), 19,20.

14.	From *Forever in Love,* 'Young Love,' by Richard Exley (Tulsa, OK: Honor Books, 1996), 62.

15.	From *1001 Love Poems,* 'A Quoi Bon Dire,' by Charlotte Mew (New York, NY: Black Dog & Leventhal, 1996), 657.

16.	From *Valentine Ideals,* 'St. Valentine's Day,' by Edgar A. Guest (Milwaukee, WI: Ideals Publishing Corp., Vol 40, No. 1).

17.	From *1001 Love Poems,* 'To Love,' by C. S. Lewis (New York, NY: Black Dog & Leventhal, 1996), 245.

18.	From *Collected Poems (1909-1962),* 'A Dedication to My Wife,' by T. S. Eliot (Harcourt Brace & Co.).

19.	From *Love for a Lifetime: Building a Marriage That Will Go the Distance,* 'Ideas for Anniversary Conversation Starters,' by Dr. James Dobson.

20.	'When I Was One and Twenty,' by A. E. Housman (Henry Holt & Co.).

21.	From *One Thousand Beautiful Things,* 'The Highway Man,' by Alfred Noyes (New York, NY: Peoples Book Club, Inc., 1947), 36.

22.	From *The Book of Love* (Diane Ackerman & Jeanne Mackin, Eds.), 'Love's Philosophy,' by Percy Bysshe Shelley (New York, NY: W. W. Norton & Co., Inc., 1998), 333.

23.	From *Jane Eyre,* 'Mr. Rochester Proposes to Jane,' by Charlotte Bronte (New York, NY: Random House, 1943).

24.	From *Cyrano de Bergerac, 1001 Beautiful Things,* 'A Kiss,' by Edmond Rostand (New York, NY: Peoples Book Club, Inc., 1942), 35.

25.	From *A Man Called Peter,* 'The Halls of Highest Human Happiness,' by Catherine Marshall (New York, NY: Avon Books, 1951).

26.	From *1001 Love Poems,* 'On the Road to the Sea,' by Charlotte Mew (New York, NY: Black Dog & Leventhal, 1996), 467.

27. From *1001 Love Poems*, 'My Better Half,' by Ike Muila & Isabella Motadinyane (New York, NY: Black Dog & Leventhal, 1996), 557.

28. From *Just As I Am*, 'Ruth and Billy's Courtship and Marriage,' by Billy Graham (New York, NY: HarperSan Francisco/Zondervan, 1997), 71 ff.

29. From *1001 Love Poems* (Beck & Wakeman, Eds.), 'Special Pleading,' by Sidney Lanier (New York, NY: Black Dog & Leventhal, 1996), 480.

30. From *1001 Love Poems*, 'Poem In Praise of My Husband (Taos),' by Diane Di Prima (New York, NY: Black Dog & Leventhal, 1996), 359.

31. From *Masterpieces of Religious Verse*, 'Prayer of Any Husband,' by Mazie V. Caruthers (Harper & Brothers, 1948), 1056.

32. From *Collected Poems*, 'The Concert,' by Edna St. Vincent Millay (New York, NY: Harper & Row Publishers, Inc., 1949), 186.

33. From *A Book of Children's Literature*, 'The Steadfast Tin Soldier,' by Hans Christian Anderson (Holt, Rinehart, & Winston, 1925), 214-216.

34. From *Poems of Emily Dickinson*, 'Why Do I Love You, Sir?' by Emily Dickinson (Boston, MA: Little, Brown, & Co., 1960), 480.

35. From *The Finishing Touch*, 'A Month for Love,' by Charles R. Swindoll (Dallas, TX: Word Publishing, 1994), 58.

36. From *Voices From the Heart* (Landin & Noll, Eds.), 'A Letter to His Wife' by Obediah Holmes (Grand Rapids, MI: William Eerdmans, 1987), 95-98.

37. From *The Collected Poems* by Rupert Brooke, 'The Great Lover' (Dodd, Mead, & Co., 1915), 114.

38. From *Whispers of the Heart for the One I Love*, 'Did I Ever Tell You?' by Richard Exley. (Tulsa, Oklahoma: Honor Books, 1996), 62.

39. From *Christy*, 'Can This Really Be Love?' by Catherine Marshall (New York, NY: McGraw-Hill Book Co.), 396 ff, 495.

40. From *Collected Poems*, 'Recuerdo,' by Edna St. Vincent Millay (New York, NY: Harper & Row Publishers, Inc., 1949), 128.

41. From *Little Women*, 'The First Wedding,' by Louisa May Alcott (Reader's Digest Edition, 1985, first published in 1868-69), 218-225.

42. From *Truman*, 'Bess and Harry Truman's Courtship and Marriage,' by David McCullough (New York, NY: Simon & Schuster, 1992), 80 ff.

43. *Ibid.*, 'Bess and Harry's Wedding,' 137 ff.

44. From *The Book of Common Prayer*, 'A Marriage Blessing' (New York, NY: The Church Hymnal Corp.), 429,430.

45. *Ibid.*, 'Four Marriage Prayers.'

46. From *1001 Love Poems* (Berk & Wakeman, Eds.), 'This Marriage,' by Jal'al U'ddin Rumi (New York, NY: Black Dog & Leventhal, 1996), 356.

47. From *The Book of Love* (D. Ackerman & J. Mackin, Eds.), 'The Gift of the Magi,' by O. Henry (New York, NY: W. w. Norton & Co., Inc., 1998), 171.

48. From *Masterpieces of Religious Verse* (James Dalton Morrison, Ed.), 'A Wedding Hymn,' Thomas Tiplady (Grand Rapids, MI: Baker Book House, 1977).

49. From *I Thee Wed* by Pat Ross, 'Miss Margaret E. Sangster on Love,' by Margaret E. Sangster (New York, NY: The Penguin Group, Viking Studio Books, 1991).

50. From *I Thee Wed* by Pat Ross, 'Miss Emily Post on the Bride,' by Emily Post (New York, NY: The Penguin Group, Viking Studio Books, 1991).

51. 'The Word,' by John Masefield.

52. From *This Incredible Century*, 'Marriage,' by Norman Vincent Peale (Wheaton, IL: Tyndale House Publishers, Inc., 1991), 204.

53. From *An American Life*, 'Nancy & Ronald Reagan,' by Ronald Reagan (New York, NY: Simon & Schuster), 121 ff.

54. From *Saving Your Marriage Before It Starts*, 'How to Predict a Happy Marriage,' by Les Parrott III and Leslie Parrott (Grand Rapids, MI: Zondervan Publishing House, 1995).

55. From *The Finishing Touch*, 'From a Dad to a Daughter,' by Charles Swindoll (Dallas, TX: Word Publishing, 1994), 54.

56. Parrott & Parrott., *Op. Cit.*, 'Where There Is Hope: C. S. Lewis and Joy Davidson.'

57. 'Remembering Joy,' C. S. Lewis.

58. From *The Applause of Heaven* 'The Kingdom of the Absurd,' by Max Lucado. (Dallas, TX: Word, 1990), 37.

59. From *The Book of Love* (D. Ackerman & J. Mackin, Eds.), 'A Resurrection,' by Willa Cather (New York, NY: W. W. Norton & Co., Inc., 1998), 150.

60. From *1001 Love Poems* (Berk & Wakeman, Eds.), 'Lonesome Dove,' Traditional American (New York, NY: Black Dog & Leventhal, 1996).

61. From *The Love Book* (D. Ackerman & J. Mackin, Eds.), 'When You Are Old,' by William Butler Yeats (New York, NY: W. W. Norton & Co., Inc., 1998), 362.

62. 'The Happy Prince,' by Oscar Wilde (London, England: Tiger Books International), 7 ff.

63. From *1001 Love Poems* (Berk & Wakeman, Eds.), 'Love In the Valley,' by George Meredith (New York, NY: Black Dog & Leventhal), 149.

64. From *The Book of Love* (D. Ackerman & J. Mackin, Eds.), 'Ulysses Returns to Penelope,' Translated by Samuel Butler (New York, NY: W. W. Norton & Co., Inc., 1998), 283.

65. From *A Book of Children's Literature*, 'Daphne,' by Ovid (Holt, Rinehart & Winston, Inc., 1925), 119,120.

66. From *Team Mates*, 'Team Building God's Way,' by Bob & Yvonne Turnbull (Kansas City, MO: Beacon Hill Press of Kansas City, 1998).

67. From *1001 Love Poems* (Berk & Wakeman, Eds.), 'Symptoms of Love,' by Robert Graves (New York, NY: Black Dog & Leventhal, 1996), 36.

68. From *More Heart Throbs*, 'The Old Bachelors' Sale,' Anonymous (New York, NY: Grosset & Dunlap, 1911), 66.

69. From *1001 Love Poems* (Berk & Wakeman, Eds.), 'Sally in Our Alley,' by Henry Carey (New York, NY: Black Dog & Leventhal, 1996), 294,295.

70. *Ibid.*, 'When We Fight,' by Leslie Newman, 83.

71. From *More Heart Throbs*, 'Kissin',' A Scottish Saying (Grosset & Dunlap), 250.

72. From *The World's Shortest Short Stories* (Steve Moss, Ed.), 'A Second Chance,' by Jay Bonestell; 'Rites of Passage,' by Mark Turner; 'The Dance,' Joy Jolissant; 'You Can Never Go Back,' Jay Bonestell (Philadelphia, PA: Running Press Book Publishers, 1995, 1998).

73. From 'Observations on Marriage,' by Robert G. Lee (New York, NY: Crown Trade Paperbacks, 1996).

74. From *More Heart Throbs*, 'The Bewitched Clock' (A Folk Tale) (Grosset & Dunlap).

75. From *What Makes a Man?* 'The Sensitive Man and Romance,' by Charles Stanley (Colorado Springs, CO: NavPress, 1992).

76. 'The Creation,' by James Weldon Johnson.

77. From *The Dairy of Adam and Eve,* 'Created in the Image of God,' by Mark Twain (New York, NY: W. W. Norton & Co., Inc., 1998), 104.

78. 'Hosea and Gomer, A Love That Will Not Let Go,' by Paul Medford.

79. From *1000 Beautiful Things,* 'Was This the Face?' by Christopher Marlowe (People's Book Club, Inc.), 143.

80. From *The Literature of the United States, Vol. I,* (Blair, Hornberger & Stewart), The Courtship of Miles Standish, 'If I'm not Worth the Wooing...' by Henry Wadsworth Longfellow (Scott, Foresman, & Co., 1946), 780.

81. From *The Beloved,* 'The Life of Love,' by Kahlil Gibran (Ashland, OR: White Cloud Press, 1994. Translation by John Waldbridge).

82. From *Famous Love Letters,* 'Absence and the Heart,' Clementine & Winston Churchill Letters (Reader's Digest, 1995).

83. 'Music I Heard,' by Conrad Aiken.

84. From *The Love Book* (D. Ackerman & J. Mackin, Eds.), 'Barter,' by Sara Teasdale (New York, NY: W. W. Norton & Co., Inc., 1998), 377.

85. From *A Book of Children's Literature,* 'The Real Princess,' by Hans Christian Anderson (Holt, Rinehart & Winston, Inc., 1925), 190.

86. From *The Finishing Touch,* 'The Final Toll,' by Charles R. Swindoll (Dallas, TX: Word Publishing, 1994), 88.

87. From *The Greatest Thing in the World,* 'Love, Faith and Eternal Life,' by Henry Drummond (Uhrichsville, OH: Barbour & Co., Inc., 1994).

88. From *Bambi,* 'The Two Leaves,' by Felix Salten (New York, NY: Simon & Schuster, Inc., 1929).

89. From *The Prophet,* 'On Love,' by Kahlil Gibran (New York, NY: Alfred A. Knopf, Inc., 1923, 1951, 1995).

Author Index

TITLE INDEX

Additional copies of this book
are available from your
local bookstore

Honor Books
Tulsa, Oklahoma